MW01011711

Lebanon Valley College
Science Education Partnership
Garber Science Center - Room 122
North White Oak Street
Annville, PA 17003

1-800-555-8802

Prentice Hall Guide To
SCHOLARSHIPS
AND
FELLOWSHIPS
FOR
MATH AND SCIENCE
STUDENTS

A Resource
for Students Pursuing Careers
in Mathematics, Science and Engineering

Mark Kantrowitz
Joann P. DiGennaro

PRENTICE HALL
Englewood Cliffs, New Jersey 07632

Prentice-Hall International (UK) Limited, *London*
Prentice-Hall of Australia, Pty. Limited, *Sydney*
Prentice-Hall of Canada, Inc., *Toronto*
Prentice-Hall Hispanoamericana, S.A., *Mexico*
Prentice-Hall of India Private Limited, *New Delhi*
Prentice-Hall of Japan, Inc., *Tokyo*
Prentice-Hall of Southeast Asia Pte. Ltd., *Singapore*
Editora Prentice-Hall do Brasil, Ltda., *Rio de Janeiro*

Library of Congress Cataloging-in-Publication Data

Kantrowitz, Mark.
   Prentice Hall guide to scholarships and fellowships for math & science students : a resource
guide for students pursuing careers in mathematics, science, and engineering / Mark Kantrowitz and
Joann P. DiGennaro. — 1st ed.
      p.   cm.
   Includes index.
   ISBN 0-13-045337-4. — ISBN 0-13-045345-5 (pbk.)
   1. Mathematics—Scholarships, fellowships, etc.—United States—Directories. 2. Science—
Scholarships, fellowships, etc.—United States—Directories. 3. Engineering—Scholarships, fellowships,
etc.—United States—Directories. I. DiGennaro, Joann P. II. Title.
QA13.K36   1993
507'.973—dc20   93-18449
                                                                                                          CIP

ISBN 0-13-045345-5 (P)

ISBN 0-13-045337-4

PRENTICE HALL
Career & Personal Development
Englewood Cliffs, NJ 07632

Simon & Schuster, A Paramount Communications Company

PRINTED IN THE UNITED STATES OF AMERICA

Acknowledgments

We'd like to thank all the organizations that provided information about their programs and all the parents and students who have suggested additional programs, especially new ones. We'd also like to thank the CEE staff — Medi Hoover, Maite Ballestero, Mariana Pestana, Ann Mathison, and Kevin Karp — who contributed time and effort toward researching the book and sending out hundreds of query letters. Finally, thanks to the CEE's Board of Trustees and others too numerous to mention for enthusiastically supporting this effort from its inception.

We are grateful to all the reviewers who contributed helpful comments on drafts of the book. Suggestions, corrections, and advice were provided by Jade Goldstein, Dr. Barbara Lazarus, Michael C. Behnke, Sterling Hudson, Bill Fitzsimmons, Janet A. Lavin, Mary L. Walshok, George Stoner, Vicki Baker, Lori Heberley, Nadine L. Romstedt, Sharona Gordon, Betty Kantrowitz, William Kantrowitz and Dr. Myles R. DiGennaro. Any remaining errors are, of course, our own.

Thanks to Tom Power, our editor at Prentice Hall, Barbara Palumbo, desktop publishing manager, and Louise Rothman, production editor, for their assistance in completing this project.

MARK KANTROWITZ AND JOANN P. DIGENNARO

Corrections and Comments

Corrections, comments, suggestions, and information about programs appropriate for this guide should be sent to:

Center for Excellence in Education
7710 Old Springhouse Road
McLean, VA 22102

Tel: (703) 448-9062
Fax: (703) 442-9513

E-mail: scholarship-book@rsi.cee.org

In memory of *The Admiral*:

> Late to bed
> Early to rise
> Work hard as hell
> And you'll be wise.
>   – Admiral H.G. Rickover (1900–1985)

Foreword

This book was written by Mark Kantrowitz and Joann P. DiGennaro, President of the Center for Excellence in Education. The CENTER FOR EXCELLENCE IN EDUCATION (CEE) was founded in 1983 by Admiral H.G. Rickover, the father of the nuclear Navy and developer of civilian nuclear power, to help our best students and teachers keep the United States competitive in science and technology. The Center is a private, nonprofit organization, not subject to federal and state mandates or political pressures.

The Center provides programs and opportunities for an often-neglected group of students, the academically talented. For example, in the years the Center has sponsored its summer RESEARCH SCIENCE INSTITUTE (RSI), the organization has had more of its students chosen as Westinghouse Science Talent Search honorees and winners than any other educational organization in the country.

The RESEARCH SCIENCE INSTITUTE (RSI) program was developed with leading educators from the United States and several other nations. The six-week, highly intensive program is offered to academically talented students in mathematics and science who have completed their third year of high school or the equivalent. It combines one week of intensive classroom lectures and four weeks of off-campus internships in scientific research with scientists from private corporations and academic institutions. Classroom instruction by leading university professors during the first week provides theoretical background in mathematics and the biological and physical sciences. High school teachers noted for their excellence in teaching highly precocious students present courses in scientific communications, computer use, and research methods. For four weeks, students gain practical experience in scientific research as they work with scientists five hours daily, five days a week. During the evening, the students participate in tutorials led by the teachers and lectures by distinguished scientists. The final week is spent preparing the research reports, which are presented in oral and written form. Subsequently the reports are published by the Center.

This book was originally developed in 1985 by Mark Kantrowitz (a 1984 RSI alumnus) as a scholarship guide for RSI students and alumni/ae. Over the years it has continually been revised and updated by Joann P. DiGennaro, CEE President, and Mark Kantrowitz. When RSI alumni and alumnae began entering graduate schools in 1989, we added fellowship programs to the listings. Alumni/ae and their parents have often mentioned to us that this is the only book to focus on opportunities for mathematics, science, and engineering students at the high school, undergraduate, and graduate levels. Accordingly, we decided to publish the book to make it accessible to a much greater audience.

The Center also sponsors the ROLE MODELS AND LEADERS PROJECT for minority students in urban cities throughout the United States. During their junior and senior years in high school, these students meet with adult leaders and role models to broaden their vision of the fields of science and technology. The program helps the students find and reinforce their career interests, acquaints them with the college admissions process and sources of financial aid, and gives them opportunities to be mentored by professionals in their field of interest. The students also participate in field trips and enrichment activities and receive guidance on practical matters, such as résumés and job interviews. So we've included programs in this book which are targeted toward minority mathematics, science, and engineering students. We've also included programs directed toward female students.

For more information on the programs and activities of the Center, please call or write:

Center for Excellence in Education
7710 Old Springhouse Road
McLean, VA 22102

Tel: (703) 448-9062
Fax: (703) 442-9513
E-mail: center@rsi.cee.org

About the Authors

MARK KANTROWITZ has two Bachelor of Science degrees from the Massachusetts Institute of Technology (MIT), one in Mathematics and one in Philosophy, and a Master of Science degree in Computer Science from Carnegie Mellon University (CMU). He is currently pursuing a Ph.D. in Computer Science at CMU. While in high school, he was ranked first in several mathematics and science competitions and received numerous merit-based college scholarships, including a Westinghouse Science Talent Search scholarship. He is currently a recipient of a National Science Foundation Graduate Fellowship and a Hertz Foundation Research Fellowship Grant and is a member of nine professional organizations in mathematics and science.

JOANN P. DIGENNARO is President of the Center for Excellence in Education and serves as a member of its board of trustees. The Center is a nonprofit educational foundation dedicated to improving United States science and mathematics education through innovative programs. Ms. DiGennaro established the Center (formerly the Admiral H.G. Rickover Foundation) with Admiral Rickover in 1983.

She received her B.A. from Purdue University, attended the University of Rome and holds an M.A. with honors from the University of Maryland. She was awarded a scholarship to read the law at Oxford University and received her J.D. from the George Mason University School of Law with the award for outstanding student of international law. She subsequently was named outstanding alumna of George Mason University. She has been an instructor at the University of Maryland and at Purdue University.

Ms. DiGennaro is a member of the American Bar Association and the Virginia Bar Association, and is listed in *Who's Who in American Women*. She has served as an officer and member of numerous national, state, and local boards. She is a frequent lecturer in the United States and abroad about increasing educational opportunities for academically precocious students and also about gender and ethnic issues as they concern careers in mathematics and science. She has negotiated several bilateral scientific youth exchanges for high school students between the United States and other nations, several under the auspices of the U.S. Information Agency. These exchanges include the first with the People's Republic of China and India, and the first exchanges between the United States and Eastern European countries since World War II.

Contents

Contents

6. Fellowships   139

7. Contents and Competitions   **201**

Contents   xix

Introduction

This is the first book to focus on opportunities for science and mathematics students at the high school, undergraduate, and graduate levels. Ever since we started compiling this guide, the number of programs listed has grown to greater than 300, including over 200 scholarships and fellowships. Most of the scholarships, fellowships, and grants described in this book are merit based, though a few take financial need into account.

We hope that this guide to scholarships and fellowships for mathematics and science students can reduce the role that finances play in decisions about which university to attend. Our goal is to eliminate some of the barriers that discourage students from seeking careers in science and technology.

Who Should Read This Book?

This book is targeted at mathematics, science, and engineering students and their parents. It is also of interest to guidance counselors, mathematics and science teachers, school principals, financial aid officers, and educational organizations. It is unique — no similar publication serves this audience. The other available guides, most of which are listed in the annotated bibliography (Chapter 12, pages 301–312), either neglect mathematics and science students, or are so general and so undiscriminating in their selection that the relevant worthwhile programs are buried among the irrelevant ones. The book also lists many scholarship and fellowship programs directed toward women and minorities.

To put it simply — if you are seeking information about resources for math and science students, whether for yourself or for advising others, you should read this book.

What Kinds of Programs Are Listed?

This book lists two kinds of programs:

- Programs that focus on mathematics, science, and engineering.
- Programs of a more general nature that do not restrict the student's field of study.

Although we've concentrated on the former, there are enough of the latter to interest students who plan careers outside of the math and science realm. There are also a considerable number of programs directed toward female and minority students.

For a program to be included, it couldn't have very strict and limited requirements. For example, we haven't listed school-specific programs (except where more than one or two schools are involved), because you can get that sort of information by calling the school's financial aid office.

The types of programs include:

- Undergraduate Scholarships
- Graduate Fellowships
- Contests and Competitions
- Internships and Summer Employment
- Summer Research Programs
- Study Abroad
- Science and Mathematics Honor Societies

Some sponsoring organizations use the terms scholarship, fellowship, grant, and award very loosely, especially when both undergraduate and graduate students are eligible. We define our use of the terms in the following paragraph. Undergraduate scholarships are listed in Chapter 5 and graduate fellowships in Chapter 6. When a program allows both undergraduate students and graduate students to apply, we have listed it only in Chapter 5, but have indexed it as both a scholarship and a fellowship.

Scholarships provide financial aid for undergraduate study and cover tuition and fees. *Fellowships* support graduate and professional study and most often include a stipend to defray living expenses. Fellowships may also include an allowance for travel and research expenses and/or tuition and fees. A *dissertation fellowship* provides support for students who have passed the comprehensive qualifying exams and have started writing the thesis. Dissertation fellowships may cover thesis publication costs as well. Most fellowships are for research and study at the institution of the recipient's choice. *Residential fellowships*, however, support work in residence at a research facility of the sponsor, such as a library or museum. Residential fellowships pay transportation costs to the institution and living costs during the stay. *Grants* fund research expenses and special projects and usually do not include stipend and tuition support. They are intended to pay for the expenses directly related to the project, such as materials, equipment, and facilities usage. *Grants-in-aid* are smaller grants that pay only a portion of the costs of the project. *Awards* and *prizes* are presented after the fact to recognize outstanding performance and often include a small honorarium. *Travel awards* are often associated with a technical conference and enable students to attend the conference by providing funds for transportation, lodging, and registration fees. Sometimes they require that the student have written a paper which was accepted for presentation at the conference.

A Word About Financial Aid

Many students make the mistake of prejudging their academic options according to the price tag. They are scared away from the big name universities by the high costs of tuition, room, and board.

Don't make such a hasty decision!

For undergraduate education, many schools offer financial aid in the forms of scholarships, grants, low-interest or interest-free loans (e.g., PLUS, GSL, and Perkins loans), and part-time employment. Some will meet all of your demonstrated financial need, and some may even offer you a merit-based scholarship to convince you to matriculate.

For graduate education, many schools will offer you full financial support — a tuition waiver and a monthly stipend — in the form of a fellowship, research assistantship, or teaching assistantship. Some will give you additional income for grading papers. This is especially true for students studying mathematics, science, and engineering.

Be sure to exhaust all avenues of financial aid before you decide that a certain school is beyond your means. Visit or call the financial aid offices at the schools you wish to attend. Many have peculiar and rather specific scholarships for which you just might qualify. They can also help explain just how you can really afford to attend the school. We discuss this in greater detail in Chapter 4.

How to Use This Book

This book contains information about a variety of programs and resources available to high school, undergraduate, and graduate students in mathematics, science, and engineering. Whether you are interested in contests and competitions, summer programs, college scholarships, graduate fellowships, or research programs, the information contained in this book provides a good place to start your search. If the listings aren't enough, continue your search with the extensive bibliography of related publications and other sources of information. Most of these books can be found in your local library or ordered through the mail.

The majority of the financial aid programs included in this listing are merit based and not college-controlled. College-controlled scholarship programs have been included only if they apply to several schools, such as all schools in an educational district or state. For information on collegiate grants and awards, call or visit the financial aid office of the particular college or university.

In presenting information about each scholarship, we've tried to keep the layout compact but easy to read. The following diagram illustrates the general structure of the entries. More detailed information about each program can always be obtained by writing to the address listed in the entry. Scholarships are listed in alphabetical order.

NAME OF THE PROGRAM	1

Type:	The category of the program: Scholarship, Fellowship, Contest, Research Grant, Intership, Award.
Focus:	The major theme or topic area of the program.
Eligibility:	Who can apply or enter.
Description:	A description of the program and the application process.
Awards:	What you win.
Deadline:	When you must enter.
Address:	Where to write for more information. Be sure to enclose a stamped self-addressed envelope with your request to facilitate their reply.
Telephone:	Where to call for more information.

If you want to find a particular scholarship, look for its name in the table of contents. If you don't know the name of the scholarship, look in the index. The index lists scholarships and fellowships by category, topic or focus, eligibility restrictions, and deadline date. Programs are also indexed according to other keywords, such as sponsoring company, as appropriate. Note that some programs are indexed under general categories, like Science and Mathematics, so if you're interested in a specific field like Chemistry or Statistics, be sure to also check the superordinate categories that include it.

Overview

The rest of the book is organized as follows:

- Chapter 1 gives a few helpful hints about searching for financial aid and completing applications. You should read this chapter if you are applying for any of the programs listed in this book.

- Chapter 2 gives advice on applying undergraduate school. If you are applying to college, you should also read Chapter 1.

- Chapter 3 gives advice on applying to graduate school. As with any application, you should also read Chapter 1.

- Chapter 4 discusses methods for estimating financial need. Although it is directed primarily toward students who are about to begin their undergraduate education, some of the material is also appropriate for graduate students.

- Chapter 5 contains listings of undergraduate scholarships. It also contains programs that are directed toward both undergraduate and graduate students.

- Chapter 6 contains listings of graduate fellowship programs.

- Chapter 7 contains listings of contests and competitions, targeted mainly at high school students, but some also allow undergraduate and graduate students to enter.

- Chapter 8 contains listings of internship and summer employment programs aimed at science and mathematics students.

- Chapter 9 contains listings of study and travel abroad programs.

- Chapter 10 summarizes other resources such as honor societies, talent searches, professional organizations, government aid programs, and so on.

- Chapter 11 discusses the taxability status of scholarships and fellowships.

- Chapter 12 is an annotated bibliography describing most other sources of academic and career information of interest to mathematics and science students.

The index begins on page 313.

Chapter 1

A Few Helpful Hints in Applying for Financial Aid

This chapter gives advice on searching for financial aid and filling out application forms. It concludes with a listing of some of the more noteworthy programs listed in this book.

Start the Search for Aid Early

Don't underestimate the amount of time it will take you to identify appropriate programs, send away for application forms, and complete the applications. Writing essays takes a lot of time, so the sooner you start, the better.

Some programs have very early deadlines. If you miss the deadline, you won't get any money, even if you're the perfect candidate. Moreover, some programs review applications on a rolling basis, so applications received closer to the deadline have a poorer chance of getting selected.

At a bare minimum, you should start your search for aid the summer before your senior year. You can do the research to find the programs for which you are eligible, send away for application materials, and start working on your essays all before the semester begins. But nothing stops you from thinking about financial aid and related issues in your freshman year of high school. The sooner you start thinking about financial aid and your academic and career goals, the more likely you are to be eligible to apply for aid. Some programs start at an early age, or require work, such as a science fair project, which is best done well in advance of the deadline. If you have clearly defined goals for yourself, you'll be better able to plan for your future.

Whatever you do, *don't procrastinate!* Applying to undergraduate or graduate school is time-consuming. Add applications for scholarships and fellowships to the load, and you have a tremendous amount of work to do in very little time. Doing all this work takes a lot of effort, so you may be tempted to put if off. Don't. You will write a better application if you have enough time to think before you write and revise your essays. If you wait until the last possible minute, your application will be rushed and your essays shallow. Plan ahead, spread out your work over time, and pace yourself.

1

Assess Your Financial Needs and Preferences

How much money will you need? Chapter 4 discusses methods for estimating college costs and the amount of your family contribution.

Do you want only grants, or are you willing to accept loans and part-time employment during the school year? Most schools assume that you will be earning money during the summer from a job.

It is impossible to fully finance an education through summer employment and a part-time on-campus job during the semester. It is therefore important to secure as much scholarship money as possible. Such aid comes from the federal and state government, and private sources, such as corporations, unions, fraternal organizations, and foundations. Although colleges also have grant aid, it is seldom merit-based. Colleges rely heavily on loans and part-time employment to flesh out their aid packages. You'll need to apply to scholarship grant programs, such as those listed in this book.

Be Resourceful

No book can list every scholarship for which you are eligible. Had we attempted to do so, this book would have become unwieldly. Instead, we've focused on programs of interest to most students of mathematics, science, and engineering, and omitted many of the more random and specialized programs.

As you can see from the bibliography on pages 301–312, there is an overwhelming number of programs available. Most have very specific and sometimes peculiar restrictions, but if you look long and hard enough, you're sure to find some for which you qualify. Those books which are particularly good places to start your search have a diamond ($\diamond$) at the end of their entry in the bibliography. You can find the books described in the bibliography at your guidance counselor's office, or in your local library's reference section.

The listings in this book and the books described in the bibliography should serve as a good starting point for your search. Your town librarian may also know of some programs which are local to where you live, such as a local chapter of DOLLARS FOR SCHOLARS^{TM} (page 82). Check the bulletin board in the library, school or town hall, and also look in the local newspapers. Ask everyone you know for information on scholarship and fellowship programs for which you might qualify.

Avoid companies that say they will match you with "the millions of dollars of scholarship money that go unclaimed each year." These companies have you fill out a form and charge you a hefty fee for a list of potential scholarship sources that supposedly match your profile. You must then write to the scholarship programs yourself for an application form. That's if the list you receive has the sponsor's current addresses and the deadlines haven't already passed. It may also turn out that you aren't eligible for most of the programs on your list. Most of these companies are run by people who have no qualifications or knowledge of financial aid. They simply forward your profile to a parent company that retrieves a list of addresses from a database. The quality of these databases is questionable, since the entries are often old and inaccurate. If you use one of these companies, you probably won't receive any aid and their guarantees are worthless.

You are much better off going to your local public library. If you're considering using one of these companies, check first with the Better Business Bureau or the State Bureau of Consumer Protection.

Be resourceful! Check with the organizations to which you belong — fraternities, professional organizations, hobbyist groups, church/synagogue — to discover if they have any scholarship programs. Ask your employer and your parents' employer if they have a scholarship program. Many corporations will pay for all or part of the educational expenses of their employees and their employees' dependents. If you are a veteran or a dependent of a veteran, check with local veterans groups and the Veterans Administration.

The scholarships may be small, but every penny counts. Don't eliminate a program simply because the amount of the award is small ($1,000–$2,000). If you get many small scholarships they can add up to a sizable chunk of money. Moreover, your success in getting a small scholarship now may lead to your getting a larger one later if you add the name of the small scholarship to your résumé. Winning an award, even a small one, adds to your prestige.

Identify those special qualifications which might make you eligible for some of the more restricted and targeted aid programs, such as

- ☐ Sex (female or male)
- ☐ Race or ethnic group
- ☐ Minority status
- ☐ Handicapped status
- ☐ Place of residence
- ☐ Citizenship
- ☐ Membership in an association, group, organization, or club
- ☐ Membership in a fraternal group (fraternity or sorority)
- ☐ Employer
- ☐ Union membership
- ☐ Religious affiliation (both local church/synagogue and the national organization)[1]
- ☐ Military or veteran status
- ☐ Creative or professional achievement (e.g., publications)
- ☐ Athletic achievements
- ☐ Hobbies and musical instruments
- ☐ Academic merit
- ☐ Special skills
- ☐ Financial need
- ☐ Field of study

Even if one of the categories doesn't apply to you, if it applies to your parents, step-parents, guardians, or your spouse, you could still qualify. Don't eliminate a program from consideration just because your parents are divorced, separated, remarried, or

---

[1] For example, Methodists should write to Board of Higher Education and Ministry, United Methodist Church, P.O. Box 871, 1001 Nineteenth Avenue South, Nashville, TN 37202-0871, (615) 340-7344 and Presbyterians should write to Presbyterian Church (USA), Office of Financial Aid for Studies, 100 Witherspoon Street, Louisville, KY 40202-1396, (502) 569-5736/5745/5735.

deceased — you may still be eligible. Even the most remote connection is worth pursuing. Given enough lead time, you or your parents could even join an organization or establish residency in order to be eligible for some programs.

Use the index to quickly find the programs that match your qualifications, or leaf through the book page by page. Entries are structured to make it easy to identify the restrictions.

The table of contents of this book contains check boxes next to the name of each scholarship program. Mark off the boxes of the programs you are considering.

Eliminate Unlikely Programs

At this point you've probably amassed a long list of programs. Pay attention to the restrictions and cross off any for which you don't qualify. Read the detailed descriptions for any other potential restrictions and eliminate the least likely ones. Eliminate awards which can't be used at your current level of study, but keep note of them for future use. Applying takes time and money, so you don't want to waste it on programs for which you aren't eligible.

Contact the Schools' Financial Aid Offices

Visit or call the financial aid offices of the schools you are considering even if you think you don't qualify for anything. Although most schools sponsor need-based financial aid programs in an effort to enable all students to attend, some also have merit-based programs to encourage the most academically talented students to matriculate. Others will determine the proportion of grant money in your aid package according to your GPA. Some colleges have extremely specialized, eccentric, and esoteric scholarships for which you might happen to qualify, regardless of your financial need. For example, alumni sometimes attach the strangest of strings to their contributions. Several programs depend on your having a particular last name (e.g., Murphy or Gatlin) or having grown up in a particular town (e.g., Rochester or Dorchester). Some schools also administer external programs which don't depend on need. So contact the financial aid office at every school you're considering and ask for information on all the programs they have available.

This book lists mainly those aid programs which aren't college-controlled (the exception being those programs which are common to several colleges). For example, we excluded the North Carolina State University's Merit Awards Program because it was school-specific.[2] So for information on merit-based scholarship programs, you must write, call, or visit the financial aid offices of the schools you are considering. Several books describing college-controlled merit-based aid programs are also listed on page 308 of the bibliography.

Although most schools maintain the fiction that they will meet your full demonstrated financial need, the realities of budget pressures often ensure that their conception of

---

[2]For information on NCSU's Merit Awards Program, write to Merit Awards Program, North Carolina State University, Box 7342, Pullen Hall, Raleigh, NC 27695-7342, or call (919) 515-3671.

financial need doesn't match yours. There's a big difference between giving you a grant and expecting you to mortgage your future and your parents' home. On the other hand, your education is an investment in your future, not a frill, so consider your tuition as the cost of that investment.[3]

If during your education your financial circumstances change, visit your financial aid office. Most schools have emergency funds to handle parental death, unemployment, or major disability. Sometimes they'll be able to increase your aid package. Most schools would rather try to find you an extra $400 than see you drop out of school during your last semester because of money problems.

Get Current Application Materials

To be certain that the data given in this book is correct and complete, you should always write or call the sponsoring organization for complete current information and application materials. Some change the application form or the deadlines from year to year. Because foundations do move on occasion, if your mail is returned marked "Addressee Unknown," try calling one of the listed phone numbers for the current address. All listings have been verified within the past six months, but in any undertaking of this magnitude, at least one program will change between the final edit and the time the first book appears on the shelves in your local bookstore.

In your information request letter, first identify who you are, then ask for the information you need, and close with a line that expresses your gratitude. A sample letter for requesting information and an application appears in Figure 1.1.

Dear Program Director,

I am a student at *Anytown High School* and will be applying for admission to *Big City College*.

I am interested in receiving information about your *Lots O'Money Scholarship* program. Please also send current application forms when they are ready.

Enclosed is a self-addressed, stamped business-size envelope for your convenience.

Thank you for your time.

Sincerely,
John Q. Student

Figure 1.1: Sample Information Request Letter

---

[3] According to a 1993 Census Bureau study, people with bachelor's degrees earn $2,116 a month on average, with a high of $2,953 for engineering and a low of $1,592 for the humanities and liberal arts. People with just a high school diploma earn $1,077 a month on average.

List Your Accomplishments

Before filling out scholarship and college application forms, make a detailed resume of your academic and nonacademic honors, awards, and activities. Good things to include are:

- ☐ Major school activities
- ☐ Volunteer/Community activities
- ☐ Skills and talents developed outside of school
- ☐ Athletic participation
- ☐ Musical instruments
- ☐ Hobbies and leisure time activities
- ☐ Special summer programs attended
- ☐ Employment during school and summer
- ☐ Prizes and awards received from competitions
- ☐ Publications
- ☐ Anything you find unique or special about yourself

This will help you organize your thoughts and make sure that you do not accidentally omit an important qualification. In addition, often the best way to see where you're headed is to look where you've been. Writing this list of accomplishments will help you think about what you want to do in the future. You should also give a copy of this resume, possibly abbreviated, to the people who will be writing letters of recommendation for you.

Assess Your Career Goals

Think about your career goals. It may sound trite, but you need to think about what you want to be when you grow up. Adulthood comes quickly. How far do you plan to pursue your education? Will you want to go to graduate school, or just to undergraduate school for a bachelor's degree? If you want to go to graduate school, is it to receive professional training (typically a master's degree) or is it to become prepared for an academic career (typically a Ph.D. or other doctoral degree)? Or perhaps a professional school (medical school, dental school, or law school) is in your future?

To obtain information on career opportunities in a particular field, write to some of the organizations listed starting on page 276.

Think about other considerations that may affect your academic and career goals. For example, are there any geographic limits on where you can live, study, work?

Determine Your Academic Interests

What field of study do you want to pursue? What are your favorite subjects in school? Often the best area to work in is the one you like the most. But don't make too firm a choice, because you may encounter new fields in college to which you hadn't been exposed in your previous academic experiences.

Some of the fields covered by this book are listed in Table 1.1.

☐ Accounting	☐ Earth Sciences	☐ Mechanical Engineering
☐ Acoustics	☐ Ecology	☐ Medical Technology
☐ Actuarial Science	☐ Economics	☐ Medicine
☐ Aeronautics	☐ Education	☐ Metallurgy
☐ Aerospace	☐ Electrical Engineering	☐ Meteorology
☐ Agriculture	☐ Electronics	☐ Microbiology
☐ Agronomy	☐ Electron Microscopy	☐ Mycology
☐ Animal Science	☐ Energy	☐ Neontology
☐ Anthropology	☐ Engineering	☐ Neuroscience
☐ Archaeology	☐ Enology	☐ Nuclear Engineering
☐ Architecture	☐ Entomology	☐ Ocean Engineering
☐ Artificial Intelligence	☐ Environmental Science	☐ Oceanography
☐ Astronautics	☐ Epidemiology	☐ Optics
☐ Astronomy	☐ Fluid Mechanics	☐ Optometry
☐ Atmospheric Science	☐ Food Science & Technology	☐ Ornithology
☐ Avionics	☐ Forensic Sciences	☐ Paleontology
☐ Behavioral Sciences	☐ Genetics	☐ Pharmacology
☐ Biochemistry	☐ Geography	☐ Physics
☐ Biology	☐ Geology	☐ Planetary Science
☐ Biostatistics	☐ Geophysics	☐ Psychiatry
☐ Biotechnology	☐ Government	☐ Psychology
☐ Botany	☐ Health Sciences	☐ Public Service
☐ Business	☐ History of Science	☐ Robotics
☐ Chemical Engineering	☐ Horticulture	☐ Safety Engineering
☐ Chemistry	☐ Human Factors	☐ Science Journalism
☐ Civil Engineering	☐ Hydrology	☐ Seismology
☐ Climatology	☐ Icthyology	☐ Sociology
☐ Cognitive Science	☐ Immunology	☐ Solar Energy
☐ Communication Science	☐ Law	☐ Space Science
☐ Computer Engineering	☐ Library Science	☐ Speleology
☐ Computer Graphics	☐ Linguistics	☐ Statistics
☐ Computer Science	☐ Marine Biology	☐ Toxicology
☐ Conservation	☐ Materials Sciences	☐ Veterinary Medicine
☐ Dental Lab Technology	☐ Mathematics — Applied	☐ Viticulture
☐ Dentistry	☐ Mathematics — Pure	☐ Zoology

Table 1.1: Fields of Study

Letters of Recommendation

Choose your teacher recommendations carefully. Be sure to use only people who know you well and can write well. Pick teachers who think you're among the best students they've ever taught. Don't be afraid to ask the teacher if they can write you a *good* letter of recommendation. If they say they can't or won't, ask them for suggestions of other people to approach.

Give your references enough time to write. Teachers tend to get swamped with many requests as deadlines approach and will appreciate reasonable advance warning.

Some will refuse to write a letter just a week before the deadline. Ask for a letter of recommendation at least two months in advance of the deadline, if not earlier.

You should write a two or three page autobiography to give to guidance counselors and teachers who are writing recommendations for you. As a matter of courtesy, when asking someone to write you a letter of recommendation, provide him or her with a stamped, addressed envelope.

Getting Nominated

Some scholarship and fellowship programs require that you be nominated — by your advisor, by a faculty member, by your high school principal, by your department chairman or by a member of the professional society that selects the grant recipient. If the nominator isn't already familiar with your qualifications, they probably won't nominate you. So it can sometimes pay to be a *little* aggressive.

Make an appointment to see the appropriate person, and bring along a copy of your résumé and a description of the program. Tell him or her that you'd like to be considered for nomination, and give him or her your résumé and the program description. Be prepared for an impromptu interview. Be *extremely* polite or you'll come across as too pushy. There's no guarantee you'll be nominated, but chances are they'll remember you. (And if they've forgotten about the program until the last minute, you become the default nominee.)

Log All Correspondence

Keep a log of all incoming and outgoing correspondence. This will help you quickly determine the status of any of your applications and let you choose which application to work on next. A chart similar to the one in Table 1.2 on page 9 is a good start. When you list the programs on the chart, write them in deadline order, so the ones near the top are the ones you must finish first. In the chart's headings, *Info Inquiry* is the date you wrote away for current information and an application and *Info Received* is the date you received this information. *Deadline* is the date the materials are due and *Notification* is the date winners are announced. *References* is the date you asked your teachers to write you letters of recommendation and *Application Mailed* is the date you mailed the completed application.

General Hints

- Deadlines are often the last date for the *receipt* of application materials by the grant sponsor. Allow several days for the U.S. postal service to deliver your application, or use an overnight delivery service such as Federal Express or Airborne. Write to the organization well in advance of the deadline; the sooner, the better.

- Enclose a self-addressed, stamped business-size envelope (SASE) when requesting information about a program for a faster reply.

Program Name	Info Inquiry	Info Received	Deadline	Notification	References	Application Mailed

Table 1.2: Correspondence Log

- Keep a separate file folder for each program. Put photocopies of all papers, forms, applications, and correspondence in the file. Write deadlines on the front of the file folder.

- Create checklists and to-do lists and check off the entries as you complete them.

- Read the instructions carefully. Double-check all forms and applications for accuracy and completeness.

- When writing an essay for a scholarship or fellowship, consider the sponsor's goals in granting the award. Try to position your application to meet some or all of their needs. But don't stretch too far, or the result will seem unnatural.

- Proofread your essays for spelling and grammatical errors. Have others read your essays. If possible, look at essays written by people who have been admitted to schools you respect, but be careful to not copy any of their ideas. (Don't let it discourage you either.)

- Make a note of the deadlines. Deadlines have a habit of creeping up on you when you least expect them.

- Type every essay and application, even if your handwriting is extraordinarily good. Double-space if possible. Practice first by typing on a photocopy of the application form.

- Don't be modest. If you don't tell them you were captain of the math team, how do you expect them to know it? You've got to sell yourself, to persuade them to give the scholarship to you and not to someone else.

- Always make a photocopy of all your application materials in case they are lost in the mail.

- Document every conversation you have with a financial aid officer. Confirm your conversation in writing and keep a copy, since financial aid offices are notorious for losing things. This will help protect you against receiving incorrect information from a financial aid officer.

- Send important correspondence "return receipt requested." Though this costs more, it lets you know that your mail has been received and on what date. If money is short, enclose a stamped, self-addressed postcard with your application. Write the name of the program and "Date Received: _____" on the back of the postcard.

- Beware of any organization that asks you for a nontrivial amount of money to receive a scholarship application or to enter a competition. There are many scams which prey on unsuspecting students and their parents. If you are unsure about any program, show the description to your teachers and guidance counselor and ask them for their opinion.

Hints for High School Students

- The initial screening of the Presidential Scholars program and other scholarships is by your ACT/SAT national test scores. Be sure to check the yes box on the Student Search Service (ETS/SAT) or the Student Profile Section (ACT) registration form to release your information to the Commission on Presidential Scholars and other scholarship programs.

- On a financial aid form, always apply for the Pell Grant.

- Look for local scholarships, which, although smaller, tend to be more abundant (and sometimes, though not always, easier to get!).

Hints for Graduate Students

- First year graduate students are eligible to apply for the Hertz and NSF fellowships even if they applied the previous year as college seniors. If you don't get the NSF Fellowship the first time you apply, ask for a copy of your evaluation forms. The evaluation forms will point out your weak areas and will be useful when you redo your application.

- For a statement of purpose or statement of research objectives, try to be as specific as possible. If you are interested in a particular research problem, describe it and tell them what interested you in the problem. Tell them how you became interested in the field. If you don't know what you're interested in beyond vague generalities, say something anyway. If you sound wishy-washy and not focused, you probably won't get a fellowship. It isn't a big deal if you change your mind later. If you've published any papers or technical reports, cite them and note whether they were refereed. Tell them what you intend to do after you get your Ph.D. — go into academia or industry, or start your own company?

- *The Chronicle of Higher Education*, a weekly newspaper for college and university administrators, is a good source of information about new fellowship programs. Your university library should have a copy.

Programs of Note

This section lists some of the more prestigious and well-known general grant programs and their page numbers. Every student should consider applying to these programs.

Scholarship Programs:

Fellowship Programs:

Study Abroad:

Medicine:

Programs for Female Students:

Minority Programs:

Humanities:

Chapter 2

Undergraduate School

You can't go to heaven if you die dumb.
— Admiral H.G. Rickover

This chapter describes a common sense approach to choosing a college or university. It doesn't present the only method of selecting a school, but covers many of the key considerations that go into making a solid decision about postsecondary education. With these factors in mind, you will be able to decide in a careful and intelligent manner where to apply and which school you will eventually attend.

Much of the advice in the previous chapter about applying for scholarships and fellowships also holds true for applying to undergraduate schools.

Know Yourself

Money is frequently the first thing students and their families think about when they consider colleges. Financial obligations are certainly important issues, but college costs should not play such a primary role in the initial selection process. Don't rule out any school ahead of time because of the costs. Let's not put the buggy before the horse.

You are going to college to get an education. You need to decide what you want to be and then determine where you can go in order to achieve your goals. Only after you've thought about your needs should you weigh your options according to cost. Even then, costs need not constrain your choices. As we will discuss in Chapter 4, a school's tuition has little to do with whether you can afford to attend that school. A hasty decision to limit your alternatives based on price could cause you to overlook some of the best opportunities.

A careful evaluation of "Who I am" is the key to assessing the right school. Before jumping into the fray of the application process, make a list of what you think you want to accomplish during your university studies. In other words, what environment will be the most conducive to assisting you to successfully complete your undergraduate and graduate studies?

If you aren't sure about what you want to do, talk to your guidance counselor about career choices. Taking a vocational test can help you identify your strengths and weaknesses and will suggest a career path that you'll find interesting and satisfying. The best career is in a field you like — if you enjoy the work, are intellectually stimulated, and they pay you well, what more could you ask for? For information on career opportunities in specific fields, see the listing that begins on page 276. You should also ask people you know if they know anyone who works in the field that interests you and visit that person. Similarly, if you're interested in medicine, you should try volunteering at a local hospital. You may discover that your favorite career doesn't match your expectations.

Peer influence among classmates is common. You will have your eye on many of the same institutions as your friends and competitors, especially when you are planning similar careers. Often these schools are pretty good places to begin your evaluation. A word of caution is in order here, however. Do not give short shrift to the many very fine but less popular schools, just because you didn't take the time to do a thorough assessment of professors and departments. Don't go to a school just because your friends (or girlfriend or boyfriend) plan to attend it.[1] A school which is excellent in your friend's favorite field may not be as good in your chosen career.

Don't limit your search to one school based on its strength in a particular department, a professor you admire and respect,[2] or any other single factor. Your interests may change as you encounter subjects you hadn't even heard of while in high school. Leave yourself room in which to grow and change.

Criteria to Consider

This section analyzes several aspects of a college or university which you should consider in deciding what school is best for you.

Academics

Get a copy of the catalog from each school and read it carefully. If possible, get a description of the typical path taken by majors in the department that interests you. Concentrate on the core courses and any auxiliary courses related to your major. When core prerequisites have been successfully completed in your major, breadth and depth in other related departments become crucial. A successful career is contingent on the interplay of both scientific and humanistic coursework, so good science and mathematics students should look beyond the upper division courses of a scientific or mathematical bent to select several good electives in the humanities. Although an economics course is certainly worth taking, your program should also include humanities subjects of a nontechnical nature.

---

[1] You're not going to school to get married — get your priorities straight. If your friendship isn't strong enough to survive a long-distance relationship, it isn't worth staying nearby to preserve it. People change in new environments, so there is a good chance you'll make new friends in college.

[2] Note: On a graduate level, basing your choice of school on a single professor can be a valid criterion, assuming that he/she has tenure and will be your advisor. But even faculty with tenure can decide to leave for a better opportunity elsewhere, or you may develop a personality conflict with your advisor. So it is always best to select a school that has several people with research interests you like.

Above all else, in college you will learn how to reason, communicate, and learn. Writing and thinking skills are developed in different ways by the sciences and the humanities; you need a bit of both. By experiencing the different kinds of approaches to seeking solutions to problems, you will become prepared for a diverse spectrum of challenges later in life. No matter what your field, see to it that you learn basic computer skills, including word processing and elementary computer programming, some quantitative analysis methods (e.g., statistics), and oral and written communication skills.

Faculty

How many tenured professors are associated with the department of your particular major? How many untenured or part time? What courses do they teach? Are there any Nobel Laureates, Field's medalists, or other "gurus" in the department? If they teach, do they teach only advanced subjects, or also introductory classes? How much attention is given to teaching ability in the tenure-granting process?[3] Are undergraduates assigned to different faculty as advisees, or is one professor responsible for advising all the students?

Do professors or graduate teaching assistants (TAs) teach most courses? What is the student/instructor ratio in the major courses? How many graduate students are in your department? Which undergraduate schools did the graduate students attend? How many research assistants (RAs) are assigned to each professor? How many TA positions are there? Does your department collaborate with other departments at the university and with the corporate and governmental research communities? Do the faculty have joint appointments in other departments?

Students

Ask questions of students enrolled in your proposed major. How much mentoring and advice are they offered? Learn how many female faculty and RAs are in your department, particularly if you are a female or underrepresented minority graduate student in mathematics or the physical sciences. Mentoring alleviates loneliness, and the comradery is of nurturing significance. It should not be an overriding consideration, but the lack of a female or underrepresented minority mentor in your graduate department or in your upper level classes can impede your progress, especially if you are not comfortable working in a competitive atmosphere. Just having someone to talk to occasionally can help a lot.

Social Atmosphere

What social activities are available to promote friendships among students with similar interests? Can you participate in intramural and extramural sports, music, art, dance, and

---

[3]Research universities often place higher priority on research ability than on teaching skills, and small liberals arts colleges the reverse. But at a research university teaching can benefit from faculty research, and if you want to participate in research as an undergraduate, you're more likely to find opportunities at a research university.

hobbies? Extracurricular activities like these can help clear out the cobwebs during the sometimes grueling and intense loads of coursework. When you're nearing the breaking point, a good game of rugby or ultimate frisbee can help you release some steam and relieve your frustration, or at least burn off some of the freshman fifteen. Do you think you'd like fraternity or sorority living? Does the campus have a reputation of being heavily Greek or Preppie? In what kind of atmosphere will you best thrive?

Curriculum Beyond the Major

The core requirements for a particular major in mathematics or science do not differ very much from school to school. However, the breadth and depth of what is available beyond the core courses can vary considerably. What electives are suggested by the departmental advisors, and how many are permitted/required for graduation? How many semester hours or units are required for your major? Is the degree considered a traditional one — one that requires expository writing and a foreign language — and hence in all likelihood more difficult and classical? If you are an underrepresented minority, is there an unacceptable attrition rate among minorities in your particular major?

Weather

Some people profess that weather does have a psychological impact on studying performance. Students and many adults simply do not study as well in a setting of sub-zero weather conditions. Birds chirping, squirrels frolicking on a green lawn, beautiful flowering plants, and a gorgeous panorama are, for many, most conducive conditions for a healthy attitude. Indeed, California does offer much of this setting, but your choice of a school should not set too high a priority on sun and fun. Cold weather does have its compensations, such as snow skiing, ice skating, sledding and snowball fights. Nevertheless, if you suffer from allergies or hay fever, you should definitely find out what the pollen count index is for the location near the school. Rand McNally's *Places Rated Almanac* is a good source of general information about the surrounding neighborhood.

Campus Visits

Visiting the campuses is probably the most important method you can use to help decide where to apply and where to matriculate. Don't buy blind.

Visit several colleges and universities during your junior year in high school, if at all possible. You will get a much more realistic impression of the campus if you visit during the academic year. During the summer most regular undergraduate students and many graduate students are away on vacation or working. For example, Columbia University is deserted during the summer. Classes also aren't in session, or if there are any classes, many times they aren't comparable to those taught during the school year. The grass looks greener, the classrooms have been recently painted, and there's no snow on the ground. If you must visit during the summer, realize that you may be getting a distorted picture of the campus.

When you visit the campus, try to leave your parents behind. You'll be attending the school, not them. If your parents do tag along, you may feel inhibited from asking the questions you'd ask if they were absent. On the other hand, they may ask questions you'd never think to ask. So there are some benefits to taking your parents with you when you go. But you need to start learning to stand on your own sometime, and the college transition is a good place to start. If your parents insist on seeing the campus before they pay a shilling, we'd suggest exploring the campus separately. Tell them that this will let you cover twice as much ground, if they need convincing.

During your visit, you should:

- ☐ Take a campus tour.
- ☐ Talk with students.
- ☐ Drop by the student union, library, admissions office, and financial aid office.
- ☐ Sit in on classes.
- ☐ Wander downtown to see what's nearby, in terms of restaurants, entertainment, shopping, and other things of potential interest to you.
- ☐ If the students have written a guidebook to the school and the downtown area, buy a copy to read later.
- ☐ Eat a meal in the cafeteria and at a nearby restaurant.
- ☐ Stay overnight in the dorm with a student. (The admissions office can help arrange this for you.)
- ☐ Make an appointment to see a professor in your field.
- ☐ If you're interested in athletics, meet with a coach.
- ☐ Explore the campus on your own.

As soon as you return home, record your observations and impressions for future reference. Memories will fade and blur rapidly, especially if you visit many schools in rapid succession.

Don't be shy in asking questions of students — stop them in the corridors or sit with them in the cafeteria, if you can't think of a better way. Talk to at least two students, to get a somewhat balanced picture. Ask them about courses, professors, and things that are important to you. Admissions officers and staff may not be as forthcoming during a meeting or on a scheduled campus tour. If a student loves or hates the school, they'll give you their opinion, at length. Students from underrepresented populations should be particularly keen to ask questions during college and university visits.

Solicit Everybody's Opinion

If it is not financially feasible for you to visit several colleges and universities, it certainly is possible to locate several alumni/ae and graduate students within your community who attended the school as undergraduates. Track them down and milk them for all the information and impressions they've got. Use the alumni interview to ask questions. Ask your guidance counselor, your parents, your relatives, the admissions representatives, and current students for their opinions. You'll get a lot of input, but ultimately you have to make a decision you'll be happy with.

Several schools host receptions where alumni and alumnae meet with candidates applying to their alma maters. Sometimes these involve an interview as part of the admissions process. These information receptions are not usually crucial to admission, but you should make an effort to put your best foot forward. Consider them a chance to practice for the real interview. Dress appropriately. Do not stand or sit in a corner at the reception as lively as a bump on a pickle, even if the soirée is very boring. Use the reception as an opportunity to add to your stock of information about the school.

Books to Read

Two particularly good books about choosing a college are Edward B. Fiske's *Selective Guide to Colleges* (previously published as the *New York Times Selective Guide to Colleges*), Times Books, New York, 1988, and *Lisa Birnbach's College Book*, Ballantine Books, New York, 1984. Both books are updated periodically, so more recent editions are almost certainly available. They are quite entertaining to read. Fiske has also written with Joseph Michalak *The Best Buys in College Education*, Times Books, New York, 1987.

The Application Process

Getting into the college of his or her choice is the dream of every college-bound senior. You can help your chances by being realistic in your evaluation of yourself and by carefully completing the application process.

Before the Senior Year

If you start thinking about your future before your senior year is upon you, you can optimize your chances through careful advance planning.

When you enter high school, begin thinking about college or university possibilities. Participate in a consistent pattern of extracurricular activities and leadership roles, establish good rapport with your teachers and guidance counselors, and enroll in a solid set of courses. Take academic competitions and contests (see Chapter 7) and practice on copies of the exams from previous years. During the summer, participate in enrichment programs such as the CEE's Research Science Institute, the Duke University Talent Identification Program, the Hampshire College Summer Studies in Mathematics, or Ohio State University's Arnold Ross Young Scholars Program.

Exercise your weaknesses and build your strengths. For example, if you have a poor vocabulary, try learning and using a new word each day. By working over a long period of time, instead of cramming for exams, the new vocabulary will become a part of you and you will learn to unconsciously use it correctly. Likewise, if you're weak in math, practice some math problems every day.

When deciding what classes to take, enroll in as many advanced chemistry, physics, biology, mathematics, and computer science courses as your high school offers. You should also take four years of English, because good communication skills are important to the budding scientist. One or two foreign languages will also be useful.

Similarly, when you're in college, if you intend to go to graduate school, you should think about graduate school when selecting your courses or even which school to attend. Your chances of being admitted to a good graduate school might be better served by doing well at a low-ranked school than mediocre at a school with a higher ranking. Participating in research as an undergraduate can help you get into graduate school.

A timetable for the application process during your senior year appears in Figure 2.1.

AUGUST	SEPTEMBER	OCTOBER
☐ Develop an initial list of colleges and scholarship programs. ☐ Write away for current application materials and catalogs. ☐ Write up a résumé of your accomplishments.	☐ Plan out the rest of your senior year. ☐ Ask teachers to write recommendations, if you haven't already. ☐ Meet with your guidance counselor. ☐ Register for the October ACT test dates, if appropriate.	☐ Register for the November and/or December SAT and Achievement test dates. ☐ Start writing your essays. ☐ Visit colleges. ☐ Take the SAT or ACT test.

NOVEMBER	DECEMBER	JANUARY
☐ Register for the December ACT test date, if applicable. ☐ Take the SAT or ACT test. ☐ Finish writing your essays. ☐ Submit early action applications (by November 15). ☐ Check that your recommendations have been written and mailed.	☐ Take the SAT or ACT test. ☐ You should hear from colleges about early action around December 15. ☐ Mail your regular applications, if necessary. ☐ Start filling out a FAF, but do not mail it before January 1.	☐ All applications should have been submitted by now. ☐ Communicate any new information (e.g., honors and awards) to the schools. ☐ Consider taking AP (Advanced Placement) classes in the spring.

FEBRUARY/MARCH: THE BIG WAIT		
APRIL	**MAY**	**JUNE**
☐ You should hear from schools about regular admissions by April 15. ☐ Review the financial aid packages. ☐ Decide which school to attend. ☐ If you are wait-listed at a school you want to attend, write to the admissions office.	☐ Notify the school you chose that you've decided to attend. Write letters to the other schools declining their offers. ☐ Tell your guidance counselor of your decision and write thank you letters to everybody who helped you, especially the teachers who wrote letters of recommendation. ☐ Take AP exams.	☐ Get a summer job. ☐ Relax.

Figure 2.1: College Application Calendar

Setting Realistic Goals

Burns wrote that "A man's grasp must exceed his reach or *ah*, what's a heaven for," but poetry has never been grounded entirely in reality. You should be brutally frank with yourself about your preparation and capacity for successfully completing a particular course of study at the college or university you wish to enter. If you have not taken adequate courses in high school to pursue a science or mathematics curriculum, have below average SAT scores or mediocre scores on other quantitative indicators, and have demonstrated only run-of-the-mill high school ability, then you are probably not a likely candidate to graduate in the mathematical, physical, or biological sciences at a school such as MIT or Harvard. The most important criteria to completing your degree is to look for an institution where you have a high probability of successfully completing the course work. If you covet an undergraduate degree in physics from Princeton, then you should realize that Princeton's undergraduates in physics have usually excelled on the Advanced Placement (AP) tests in physics. If you haven't been a very strong physics student in high school, it shouldn't be surprising that you'll have to struggle to succeed in physics at Princeton. On other hand, if you work very hard, you can make up for a somewhat deficient background.

A high grade point average or excellent scores on any one quantitative indicator does not by itself assure admission to a school. Your complete record, including SAT and achievement scores, consistent improvement and high academic achievement in challenging courses over a four year period, school and community activities, leadership positions, awards and honors, and, increasingly, high scores on AP exams — if AP exams are available in your high school — is used to assess your candidacy for admission. The essay submitted with your application is also given weight if one is required. Your application folder should demonstrate how you'll contribute to the campus community, whether through talent, uniqueness, or other factors.

But no matter how good your record, there is always an element of luck in any admission decision. Even the best students are sometimes rejected by some of the top schools. Despite what anybody may tell you, you don't have an 'in'. It is not unheard of for a student to be rejected by a school he or she considered an easy mark and be accepted by a reaching school.

The schools you want to attend and the schools that will accept you are two different sets. If you're lucky, these sets will overlap. You can never be sure that they will, so you should classify schools into three lists:

- *Reaching Schools.* These schools are so selective that your chances of being admitted are slim, but if they did accept you, you'd go on a moment's notice.
- *Possible Schools.* You like these schools and think you will probably get in.
- *Safety Schools.* You are absolutely certain you can get into these schools, and if they were your only option, you wouldn't mind attending. Another criterion for placing a school in the safety category is the likelihood that you'll get a merit scholarship from the school to entice you to attend.[4]

Be realistic in the range of schools you apply to. If you apply only to reaches, you might not get in to any. If you apply only to safeties, you'll get in, but you might not be as happy as you would be had you applied to a few reaches or at least a possible. Balance in your selection is the key. You should narrow your choice to about two schools in

---

[4]Schools like Washington University, Rice, Purdue, and Emory are very good. You may get a better financial deal and a better education from one of them than you would from an Ivy League school.

each category. Unlike applications to medical or law school, you only need to submit applications to five or six schools.

Early Action and Early Decision

An *early action* application has an earlier deadline, but also has an earlier notification date. If you are accepted, you can still apply to other schools. An *early decision* application is similar, but includes a contractual obligation to attend the school if they admit you in the early group. Don't confuse the two.

It is important to carefully consider whether you should apply for early action or early decision to a school. If you are accepted early, you can save a considerable sum of money on application fees. At some institutions, early applications sometimes seem to fare better than applications submitted during the regular deadlines. If you are an excellent student, you should definitely apply early action to a school. On the other hand, an early decision application commits you into attending a particular school, before you have a chance to examine the aid package. This precludes acceptance at other schools, where the financial aid packages might be better. However, some schools will allow you to back out of an early decision application after the fact if the financial aid package poses a serious problem, and will send you an estimate of your aid package before you must commit. Other early decision schools, like CalTech, will allow you to accept or reject their offer by mid-January, instead of committing you when you submit the early decision application. It behooves you to check on this particular policy before submitting an early decision application. You should only apply early decision if you are really, really sure, and then you should think twice before mailing in the application. When the admissions letters start rolling in, you may find yourself wanting to change your mind. Another drawback to early applications is the requirement to complete your admissions folder sooner.

One possible strategy is to apply early action to the "best" of your "possible" schools — a school you like and which will probably admit you, but not number one on your list. This ensures that you'll get in to at least one school, eliminating the need to apply to any safety schools and saving you all those application fees. If you apply early to one of your reaching schools, you may not get in, forcing you to also apply to safety schools. On the other hand, if you apply to your top choice and get in, you don't need to apply to any other schools. Which strategy you use depends on your personal preferences and a realistic assessment of your chances of being admitted early to your favorite school. But whatever you do, you shouldn't assume you'll be admitted early — even the strongest candidates are sometimes deferred to the regular admissions pool — so you should prepare your other applications in case you need them.

It may be possible to apply early action to more than one school. But some of the schools want you to apply to only one school early, whether or not they have any way of enforcing the restriction. For example, the Ivy League schools — Brown, Cornell, Dartmouth, Harvard, Princeton, and Yale — each request that you apply early to at most one school. Other schools have similar policies. MIT and the University of Chicago, however, have no such restriction, and do not exchange early admission candidate lists with the Ivies. So you could apply early to MIT and the University of Chicago in addition to an Ivy league school (with the exception of Dartmouth and Cornell, which are early decision). It is important to check the guidelines of each university. Some allow you to submit early applications to multiple schools, and some don't.

Special Admission Categories

Having a family member as an alumnus/a of the college or university may give you a slight advantage in the admissions process. At the very least, they'll look twice before rejecting you. But do not ask friends or family for a recommendation to the school just because they happen to be alumni/ae. Vacuous letters from alumni/ae don't help your chances of admission, and serve only to annoy the school's admissions staff.

Are you an all-American athlete? Are you a concert musician? Are you a member of an underrepresented minority? Do not be ashamed or embarrassed to use your special strengths to your advantage.

Recommendation Letters

Most schools are looking for a recommendation from a teacher who knows of your academic performance, or one with whom you have worked in an extracurricular activity. If you plan an engineering career, it isn't absolutely necessary to have a science or math teacher write a recommendation, but certainly that will be preferable to a Spanish teacher's recommendation based on a single course taken during your freshman or sophomore year of high school. Your recommenders are people who know of your exemplary capabilities and special personal qualities and who will be excited to share this information.

If you've taken courses at a local university, consider asking one of your professors to write you a recommendation. Such letters can be noteworthy, especially if you are applying to the same school and the professor is well known and respected. But you should only ask for a letter if the professor really knows you and can compare you with undergraduate students who took the same class. However, it may not necessarily be wise to substitute a letter from a professor for a letter from a high school teacher who has known you for several years. This is one of the few circumstances in which submitting an "extra" letter of recommendation might be warranted.

It is regrettable that many magnet schools assign a student to just one guidance counselor who is responsible for the student throughout his or her four years of study. Perhaps this system is easier to administer; however, it isn't in the student's best interest if the guidance counselor has little contact with the student, or the relationship goes sour. A student/counselor relationship should not be fixed from entrance into high school unless it is the mutual decision of the student and counselor.

Learn from your peers and the upperclassmen which teachers write good recommendations in a timely fashion. Recommendations from a teacher or school which arrive late or are written in a shoddy manner (or both) can cause damage to an admissions folder. This happens more often than one would think. A teacher may be a fine and grand person in class, but it doesn't follow that he or she is reliable or can write well. A good recommendation expresses your strengths and gives examples. If a weakness is mentioned, it is included to explain and minimize it, or better yet, to characterize it as a strength, in order to reduce the deleterious effects it might have on your application.

Think about asking particular teachers to write recommendations prior to the first semester of your senior year, even if you will take a course with them during your senior year. This lets them avoid the peak recommendation-writing period, spend more time writing it, and collect better examples to include. It is best for them to write the letter when you're fresh in their minds. They can always revise it later, when you need it for your application.

When you ask a teacher to write you a letter of recommendation, ask him or her if the letter will be a good one. Most teachers will be frank with you about the kind of letter they'll write. If it won't be a good one, they'll suggest that you ask somebody else.

Always waive your rights to read the letter under the Buckley Amendment. A teacher will be less open in a letter if you don't waive your rights, and admissions staff may not consider such an endorsement as seriously as a fully confidential one.

Don't solicit letters from people who have little knowledge of you. A stack of recommendations from influential people with impressive letterheads can be thought of as "overkill" as much as pressure from overzealous parents. But, because the teachers you select may not know everything about you, you should prepare a short summary of your accomplishments and give it to them with the reference forms and the stamped, addressed envelope. Teachers are also sometimes forgetful, so the summary can help remind them of your better attributes. See page 6 for advice on compiling a résumé of your accomplishments.

The Essay

An essay is normally required as part of the application. Readers are not looking for a particular topic for discussion in your essay, or a particular kind of essay. They want to see evidence of your ability to write clear, concise, cogent sentences that show a flow of information which expresses an idea. Indirectly, this lets them get to know you better. Although good essays often have a "hook" or a fresh angle, there aren't any magic ingredients you can add to a bad essay to spice it up into a good essay.

Satire and comedy are difficult to execute successfully in the few paragraphs allowed. You can fall flat on your face in attempting to write in a new and unique and different style of writing. Don't do this just to get the attention of the person reading your folder. You'll get their attention, but in a negative way. For similar reasons, avoid controversial topics, such as religion and politics. You want your essay to be catchy but appropriate.

The best essay is one which is written about something familiar to you. The essay should be yours and not that of your friend, your relative, or your parents. It should not be edited to the point where the heart has been gutted out. Be a little daring, but not too daring. Write about what you find interesting; if you find a topic interesting, you can probably write well about it. If you make claims about yourself, substantiate them with specific evidence from your personal history.

Try to tell a story in your essay. Grab the reader's attention in your opening paragraph, and sustain their interest throughout the remainder of the essay. Try to avoid trite topics. Admissions officers must read hundreds of essays each year. An articulate story that is lively and fresh will make your application much more memorable than a tired cliché.

Weigh each word and idea carefully, selecting only those items that contribute to the meaning of the essay as a whole. Consider what you want to say, how you want to say it, and why you want to say it. Make your key points clearly and progress smoothly from one to the next.

If the essay is supposed to answer a question, review your essay to verify that it addresses the question. Likewise if the application asks you to write on a particular topic. You can occasionally get away with subverting the topic or question, but only if it seems natural in your particular case and the resulting essay is well-executed. Don't ignore the topic just because you dislike it.

One of several good books on writing the application essays is Boykin Curry and Brian Kasbar's *Essays That Worked: 50 Essays from Successful Applications to the Nation's Top Colleges*, 1986, 144 pages, published by Mustang Publishing, New Haven, and distributed by Kampmann and Company, New York. Other similar books can be found in your local bookstore or library. They discuss what makes an essay good or bad, and give examples from actual college essays. Do not mimic any of the examples; admissions officers won't be fooled. Instead, learn what makes the examples work, so you'll be able to recognize the same qualities when they occur in your own compositions. Trying too hard to follow the advice in this and similar books can hurt an application. Don't try to do things or be someone you aren't. Write as you really are, not some idealized version of yourself. If you find yourself continually looking in a book as you write your essay, you are making a mistake.

Proofread what you write. Correct any spelling or grammatical errors. To check the flow of the essay, let it sit for a day, then read it aloud into a tape recorder. If it sounds awkward when you listen to it, try reworking the text. Have somebody else look at what you've written.

Do not submit more than the number of essays required. It is unnecessary and highly counterproductive.

The Interview

Before your interview, think about your goals, feelings, and opinions. You should be able to talk about them without bumbling about. Conducting practice interviews with your parents or friends as "interviewers" can help you improve your communication skills and put you at ease when talking about yourself.

Whatever you do at the interview, don't spew garbage about topics you know nothing about. Read current newspapers before you go and watch a TV news show. (In fact, it is worth reading the paper every day anyway, because it builds your vocabulary and keeps you in touch with the rest of the world.) Be honest. Relax.

Use the interview as an opportunity to ask any questions you may have. You do have questions — think them out in advance so you can be prepared for the interview.

Completing Your Application Folder

Your admission file and its completeness is your responsibility. Pay careful attention to those whom you have asked to write letters of recommendation. The sooner you ask someone you trust to write a recommendation, the less stress you'll have later. Provide everybody with a stamped, addressed envelope, and give them as much time as possible, to minimize any excuses for failing to send it in on time. More and more staff cuts are being made in high schools, and a low priority seems to prevail for maintaining good guidance counseling departments. So it is incumbent on you to follow through on your application and check that your recommendations, your principal's letter, and your transcripts have been mailed. If you suspect your recommendations haven't been mailed (or written!) gently remind the teacher or guidance counselor of the approaching deadline.

Most schools will send you a postcard to acknowledge receipt of your application and to let you know when your application folder is complete. If the school doesn't provide postcards for this purpose, enclose a self-addressed stamped postcard with a simple checklist written on the back, such as the following:

☐ Your application folder is now complete.
☐ Your application folder is incomplete. Please submit the following missing materials:

    ☐ Recommendations from _____
    ☐ High School Transcripts
    ☐ SAT scores
    ☐ Achievement scores
    ☐ Other _____

Signed: _____ Date: _____

If you're worried about the possibility of your application being lost in the mail, send it by certified or registered mail, return receipt requested. You'll get back a postcard from the post office, with the signature of the person who received your application. Do not telephone the school to check on your application folder; the records staff is busy enough without also having to answer thousands of telephone calls from nervous students and their parents. Professional schools, however, sometimes expect you to telephone them about the status of your file.

General

The guidelines for admission to a particular institution are based on criteria which over the years seem to work. The process is constantly being refined, as it should be. The obligation of the selection committee is to choose students who will be successful at their school. Quite simply, the committee represents the university, whose goals are to enlighten and to educate; more broadly, its existence is philosophically bound to what it believes is best for nurturing civilization.

Only in the most unusual circumstances should you apply to a college or university after having completed only three years of high school, and only with an expert consultation or two.[5] This shouldn't discourage you from taking college or university courses during your junior and senior years of high school.

The Long Wait

After your applications have been completed and mailed, you will experience a "Taste of Hell." This experience is more often than not also shared by your parents and loved ones, especially if you are the first child of college age. The waiting period before learning about acceptances and rejections is very stressful. Students should understand that a parent is often reliving a dream of postsecondary educational opportunities which they were perhaps precluded from experiencing themselves. Conversely, parents should understand the difficulty of this time for their child. With your college applications you begin a "rite of passage" which continues through the process of applying for important scholarships, admission to graduate or professional school, academic honors, and your first job. Your stress should only be exacerbated if you hadn't conducted a thorough search for materials or failed to synthesize the information to make the best decision.

The waiting is difficult, but perhaps these hints can help you deal with the stress. Activities of a relaxing and enjoyable nature should be taken seriously during the ensuing months. A good sporting match and reading several good books can help with the pressure. If you keep yourself busy, you won't have time to worry. And you should talk about your concerns with your parents and loved ones, so that they do not dwell on the topic of your possible admission or rejection every evening at the dinner table. There is nothing you can do to change your chances after your folder is complete, so it is best to get your mind off the matter until you have to make a decision.

Notification

When the mail arrives, don't despair if you get a thin letter. It isn't necessarily bad news. Open and read the letter — don't assume. Some schools send a regular letter to tell you of your acceptance and to let you know that a bigger packet of material will be arriving later. (Many graduate schools, on the other hand, will send the admissions packet by Federal Express or Express Mail.)

Rejection and Wait Listing

A proper realistic perspective about yourself is important for successfully getting through the application process with a minimum of stress. Being wait-listed is quite possible at the best college or university for your field of study. Rejections can happen. But maintaining the proper mental attitude will not allow for protracted disappointment or defeat.

---

[5]One good source for making such a determination is Dr. Julian Stanley or Dr. Linda Brody at the Study of Mathematically Precocious Youth (SMPY) at Johns Hopkins University. Other guidance is available through university Talent Search programs where precocious younger students are identified and encouraged to take college courses for credit.

There is a difference between disappointment and shame. Disappointments will be forthcoming for any achiever or one who inspires to be a leader. Shame should not play a part in this equation because it implies that the job of selecting a school that is best for you wasn't completed in the serious manner it merited. The shame of being rejected should be a very temporary feeling. If your record of behavior as a person and your academic performance have been exemplary, then any shame is ill placed. The application process, if done properly, is a cooperative one among those who care about you — parents, relatives, friends, and teachers.

If you are wait-listed after applying for early admission, reflect on the possible reasons for that decision, so you can improve the applications due around January for regular admission. The school of your choice assuredly received many other worthy applications for admission. Difficult choices were made. It is not uncommon for a student to say "I was stronger than John Smith who got in." What you are saying is that you think you were better based on some criteria than John Smith was. But you haven't seen his folder, so the admissions staff has considered variables in a composite of which you have no direct knowledge.

If you are wait-listed at your favorite school, you should call, visit, or write the school's admissions office. Tell them that you would definitely enroll if admitted, and ask what you can do to improve your chances. Let them know about any recent accomplishments (contests won, improved academic performance, etc.) which might influence their final decision.

There is not just one school which is for you. The old and worn statement about everything happening for the best may not be true, but it can be comforting at times. It's pretty good advice to take to heart if you're rejected outright. Rather than emote in a state of abrasiveness, pain and despair, let optimism prevail because you will get into one of your selected schools. A rejection is not the end of the world, and it isn't an evaluation of your worth as a human being. It is rather the time to assess the alternatives of the other schools to which you applied. You should be admitted to more than one school if you applied to a realistic and balanced selection of schools.

College admissions officers perform a difficult job. No one would say that they do not make mistakes. But they take every student's application seriously. When you telephone their offices, keep in mind that they are under a lot of pressure and that courtesy doesn't alway prevail under these conditions. It isn't easy to tell a parent — or a student — that they've been rejected.

Wherever you wind up, even if it is a safety school, if you are motivated enough you can turn even the worst of circumstances into a success.

Choices, Choices

When the acceptance letters arrive, deciding which school to attend can be a pleasant but excruciating experience. You should make your decision after consultation with a trusted high school counselor, a teacher whom you selected to write you letters of recommendation, your parents, and your peers who are in the same dilemma. But the decision about which institution to attend should be made selfishly. It is your life, not that of your friends or loved ones. Your future success is at stake, not theirs.

It is the fine distinctions which you have made in your research that will determine your choice between the schools where you are accepted. At this point, money should be considered if you find you like two or more schools equally, particularly if one has offered you a fine scholarship. No school should be chosen just for scholarship money unless the stress factor makes it impossible to cope with long-term debt. The question you should ask yourself is, "Where will I best succeed with a quality of life acceptable to me?"

If you still can't decide between two equally good schools, use idiosyncratic criteria to make a decision. Or flip a coin. It won't matter much in the long run.

Once you have made your decision, thank those who helped you in the process. Notes of gratitude are appreciated and should not be overlooked. Of course, take the time to humbly and happily pat yourself on the shoulder for a job well done. A pleasant decision may also be yours to consider — whether to accept advanced standing. But then at this point, it is best to concentrate on getting a summer job and making plans for earning your school "fun money."

Money Matters

Only after an analysis of the college or university atmosphere best suited for you, should financial considerations come to the fore. This book is meant to assist you in your search for financial aid and scholarships to alleviate the financial burden of acquiring a good education. There are also many helpful guides available from the U.S. government and other organizations for determining how one can pay for a college degree. We have listed many of them in the bibliography, pages 301–312. As we explain in Chapter 4, a price tag of $20,000 or more doesn't put the best schools beyond your reach. There are many creative and innovative ways to meet the financial obligations associated with attending the school of your choice.

A school isn't going to admit you and not try its hardest to help you overcome the obstacles that stand in the way of your matriculating. Financial aid officers are always willing to meet with you to discuss your financial situation.

Chapter 3

Graduate School

This chapter discusses life as a graduate student and the process of selecting graduate schools and completing an application to graduate school.

Is Graduate School for You?

A master's degree generally takes from one to three years to complete, and focuses on the practical application of knowledge and skills. In some sense it is a professional degree. A Ph.D. takes about four to six years or more, depending on the program and field, and signifies an ability to do original research. In most cases a Ph.D. is required for university teaching and research positions.

Graduate study for a doctorate typically has two main components, the qualifying examinations and the dissertation. Qualifiers are taken after one or two years of classes and typically focus on basic theoretical issues. They may be a combination of written and oral exams, depending on the particular requirements of the school. Some schools will also require the publication and presentation of a research paper. The final hurdle of a Ph.D. is the dissertation, which should make a substantial contribution to scientific knowledge. Before you start on your dissertation work, most schools require you to present a formal thesis proposal, in which you describe the research you intend to do and argue that it is both a worthwhile topic and a doable one. Your thesis proposal is then approved by a committee of faculty headed by your thesis advisor. When your research is completed, you present it in written form as a thesis and orally as a thesis defense.

Conducting research and writing a doctoral thesis are serious undertakings. They require a lot of ability and an even greater amount of sweat. You'll need a strong work ethic to survive as a graduate student. Receiving a Ph.D. is evidence that you've survived a roller coaster of intellectual, emotional, and social upheavals. Such an adventure isn't to be taken lightly. But the rewards of completing graduate research can be tremendous, both personally and financially. You will treasure your memories of the doctoral experience for the rest of your life.

Choosing a Graduate School

Before you start looking for a graduate school, you should have a fairly good idea of the kind of work you want to pursue. If you don't know what you want to study, graduate school may not be the right thing for you. You should at least know the general area in which you want to study and have some idea of the subtopics that interest you. Don't apply to graduate school just because you want to continue avoiding the real world.

If you aren't sure whether you want to pursue a Ph.D., consider enrolling in a master's program instead. Master's programs will give you practical advanced training in your field and expose you to some research in your area. Some schools require a master's degree from students before they allow them to enroll in a Ph.D. program. (Other schools give out master's degrees as "consolation prizes" to students who decide to leave the program after passing appropriate requirements, such as qualifying exams.)

Even though there are several rankings of graduate schools available, none of them ranks the schools by subfield. As a result, such rankings are useless for making an informed choice. A school may have received a good score for your general area of study, but if no faculty are working in the particular field that interests you, going there would probably be a waste of your time. Schools differ greatly in their strengths and weaknesses.[1]

Talk to faculty at your undergraduate school. They can tell you who's working in your area and where and which schools have a good concentration of people with interests similar to yours. They can also tell you about the general atmosphere of the department and its perspective on your field. Ask them to help you make a realistic choice of graduate schools, given your abilities and interests. Graduate students in your department are another good source of information.

Avoid applying to your undergraduate school for graduate admissions. Going to a different school for your graduate education will give you the benefit of a second perspective on your field. Some departments avoid this kind of inbreeding by refusing to accept their own undergraduates. In other departments, your undergraduate advisor may have a strong say in whether you are admitted to graduate work in the department.

If you're familiar with the literature in your field, read some recent journal papers. Of the ones that interest you, see who did the work and at which school. Check the references and see where they did their work and where they are now.

Visit the schools and talk to graduate students and faculty.[2] Find out the number of full-time graduate students and the number of Ph.D. degrees granted each year. Compare the average incoming class size with the number who eventually receive the Ph.D. What is the average amount of time it takes to complete a Ph.D.? Do the Ph.D. recipients get jobs in academia or in industry? What fraction of the new Ph.D. recipients get jobs

---

[1] The accuracy of rankings like the Gourman Report and the U.S. News and World Report for graduate school is also questionable. The National Science Foundation published a report in which they evaluated the nation's graduate schools, grouping them into the best 25, the next 25, and so on. The schools in each group did not correlate well with the commercially available rankings. Moreover, all of the available rankings are limited to U.S. institutions, ignoring some of the excellent schools in Canada and England. Don't choose one school over another, just because it ranks 0.01 higher.

[2] After you are admitted, most of the top schools will invite you to visit. If the department has a lot of cash, they'll offer to pay all your travel expenses and wine and dine you when you visit.

immediately? How many of the new Ph.D. recipients are forced to get a postdoctoral appointment to support themselves while searching for an academic position?[3]

Is the curriculum highly structured with many requirements, or is it looser and more laid back? Are qualifiers used to kick students out of the program, or are they just to ensure that you have the requisite background knowledge? Do students compete with each other for the right to continue in the program? Does the department provide help in studying for the qualifying examinations, or are you on your own? What are the language proficiency requirements? Does the department provide you with a clearly written set of requirements and a written description of the Ph.D. program? Are students grandfathered under the requirements in effect at the time of matriculation? How onerous are the requirements?

Are faculty on a first name basis with the students, or is the atmosphere a bit stuffy? Are the faculty accessible? Are graduate students respected members of the community, or are they just faculty slaves? Are the secretaries nice and helpful, or are they difficult to work with? Are the students happy there? How many graduate students are crammed into an office? Are there quiet places to study on campus? Do graduate students have access to computing facilities? Do students have workstations on their desks, or must they use machines in a computer cluster? Does the department (or the university) have a good library in your field? How many graduate students are assigned to each faculty member? (If more than four or five, investigate further.) How often do advisors meet with their students? (Once a week is good.) What is the department's social life like? If you're female, are there any female faculty or is it an all-male department? Look around the campus — could you enjoy spending the next n years of your life there? Is the surrounding neighborhood urban or suburban? Do you want to be near a big city or the countryside? Is the weather agreeable with you? How many research contracts support the faculty, and for what duration are the contracts? How likely are they to be renewed? Is the funding situation in the department improving, staying steady, or dwindling?

How will you get financial support? Will it continue for the duration of your stay? Finances should not play a big role in your decision of which school to attend. It is often easy to get fellowships in the sciences for studies leading to a doctorate. (Master's degree candidates aren't as fortunate.) If you don't get a fellowship, you almost always can get a research assistantship (RA) or teaching assistantship (TA). Often an RA position will be in work unrelated to your thesis area, but sometimes it can lead to a thesis topic. How heavy a work load do TAs and RAs carry? If you will have to spend more than 20 hours a week doing work unrelated to your education program, such as teaching, think twice about accepting the offer. A high work load will interfere with the timely completion of your degree. Most graduate departments in the sciences will guarantee you funding for three to five years. In the humanities and other nontechnical fields, however, funding is much tighter. If you can get an outside fellowship or grant, your position will be more secure. Also, all departments offer incentives for you to bring in external fellowship support.

---

[3]In some fields a postdoctoral appointment is almost a requirement to get established. Postdoctoral students have the opportunity to develop a research program without distractions from teaching courses or chasing after grants.

Applying to Graduate School

When you apply to graduate schools, most schools ask you to write a "Statement of Purpose." This is an essay which says why you want to go to graduate school, what you want to study, why you chose your field, why you want to go to that particular school, and what you hope to do there. It doesn't hurt to mention what you would like to do after you finish graduate school.

Get a copy of the faculty research guide and see which topics are being investigated. If a professor seems like a perfect match, write to him or her for more information.

Of the components of a graduate school application, the statement of purpose is the most important, after faculty recommendations. Grades and standardized test scores (GREs) aren't as important, although you should have an overall high GPA (minimum of about 3.5 on a 4.0 scale) with strong grades in subjects related to your chosen field. You won't get into graduate school just on the basis of good grades and test scores.

Writing the Statement of Purpose

Graduate admissions committees are looking primarily for evidence of your ability to do research. If you've published any papers, include their citations in your statement and possibly attach their abstracts in an appendix. If you did some research with a faculty or at a job, be sure to have that professor or your supervisor write you a letter of recommendation.

In your essay, you must have a clearly focused area of interest. Specify a concrete area in which you might like to specialize and suggest some specific projects you might like to investigate. Say what interests you and why. There is nothing wrong with changing disciplines between undergraduate and graduate school. Why did you choose this field and not some other? Did you take some graduate classes on the topic? How did you originally become interested in this field? What have you learned since then? Don't be wishy-washy — if you have multiple areas of interest, pick one field or the other, or at least something in the intersection of the two fields. Don't worry if you don't really know what you want to do — the personal statement is not a contract and you can change your mind later. The purpose of the statement is to demonstrate that you're serious about the field and have some depth of interest.

Support your interest in the field by citing your previous work. Talk about any past research projects you've completed. If they are directly relevant to your field, include a one-page abstract in an appendix, or at least summarize them in a paragraph. Have you any relevant work experience (summer employment or volunteer activities)? Did you major in the field? If you didn't major in the field, do you have sufficient depth and breadth of background to pursue graduate studies in that area? Do you have any teaching experience? Do you have any awards in the area? If you've done significant work with any faculty in the field, list their names and describe what you did. (You almost certainly should solicit letters of recommendation from them.)[4] For your other

---

[4]Don't be afraid to include one or two extra letters of recommendation, if they all say significant and important things about you. But be careful not to include any vacuous or lukewarm letters which don't

recommendations, ask faculty from the area who have taught you recently.

Next, explain why you chose this particular department. If there is a particular faculty member there who you hope to work with, say so. Explain how your interests mesh with his or her interests. If that professor decides he or she wants you as his or her student, your chances of being accepted have skyrocketed. If there's a paper published by someone in the department (even a graduate student) that you find interesting, let them know about it. If your undergraduate professors recommended the department to you, say so and say why they recommended it to you. Why is this school a good choice for you? Why are you a good choice for this school?

Tell them why you want to go to graduate school in the first place. Support this by mentioning what you intend to do after graduate school. What are your long-term career goals? Are you planning on continuing on into academia? Or do you want to work in an industrial research laboratory? Why do you want to get a Ph.D.? Why is a Ph.D. necessary for what you want to do? (Remember, this isn't fixed, so you can change your mind after you get in.)

If there are any deficiencies in your background, explain them. If you did poorly in an important class, tell them why and what you did afterward to remedy the problem. Did you later take a more advanced class in the topic and do well in it? The admissions committee shouldn't get any surprises when they look at your grades and test scores.

Keep your statement of purpose short and concise, no more than about two pages. Whatever you do, don't ramble. Be honest and don't overstate your qualifications. Don't understate them either. Where possible, support general statements with specific examples. Try to make your essay and the application as a whole into a cohesive unit that explains why you're a good candidate for doctoral research in your area at this school.

It almost goes without saying, but you should proofread your application and correct any spelling, grammar, or punctuation errors. Read your statement aloud and rework any awkwardness in the presentation. When you read your statement, tape yourself, and listen to it. If it sounds monotonous, spend some more time on it to improve the writing style. Ask a friend to read what you've written and make suggestions for improvement. Graduate students at your school can critique your statement and offer good advice, since they've been through the process recently. Ask them if they're willing to let you look at their statements, so you can see an example of a successful essay.

For more hints on writing essays, see page 23 ("The Essay" section of Chapter 2).

For examples of personal statements, read *How to Write a Winning Personal Statement for Graduate and Professional School*, by Richard J. Stelzer, Peterson's Guides, Box 2123, Princeton, NJ 08543-2123, 1-800-EDU-DATA, 1989, 112 pages, $9.95. A similar book is Donald Asher's *Graduate Admissions Essays — What Works, What Doesn't, and Why*, Ten Speed Press, Box 7123, Berkeley, CA 94707, 1991, 131 pages. Stelzer's book includes interviews with admissions officers at the top graduate and professional schools. Asher's book is punctuated with reprints of relevant comic strips and discusses the process of soliciting (and writing) letters of recommendation. Both books cover business, medical and law school applications, in addition to graduate school applications.

---

contribute to your application. Letters from faculty are usually preferred to letters from employers, though there are exceptions to this rule.

Taking the GRE and Taking Time Off

Plan ahead before taking the Graduate Record Examination (GRE) to give yourself enough time to take it twice if necessary. Everybody has a bad day every now and then, so you may find yourself wanting to retake the exam. If you have to take both the general exam and a subject exam, try not to take them on the same day. Not every school requires a subject exam and some don't require the GREs at all, so be sure to read the application requirements carefully.

Take practice tests for several months before the exam; familiarity with the style of the GREs will make you more comfortable when you take the real thing. Practice tests can also improve the speed and accuracy with which you answer the questions. When you make a mistake on a practice test, identify the trap you fell into, so you can avoid it in the future. The Educational Testing Service (ETS) publishes copies of retired GRE general tests. Get a copy and practice with it under simulated test conditions; your score on it will be a good indicator of your score when you take the GRE for real. Even if you buy *How to Prepare for the Graduate Record Examination: GRE General Test*, by Samuel C. Brownstein, Mitchel Weiner and Sharon Weiner Green, Barrons, New York, 9th edition, 1990, 659 pages, and *GRE: Graduate Record Examination General Test*, by Thomas H. Martinson, 3rd edition, Prentice Hall, New York, 1990, 564 pages, you should still test yourself on one of the old GREs.

When you take the GRE, there are several simple strategies you can follow to improve your score.

- It *always* pays to guess. The GRE doesn't have a penalty for wrong answers, unlike the SAT, but even on the SAT it pays to guess. If you can eliminate some of the choices before you make a guess, the probability of your selecting the correct answer has increased. It is very hard to design a multiple choice question with four good wrong answers. Still, on the GRE even blind guessing can improve your score.
- Every time you move on to a new question, mentally distance yourself from the question. If you're prone to panic, taking a deep breath can help. Take a few seconds to think about the techniques one uses to solve the problem and identify any shortcut methods to test for wrong answers. Pick the quickest route to the correct answer. If you have time later, you can return to the question and check your answer using the other method. Remember, you don't need to derive the correct answer, just identify it. For example, if you know that the correct answer must be odd and four of the answers are even, you just identified the right answer with very little work.
- If you find that you're spending too much time on a question, skip it and come back to it later. Answer the easy questions first, before wasting your time on the hard questions. Both count equally to your score. Often, you'll find that the question seems simpler the second time you look at it.
- Try to be organized when you write in your test booklet. After you answer each question, mark it to identify the answer you chose and how you derived it. Cross off wrong answers and circle the correct answer. If you guessed or want to check your solution later, put a question mark in the margin next to the question or circle

the question number.

- Make sure that you fill in the circles in the correct row of your answer sheet, especially if you skipped a question. (Better yet, when you skip a question, fill in a random circle anyway.) Copy the answers from your test booklet to the answer sheet a page at a time instead of one by one. You'll have fewer copying errors this way and you won't be constantly looking back and forth from test booklet to answer key.

- Try to manage your time so that you have at least a quarter of your time left after attempting every question, to let you return to the questions you skipped or marked as uncertain. Use the last minute to double check that you copied your answers correctly to the answer sheet.

Get a good night's sleep before the exam and eat a wholesome breakfast.

For more advice on test-taking strategies, get Princeton Review's *Cracking the System: The GRE*, by Adam Robinson and John Katzman, Villard Books (Random House), 201 East 50th Street, New York, NY 10022, 1993, 338 pages, $16.00. This book discusses techniques for quickly selecting the correct answer for every kind of question that appears on the GRE general test.

Sometimes students aren't sure whether they want to go to graduate school, or need to take time off between their undergraduate and graduate careers to earn money to pay off their debts. Be sure to take the GREs before you leave, just in case you later decide to go to graduate school. It is very hard to get back into the mode of studying when you've been out of the classroom for a few years. Your knowledge of the specific areas covered by the subject exams will fade very quickly, so it is best to take the tests while your memory is fresh. GRE scores remain valid for five years from the examination date. Also, if you know you'll have to take some time off, it is better to take time off between undergraduate school and graduate school than after graduate school. Work experience between undergraduate and graduate school may even enhance the quality of your graduate work.

Choosing an Advisor

Choosing an advisor is one of the most important decisions you will make during your academic career. It is a key to your successfully completing the program and it affects your chances of getting a good job after you graduate. In addition, in many departments your funding comes from your advisor.

Your advisor is responsible for helping you make your way through the graduate program and for evaluating your progress and promise. Every student has down periods at some point in their graduate studies, whether from depression due to failed qualifying exams, insufficient research progress due to personal problems, or other reasons. It is very important that your advisor be able to help you over these hurdles.

For these reasons and more, you should be extremely careful when choosing an advisor. When evaluating a prospective advisor, you should ask yourself the following questions:

1. *Do you want this professor to be your advisor?*

- Are you comfortable working with him or her? Do your personalities mesh well? Is he or she a nice person? Do you trust his or her judgment? Does he or she work the same hours you do? (Is he or she a night person or a day person?)
- Do you share the same research interests? Is he or she the only advisor working in your area, or is he or she part of a group? Does his or her style of conducting research agree with yours? Do you have the necessary background knowledge to succeed as one of his or her students?

2. *Does this professor want you to be his or her student?*

- How many students does he or she have already? Some faculty already have more students than they can handle. Advisors who have more than five or six graduate students, probably don't have enough time to meet with them more than once every two weeks. They may even have some of their older graduate students advise you on your research instead of advising you directly. Other faculty don't have very many students, but they don't want any more, because they want to concentrate on their current students.
- If a professor doesn't want you as a student, you won't be able to get him or her to be your advisor (and if you did manage that somehow, it would be a mistake). If a professor doesn't really want you, he or she won't devote enough time to you and won't defend you when you have problems.

3. *How good an advisor is this professor?*

- Does he or she work well with others, with his or her students? How many of his or her students have left the program? How many of his or her previous students have graduated? Are they successful? How long did it take them to complete their degrees? Have his or her current students produced good research and published papers? Do the professor's current students like him or her? What do they have to say about him or her? If any of his or her former students switched to a different advisor, why did they change advisors? (Talk to his or her current and former students — they are the best source of information about your potential advisor. Of course, you will have to use your own judgment with a new faculty member.)
- Is this professor responsible? Does he or she keep appointments? Will he or she read your papers (or thesis!) on time? How much time does he or she have available to spend on you? Does he or she spend a lot of time on other responsibilities, such as consulting and administrative duties? Does this professor defend his students at departmental meetings?
- How long has he or she been at your school? Does he or she have tenure? Is he or she going to stay around for a while? If this professor got a good offer from another school or a company, how likely is he or she to leave? (Faculty who have been around for a while know the ins and outs of the department, and probably have more experience advising students. New faculty, on the

other hand, have fewer commitments and more exciting research projects. Younger faculty are also less likely to be burned out.)

4. *What does this professor expect from his or her students?*

- How much independence does this professor allow his or her students? Does he or she pressure them to perform? Does this professor want you to work on his or her projects, or will he or she allow you to work on your own research? If the latter, will he or she have the time and attention span to follow your progress and guide your research?

- What are his or her expectations with respect to qualifying examinations, teaching requirements, and progress during the first few years? What will he or she do if you have problems coping with qualifiers or your research? How realistic are his or her expectations?

5. *How famous is this professor?*

- How many refereed publications does he or she have? How many are in journals and how many in conference proceedings? Is his or her work respected in the research community? Do people cite his or her papers? What fraction of his or her papers have coauthors? (If a professor has co-authored papers, this can be a sign that he or she works well with others.)

- Does this professor require you to include him or her as coauthor on all your papers, or only on those he or she was directly involved in writing? (This can be a plus and a minus. When you're a young graduate student, people haven't seen your work before, so they'll be more likely to read your papers if they see a familiar name. But later on an advisor claiming credit for your work can be quite annoying.)

6. *Funding.*

- If a professor has a lot of graduate students, funding may be tight. How many research contracts does he or she have and what are their durations? How secure are his or her prospects for future funding?

- What will happen to you if his or her funding isn't renewed?

Another consideration is whether your department lets you change advisors midway through your career. Some will let you change as many times as necessary; others will let you change only when you form your thesis committee; and in a few departments, your advisor is your thesis advisor for the duration of your stay. If your initial choice of an advisor didn't work out, change advisors if at all possible. Have another advisor in mind and get his or her support for the change. Be careful to communicate clearly with your former and new advisors and do not alienate your old advisor. Be sure that you're making the right decision. The hardest thing about changing advisors is recognizing that you need to change.

The Two-Body Problem

Graduate work can be a severe drain on a relationship, especially if you're married or engaged. The problem is exacerbated when the best opportunity for one spouse is far away from the best opportunity for the other. If at all possible, try to stay near each other. Have one work while the other completes his or her studies and then switch off. Or, if feasible, try to complete your graduate education simultaneously.

Managing with children can be a heavy burden, as can buying and maintaining a house. These things take time, which comes at a premium during your graduate years. Even just owning a house will consume your weekends and evenings. A leave of absence to raise a child can drop you out of the swing of things, and some departments may discourage you from resuming your studies later. Postpone these entanglements until after you've completed your studies, unless there are extenuating circumstances.

Surviving the Qualifying Exams

Qualifiers are usually comprehensive written exams, but sometimes also include an oral component. They are difficult, but easier than conducting thesis research. They're easier because you've at least taken classes and studied for exams before; research is often something completely new.

If you've been out of the classroom for some time, getting used to taking tests again is difficult. Qualifying exams are difficult even for students fresh out of undergraduate school. You have to read thousands of pages of papers and synthesize your knowledge into a cohesive whole. Don't despair — it is possible to pass them with a lot of hard work.

Make sure you take the right qualifier at the right time. If your advisor says to jump right into research and skip the qualifiers, seriously consider ignoring his or her advice. Don't overestimate your abilities and try to take several exams at once; there are no prizes for passing all of them during the first semester. If you proceed at the average pace for graduate students in your department, you're much more likely to pass them the first time around. Form study groups with your fellow students to help you digest the material and work through sample problems.

Don't be depressed if you fail your qualifiers. Most schools let you retake them at least one more time and some more than once. It isn't unusual to fail your first qualifier and then pass the rest the second time around.

Finding a Thesis Topic

The problem most students have with writing a thesis proposal isn't with finding a topic; it is with narrowing the topic down into something which can be completed in a few years worth of work. You have these lofty goals — you want to solve big problem X — but the problem is too large and difficult for you to finish in your lifetime, unless you're very lucky. What you need to do is find a subproblem whose solution will contribute to the understanding of the big problem. You may need to repeat this process and find a smaller subproblem of the subproblem, until you obtain a problem small enough to be attacked in one or two years. Once you have this subproblem, the main problem becomes the motivation for your work.

If you're having trouble finding a suitable subproblem, you need to conduct a methodical search for a problem. The following advice will help you find a thesis topic quickly:

1. Use the literature in your field.

   - *Read the literature critically.* Look at the "future work" sections of papers and read survey papers. If authors tend to gloss over an issue, or sweep certain problems under the rug, those problems are good candidates for thesis topics. What assumptions did they make? Were they valid? How important were the results? Some papers will explicitly itemize the unsolved problems of the field. Read the "conclusions" sections of papers — perhaps you feel you can improve on their work? Trace back references from one paper to another until you know the general shape of the field.

   - *Look for gaps in the literature.* If an area has been completely overlooked, it may have many good problems. On the other hand, if there hasn't been much work in an area, you won't have the ideas of others to build upon, or other researchers to ask for advice.

2. Get advice from people you know and respect.

   - *Ask your advisor for help.* Your advisor has been through the process at least once with his or her own thesis. So he or she will probably have many ideas for good thesis topics and can quickly judge the difficulty of a topic. But don't be afraid to argue with your advisor if you think he or she is wrong.

   - *Talk to someone about your ideas.* An idea you find trivial and obvious might not be so simple to someone else. Bouncing your ideas off someone else can help remove the bugs and outline the shape of the problem. Even simple ideas can form the basis of further work. Don't limit yourself to talking to just your advisor.

   - *Seek out criticism.* Problems others find in your work can themselves often be the kernel of new ideas. If the criticism is invalid, the critic misunderstood your work — this should tell you that your explanations can stand some improvement. Use valid criticism to identify the holes in your work and patch them up.

   - *Don't neglect your spouse and children.* Sometimes key ideas come from listening to and watching others. They can also help support you emotionally in your times of crisis and depression.

3. Avoid getting stuck in a rut.

   - *Brainstorm your ideas with your advisor.* Present them at an informal seminar to get feedback.

- *Don't get stuck doing nothing.* If you're at a loss for ideas, try to remain active. Do something — anything to keep yourself working on problems that may produce the germ of an idea. Attend seminars and lectures in your area. Keep in touch with the rest of the research community.

- *Write down your ideas.* Record all your ideas in a notebook. From time to time, reread your notebook and maybe you'll think of new ideas. Be alert for ephemeral ideas and other opportunities; catch them and preserve them for later analysis. Think through an idea while you can, but don't let it slip away unrecorded. A tape recorder can help, since you talk faster than you can write (but slower than you can think). All you need is just one good idea.

- *Trust yourself.* If you don't believe in yourself, you'll never find a topic. Trust your judgment. Convince yourself that your work is important. But don't blind yourself to legitimate criticism from others.

- *Don't be afraid of negative results.* Demonstrating that a certain method doesn't work can often be more instructive than finding a procedure that succeeds.

- *Solve a simplified toy version of the big problem.* Special case solutions are often useful in and of themselves and sometimes can lead to a solution of the big problem. At least if you solve a simplified version of the problem, you have something to build upon. Break the problem apart into independent pieces. The simplest problem often has the most elegant solution.

- *Make hypotheses.* Try to validate your ideas formally or informally. Even if you're unsuccessful, you'll discover some of the relevant issues.

4. Pick something doable.

- *Don't be too ambitious.* It might be nice to solve all the world's problems in a year, but all you need to do is graduate. Pick something which can be finished in a year or two. Start small.

- *Lower your standards.* Having lofty goals can interfere with your finding a problem. Don't reject a problem out of hand because it doesn't meet your high standards. Solve the lower quality problem first and later refine it into a higher quality solution.

5. Pick a good topic.

- *Look for a topic you like.* If you like the topic, you're less likely to become depressed when your research progress hits a stumbling block.

- *Try to find a useful topic.* If the solution of your problem has practical consequences, both you and your audience will find it more interesting.

- *Exploit synergy.* Adapt ideas from other areas, or recast your problem into a completely different domain. Sometimes you'll be able to apply new advances in the other area to your problem.

6. Avoid bad topics.

- *Avoid the anthill syndrome.* Start a new colony instead of just adding another grain of sand to the pile. Some areas of research have been so thoroughly explored that new ideas are hard to come by and often have little significance. Pick a fresh area and stick with the frontier, not the tried and true.

- *Beware of abstractions.* Abstractions may be pretty, but concrete problems and examples are much easier to work with. Try to work with a concrete instance of the problem and later generalize it into abstract principles.

7. Stay focussed.

- *Don't get distracted.* Your time as a graduate student is unstructured. Although you should continue to participate in the research community, attending talks and reading papers, you should be careful that your attention doesn't wander too far from your main goal. Don't get sidetracked by endless routine chores. On the other hand, taking occasional breaks can help refresh your creative instinct. If necessary, take a week or two vacation from your work; you'll return refreshed and with a renewed enthusiasm and energy.

Allen Newell[5] once said that a good thesis does at least one of the following:

- Opens up a new area
- Provides a unifying framework
- Resolves a long-standing question
- Thoroughly explores an area
- Contradicts existing knowledge
- Experimentally validates a theory
- Produces an ambitious system
- Provides empirical data
- Derives superior algorithms or methods
- Develops a new methodology
- Develops a new tool
- Produces a negative result

Although he was referring to computer science when he presented this list, this categorization of types of theses is equally valid for other fields.

One of the main goals of thesis research is the transformation of a student into a researcher. To do this, you need to build up your general knowledge and experience. You need to know the key issues and important questions in an area. You should become familiar with the state of the art of current research. Who is doing research in your field, and what are their interests? You also need to gain confidence in yourself and your abilities as a researcher.

---

[5] Allen Newell received the A.M. Turing Award in 1975 with Herb Simon (a Nobel Laureate) and the U.S. National Medal of Science in 1992.

Writing a Thesis Proposal

The purpose of a thesis proposal is to convince the faculty that you have found a topic that contributes to scientific knowledge and that you are capable of pursuing it in the required time-frame. The thesis proposal stakes out a region of research and makes it seem important enough to merit a degree.

A thesis proposal begins with a problem statement. The problem statement identifies in one or two sentences the question that the thesis will answer. You then need to justify the topic as good research, saying why it is interesting and worth solving. You may also need to explain why it is a difficult problem. You will need to summarize work done by others that is relevant to your topic. How do you propose to solve the problem or extend the work of others? Do you have any preliminary results? What techniques are involved? What is your magic bullet (i.e., what will you be doing that others didn't do)? Point out the potential weaknesses of your approach. What are the expected contributions of the thesis? The significance of your work? Will there be any concrete results, or only theoretical ones? Is the thesis topic doable? How will you be able to tell when you are done? Characterize the kind of solution you're seeking. Include a tentative outline of your proposed research. Give a rough plan of action for the remainder of your research, with a rough schedule of the major elements. This will help you measure your progress on an objective basis. It is also a reality-check, to verify that you've picked a topic of manageable size.

Be sure to do a thorough job on your thesis proposal. It is your plan of action for the next few years. If you do a good job, your research will progress smoothly. If you do a poor job, your work will flounder. If there is any problem with your plan, it is best to discover it now, rather than later on after you've invested a lot of time.

Forming a thesis committee involves the same considerations as go into selecting an advisor. In addition, you want to ensure that you have a person from each relevant area of expertise. This is especially true when your topic is interdisciplinary in nature. You should also have at least one "big name" so that other researchers will look at your work.

Conducting Thesis Research

Keep your committee informed about your progress during the course of your thesis research. They can help you over the rough spots and provide ideas when you get stuck. They are obligated to discuss your work with you. You don't want to surprise them later on.

Try to complete your thesis work as quickly as possible. The longer it takes, the more likely your work is to be undermined by external factors. If somebody solves your problem in the interim, you lose interest in the topic, your advisor doesn't get tenure, or your approach becomes obsolete, you'll have to find a new topic. Competition with others, family pressure, and financial pressure can force you to speed up the thesis process.

Try to do the research piecemeal, one small piece at a time. An incremental approach is easier than trying to swallow the whole problem all at once. If you can write papers on intermediate results along the way, it will help with the writing of the thesis. On the other hand, in experimental fields one often does the thesis research all at once, so an incremental approach to writing the thesis isn't possible. In experimental fields, one must design the experiment and collect and analyze the data before reporting on the findings.

When writing your thesis, look at your proposal for a basic organization. A more natural organization may arise from the nature of your results or your central theme. Write the conclusion first and work backwards from there. An outline will help. The introduction and abstract should be the last thing you write, not the first. Begin and end the document with the big picture, and let the details fill in the middle. New insights should appear near the beginning of the work. If you don't like what you've written, rewrite it, possibly with a different organization.

Try to write precisely to the point. Don't exaggerate your results, but don't understate them either. If your results are weak, you probably should do some more research. If you've been ignoring something — correctness of the results or comparison with other results — now is the time to take care of it. If at all possible, don't use jargon or coin new terms. Try to rephrase your ideas using ordinary English. This will make your results accessible to a much greater audience. If you must use jargon, at least try to use somebody else's jargon instead of creating your own. Present what you've done in a clear, concise, precise, and accurate manner.

The Defense

Before you defend your thesis, you should get final comments on your thesis from your committee. Give them the penultimate draft of the document and address *all* of their comments in the final draft. If you don't you'll have a surprise during your defense.

Most thesis defenses are formalities and an opportunity for you to formally present your results to the research community. For some researchers, this will be their first chance to see you in action and form an opinion of your work. You should know your thesis inside out and be able to rattle off the key ideas of your thesis, relating them to previous work. Most likely you've already made overhead transparencies for use in job talks and other presentations of your work, so the actual work involved in preparing for a defense is minimal. Wear a new suit or dress. Relax.

After your defense, if the thesis is of general interest, try to get it published. At the very least, you should send off a copy to University Microfilms for archival purposes. If you haven't been publishing along the way, now is the time to break up your thesis into a series of articles for journals and conference proceedings. Publication of your results is important for your academic career. Do it right away, before you get distracted by the future.

Keep in contact with your advisor after you graduate. Your advisor appreciates the work you did under his or her tutelage and is generally interested in your well-being. A really good advisor will continue to mentor you during the remainder of your career. When your advisor hears of opportunities of interest to you, he or she will pass them your way. Your advisor is the beginning of an informal network which is critical to your success in an academic career.

If you picked a really good thesis topic, you'll be able to continue working on it. Your department might hire you as a postdoctoral student, or you may be able to develop it further in your new position at another institution. You've invested several years of your life in the thesis; if you can continue to benefit from that work, so much the better.

Books to Read

For an introduction to what earning a Ph.D. is all about, read *Research Student and Supervisor: An Approach to Good Supervisory Practice* (1990, 12 pages). Copies are available for $2.50 from Council of Graduate Schools, One Dupont Circle, NW, Suite 430, Washington, DC 20036-1173, (202) 223-3791. The Council of Graduate Schools also publishes *Graduate School and You: A Guide for Prospective Graduate Students*, 2nd edition, 1991 for $2.50.

When you begin writing the thesis, the book *The Role and Nature of the Doctoral Dissertation* (1991, 41 pages) is worth reading. You can get it for $10 from the Council of Graduate Schools at the above address. The Council of Graduate Schools also has some other publications of potential interest.

When you start giving job talks, get a copy of *Academic Environment — A Handbook for Evaluating Faculty Employment Opportunities*, by Karl W. Lanks (1990, 127 pages). Copies are available for $13 from Faculty Press, 824 President Street, Brooklyn, NY 11215. Another good resource is *The Academic Job Search Handbook* by Mary M. Heiberger, University of Pennsylvania Press, 1992, 175 pages, $12.95.

For an excellent introduction to teaching and research for new faculty in science and engineering, see *The New Professor's Handbook: An Introductory Guide to Teaching and Research in Engineering and Science*, by Cliff I. Davidson and Susan A. Ambrose, Hollowbrook Publishing, Durango, Colorado, 1993.

After the Ph.D.

The prestige of your graduate institution, your thesis advisor, and your thesis topic have the greatest impact on obtaining good job offers after you graduate. Later on, the quality of your publications will be a key factor. Quality is determined by the number of citations to your papers in other works and the prestige of the journals in which they were published, not by the sheer number of your publications.

At some point you will have to decide whether you wish to teach or conduct research at a university, or to get a job in industry. There are several pros and cons to each option. Some companies and some university departments have the best features of both. Don't be scared away by all the negative comments that follow.

Working in academia gives you the opportunity to set your own research agenda, assuming your proposals get funded. If you enjoy teaching, there are more opportunities for using your teaching skills at a university, obviously. You also have the freedom to travel to conferences and share research results with other scientists. You can earn extra money by doing some consulting for industry, patenting your work, or forming a startup company. On the other hand, writing homework and tests and grading them is a pain in the neck, especially if you don't have enough TAs to delegate the work to. Designing a new course or teaching a subject for the first time can take a lot of effort, but becomes easier after you've taught it a few times. (It can also be extremely invigorating.) The political environment both inside and outside the department can be aggravating. You will be under a lot of pressure to produce, especially as you get closer to tenure. You'll work harder in academia, on the weekends and evenings, with more associated stress, but you'll be doing it because you want to. Faculty get tuition remission for themselves and often for their spouse and children. Finally, you will wind up spending a lot of time chasing grant money.

In industry, you will get to work with state of the art equipment on interesting problems. The pay is much better and covers a full year, unlike the nine-month salaries of academia. Industry jobs also include paid vacation time. You probably won't have to spend as much time writing grant proposals. But reporting to bureaucracies is a nuisance, and you will feel pressure to produce something that is potentially profitable. Given the competition in the marketplace, you will have to justify your existence to the company in terms of dollars saved, services rendered, and new products developed. If you don't like and respect your manager, you will probably grumble a lot. The politics of obtaining funding, space, staff, and time for research are similar in academia and industry. If you work for the government, the rules to avoid the mere appearance of impropriety can sometimes be quite absurd. Your job security may depend on the stability of your department within the company. Finally, if you enjoy teaching, there are some opportunities to teach in a large company, but clearly not as many as in academia.

Your advisor should be the first resource you exploit in searching for a job opening, especially in academia. He or she may already know of the job opportunities in your field. Or if he or she doesn't, he or she can call colleagues at other institutions to ask about openings. Your advisor is a conduit with which you can tap into a rich network of employment and professional information. Many employment opportunities are never advertised because they are filled through this network. You should also read the employment notices in the back of professional society magazines in your field. It also doesn't hurt to send an inquiry letter to the chairman of the department at universities of interest to you, even if they aren't actively recruiting new faculty.

If you don't find a job that suits you, consider accepting a postdoctoral appointment and trying again next year. Some schools use a postdoctoral appointment as a way of evaluating potential faculty. A postdoctoral appointment gives you the chance to formulate a solid research program and get initial funding, thereby improving your chances of getting hired.

During an interview trip you will be taken out to dinner by some of the faculty, meet with the dean and department head, be interviewed by some faculty, and give a public seminar on your research.

- Don't show up at the dinner the night before looking like a tired graduate student. Dress nicely, since a bad first impression can torpedo your chances of getting the position.
- When meeting with the dean and department head, ask about the department's strengths and weaknesses, how you fit into the department's strategic plan, and

how the department is viewed by the rest of the university. How many courses will you be required to teach? What kind of funding support and facilities are provided to new faculty? Consider how many people the department has in your area. Ask how the promotion/tenure process works at the school.

- When you meet with faculty, ask about their research and research in the department in general, and ask about the city and the university. How academically talented and motivated are the graduate and undergraduate students?
- Your seminar should be accessible to individuals who aren't experts in your field and should clearly indicate your contribution. Don't exaggerate your contribution, but don't understate it either. Start the talk with a general introduction to your specific area or a background survey of relevant work.

If you are lucky to get an offer, be prepared to negotiate for items of interest to you, including equipment, lab space, graduate students, secretarial support, travel funds, and summer support. Once you've accepted their offer, it is much more difficult to get additional support in these categories.

Chapter 4

Figuring Financial Need

In this chapter we discuss how to gauge your college expenses and calculate a ballpark estimate of the amount you and your parents will be expected to contribute each year. We then discuss some financial planning methods which could ease this burden.

Estimating College Expenses

College costs fall into six broad categories:

- Tuition and Fees
- Room and Board
- Books and Supplies
- Travel and Transportation
- Personal and Incidental
- Health Insurance

College costs can be found in the school's latest catalog, or by looking in some of the books in the bibliography, such as *Peterson's Guides*. If the figures are from a previous year, assume that they increase by about 6% per year (about 3 percentage points above the inflation rate). Just multiply by 1.06 for each year until you enter college. For example, if you're just entering your freshman year in high school and tuition is now $17,000 per year, expect to pay more than $21,462 by the time you're a freshman in college. The financial aid offices at most schools can also provide you with a "student expense budget" which itemizes typical living and educational expenses for their students.

Fees include student activities fees, orientation fees, laboratory use fees, athletic fees, and health center fees. All can be found by consulting the school's catalog. Of these, only the health center fees are likely to increase appreciably each year, by the medical inflation rate of about 9%.

You can also find the room and board costs in the school's catalog. You may be able to save by living off-campus in an apartment and by cooking your own food, if the school lets you do this. Most schools require freshmen to live on-campus, even if they allow upperclassmen to rent an apartment. If you live off-campus, don't forget to include the cost of your electricity and gas bills.

Books are expensive. Figure on $300–$400 worth of books each semester, at a minimum. You can save by buying used books or by reading the texts on reserve in the library. If you buy new books, keep them in good condition so you can sell them next semester if you don't want to keep the books for yourself after the class has ended. Most college bookstores will buy back textbooks which will be used in classes during the next semester for up to 50% of the new price. You can also try selling them yourself through campus bulletin boards.

If you live off-campus or are a commuter student, calculate your daily transportation and parking costs. If you live on-campus, include your air, bus, or train fare for trips home during breaks.

Personal items and incidentals are one of the main areas in which you can economize. These items include clothing, laundry, telephone calls, recreational activities and supplies, hobbies, gifts, snacks and eating out, dates and entertainment, haircuts, hygiene consumables and aspirin, and additional dorm furnishings. The amount you spend depends very much on your lifestyle.

One major cost area often overlooked is health insurance. Some parental health insurance policies now terminate children coverage at their 19th or 21st birthday. Others continue coverage as long as the child is single and stays in school, up to a maximum age of 25. Before purchasing a student health insurance plan, you should check the coverage provided by your current insurance policy. Most schools offer a group policy for their students, at rates of between $400 and $700 a year for an individual.

Living at Home

If your finances are tight, consider the pros and cons of living at home during college. Discuss this with your family. It is usually preferable to reside in a campus living group or dormitory, because college is for maturing socially and learning independence in a "safe" environment, in addition to academic learning. If you live at home, you'll miss much of the atmosphere and experience obtained by being immersed in the college environment.

Ballpark Estimate of Family Contribution

But when comparing colleges, don't look at just the price tag. Most schools will provide you with a financial aid package to help bridge the gap between the cost of attending and the "family contribution." The family contribution is the amount they think you and your parents can afford to pay for your college education. The more expensive schools are not necessarily beyond your means, because the size of the financial aid package increases as the gap grows. Of course, a school with a limited financial aid budget might not be able to meet your full financial need, but this can happen even at the most inexpensive of schools. So apply for aid even if you don't think you qualify, and wait until you see the aid package before dismissing a school because of cost. It may actually cost you less to attend the more expensive school.

In this section we compute a rough analysis of the student's contribution and the parental contribution. This is intended to be a ballpark estimate and may differ significantly from the actual analysis performed by the school. We assume that both parents are of the typical age for parents of unmarried children who are entering college (i.e., in their forties). This analysis does not apply to graduate students, who are considered independent of their parents.

Every college can have a different method of calculating the parental contribution. They may allow different modifications to income, have a different formula, and have different expectations for summer earnings. The contribution can also be affected by high medical expenses, two working parents, parents who are older than usual, private secondary school tuitions for younger children, and the ownership of a business or farm.

For a more accurate analysis, use the *Financial Aid Form (FAF)* of the College Scholarship Service or the *Family Financial Statement (FFS)* of the American College Testing Program. You will probably have to submit one of these forms anyway to apply for aid at the school you choose to attend. These forms also serve as the entry point to the Pell Grant selection process and most states' need-based awards. You can also apply for the Pell Grant and other federal programs using the *Free Application for Federal Student Aid (FAFSA)*. But since most schools require more information than is collected by the FAFSA, you'll probably have to fill out a FAF or FFS instead. Check with the individual schools to be sure. Some states have their own forms, such as Pennsylvania's PHEAA form and California's CSAC. Both the FAF and the FFS will charge you a fee according to the number of schools you want to receive a copy of your needs analysis. If you can't afford to pay the fee due to financial hardship, talk to your guidance counselor to arrange to have it waived.

You should always apply for financial aid from the schools, even if you "know" that you won't get any aid. Many parents mistakenly assume that they don't qualify for aid because they think they earn too much or have too much savings, or their friends tell them that they won't get any aid. But personal finances are so complex and the cost of a college education is so high these days that many parents who don't apply for aid would actually qualify. There's no stigma attached to applying for aid. Let the financial aid officers, who have seen thousands of cases, decide whether you qualify. Don't prejudge the case for them — you can't get aid if you don't apply. Even if your parents didn't qualify for aid when their first child entered college, having several children in school can affect their circumstances enough to get you some aid. If you're so convinced that you don't qualify for aid that you refuse to fill in a FAF or FFS, at least submit the FAFSA form. It's free and it can't hurt.

Student Contribution

The student contribution is relatively straightforward. The student is expected to contribute about one-third of his or her savings and about half his or her summer earnings. Figuring a (conservative) 12-week summer at 40 hours per week and $5 per hour, that works out to be a student contribution of about $1,200 for the summer. Some schools have higher expectations because of a higher prevailing wage in the area surrounding the school or a longer summer vacation, so the student contribution may be as high as

$1,900 or $2,000 for the summer. Other schools may expect the student to contribute as much as 70% of their summer earnings, yielding a student contribution of up to $3,000 for the summer. (The formula for the federal programs expects students to contribute half of their summer earnings above $1,750.)

Semester employment from a work-study program doesn't affect the aid analysis, because schools consider such employment during the school year as a form of aid. But other kinds of part-time employment during the semester will figure into the analysis for the subsequent year. If the schools don't include work-study as part of your aid package, you can always find part-time employment on campus during the academic year. Only a portion of your earnings will be used to reduce the aid package, so a part-time job during the semester can help ease the burden of paying for college. But you'll want to make sure that you have enough time to study, so you'll need to strike a proper balance between employment and schoolwork. If you're persistent and resourceful, you may be able to find a job working for a professor which will not only earn you money, but teach you how to conduct laboratory research as well.

Parental Contribution

The amount of the parental contribution for each student varies according to several factors: income, assets, family size, and the number of family members in school. Most schools consider the natural parents responsible for their children's college education, even in cases of divorce, separation, or remarriage.[1] The following formula represents a typical method for estimating the parental contribution, to give you an idea of the kind of analysis colleges use. The actual computation differs from school to school and the amount you calculate may vary considerably depending on the formula employed by the school.

Calculate your parents' combined income as their adjusted gross income (from their most recent tax return), plus any deductions for IRA/KEOGH plans, plus any nontaxable income, such as social security benefits, child support, and welfare.

Your parents' assets include their home equity, bank accounts, and any investments. Home equity is the current market value of the house less any unpaid balance on the mortgage. Bank accounts include savings and checking accounts. Investments include stocks, bonds, and the net value of any real estate other than the primary home.

The Higher Education Amendments of 1992 eliminated home equity from the federal formula for calculating the parental contribution to college costs. Also, the assets of families that earn less than a certain threshold ($50,000 per year) will not be considered in determining the family contribution. This makes it easier for families to qualify for need-based federal aid. But they won't necessarily get grants, since not everybody who qualifies gets a scholarship. The real result will be that more families will be able to borrow money at low interest rates. See page 267 for information on these federal

[1]The reauthorization of the Higher Education Act defines students to be independent if they are at least 24 years of age, a ward of the court, a veteran of the U.S. Armed Forces, a graduate student, married, or have legal dependents other than a spouse. Financial aid officers may also decide a student's status in unusual circumstances. But these definitions hold only for the federal programs. Schools may decide to use their own criteria.

aid programs. Note that many schools still use home equity in their own calculations, so you may have to fill out more than one financial aid form or provide supplemental information.

Family size includes the student under consideration, both parents, and any other dependent children.

Let n be the number of family members in college. Then the expected parental contribution (EPC) is 6% of any assets beyond the first \$30,000 in assets, plus 25% of the annual gross income beyond a basic living expense level of \$18,000, less \$900 per child in college other than the student under consideration:

$$\max(0, assets - \$30,000) \times 0.06 + \frac{income - \$18,000}{4} - (n-1) \times \$900$$

The adjusted parental contribution (APC) is then

$$\frac{EPC + (n-1) \times \$500}{n}$$

Some schools, however, may expect parents to contribute as much as 12% of their assets and 40% of their annual gross income.

If your parents earn over \$70,000 and have assets of over \$100,000, you probably won't receive any need-based aid, unless they have several children in college, or have very unusual circumstances. Colleges expect families to make some sacrifices to send their children to college, especially if they are moderately well off. College financial aid is the college's estimation of what the student needs at bare minimum to attend the college. (Of course, if the school's financial aid budget has a shortfall, the school won't be able to meet the student's full demonstrated need.)

Implications

Now that you understand how schools determine your financial need, you can use this knowledge to your advantage. There are several important consequences of the manner of calculation of student and parental contributions. In particular, you should note that

1. Schools expect parents to contribute a smaller percentage of their assets and pretax income than the student.
2. Schools base their financial aid packages on the assets and earnings for the year *before* the student enters college. Moreover, income is charged a bigger percentage than assets.

The first point implies that it may not be advantageous for parents to shift assets into their child's name[2] or pay their child a wage as a summer employee in the parent's company. The financial aid formula takes a bigger bite of the child's assets and earnings, so if the parents keep the money in their own name it will have less of an impact on the

---

[2]Likewise, parents shouldn't give their children expensive presents until after they have graduated college. Instead, let the children buy their own computers, electronic gear, and other toys using the money they have earned and saved.

child's financial aid package. On the other hand, dependents are often taxed at a lower rate. So if you expect to receive very few grants and mostly loans, the tax savings gained by transferring college funds into the child's name may outweigh any benefits from a bigger financial aid package. You may need to get the advice of an accountant to strike a proper balance between the two.

The second point suggests that parents should carefully consider any decisions that will affect their income and assets during the year before their child enters college. There are some simple rules of thumb to follow:

- Avoid creating capital gains. During the child's senior year in high school, selling stocks and bonds that have increased in value will result in a capital gain that will reduce the child's financial aid package. Sell them in the junior year or before, so that their value will be treated as an asset and not income in the financial aid formula.
- If you own a house and have any consumer loans, consolidate them with a home-equity loan. A home-equity loan will figure into your financial need picture; consumer loans usually don't. Moreover, home-equity loans are cheaper than consumer loans and the interest is deductible on your income tax return. Use the home-equity loan to pay off all your credit card and auto loan balances.
- If you expect to withdraw money from pension plans — such as IRAs, Keogh plans, deferred compensation plans, and tax-sheltered annuities — to pay college costs, wait until after the child has entered college to take it out. Money set aside for retirement is usually not included in the financial aid formulas. If you take it out before the student enters school, however, it is treated like any other monetary asset. Money withdrawn from a retirement fund may also be subject to bank and tax penalties, so borrowing money from your pension is generally an unwise move.

But college costs are just one part of a bigger picture that includes other factors, such as taxes. You should not focus on financial aid to the exclusion of all else, since those other considerations could have a significant impact. The key point here is that to get the optimal financial aid package, parents should start considering their finances before the child's senior year in high school, if not earlier. The options discussed in the preceding paragraphs are points to be considered, not hard and fast rules. Your particular financial situation may make them more or less advantageous. This is one area where consulting an accountant is definitely worthwhile.

Bottom Line Comparison

Consider a school's tuition to be a list price. Just as you almost never buy anything at list price when you go shopping, you probably won't have to pay the full amount at the school you attend. Colleges will "discount" the price according to financial need, giving you a price they think you can afford. If the schools charged you more than you could afford, you wouldn't be able to attend and they'd lose the sale. So when you compare schools from a financial perspective, always compare them based on the bottom line —

how much you'll have to pay to attend — not the list price. A chart similar to the one in Table 4.1 can help you compare aid offers.

School				
Costs:				
Tuition and Fees				
Room and Board				
Books and Supplies				
Travel/Transportation				
Personal/Incidental				
Health Insurance				
TOTAL				
Resources:				
Parental Contribution				
Student Savings				
Student Earnings				
TOTAL				
Financial Aid Package:				
Federal Pell Grant				
State Grant				
College Grants				
Federal Perkins Loan				
Federal Stafford Loan				
College Scholarships				
Federal College Work Study				
TOTAL				
Need Gap:				
Costs - Resources - Aid				
Additional Resources:				
Unsubsidized Stafford Loans				
Other Supplemental Loan Programs				
Other Employment				
Other Scholarships				
Relatives				

Table 4.1: Bottom Line Aid Offer Comparison

When you submit a financial aid application to a school, they'll give you a financial aid package composed of grants, loans, and part-time employment, and expect you to make up the difference. Grants are gifts of money; in contrast, loans are money you owe and will have to repay. If you receive outside scholarships that are paid directly to the school, most schools will reduce your aid package by the same amount (greedy little devils, aren't they?).[3] If you're lucky, they'll cut your loans; if you're unlucky, they'll cut your grants. Despite the potential for reductions in your financial aid package, the

---

[3]Even if you don't receive any aid from the school, they'll try to get the money funneled through the

more money you can bring in on your own, the better off you'll be.

Most schools require students to report all outside scholarships, because they are trying to distribute limited funds fairly. If your financial need decreases, the schools reserve the right to give you a smaller handout. On the other hand, the authors feel this undermines the purpose of the scholarship, which is to aid the student, not the school. Some graduate schools, in an effort to be more equitable to the students, reward them with a stipend increase when they get an external fellowship. This encourages the students to bring in outside support. When a school requires you to report all your scholarships, there isn't much you can do. Failure to comply will get you into trouble later when the school finds out, and may actually be illegal (in addition to being dishonest) if your financial aid package includes federal aid.

If there are significant discrepancies among the aid packages you've received from the different schools, especially in the parental contribution, and you strongly feel that the financial aid offer would prevent you from enrolling, or your family's financial situation has taken a sudden change for the worse, talk to the financial aid administrators at the schools that interest you the most. If your argument is compelling, they may increase your aid. Most schools have emergency funds to handle contingencies like the death, major disability, or unemployment of a parent. Schools expect you to make some sacrifices to attend college, but not ridiculous ones.

State schools are usually much cheaper than private schools because they're funded by taxes. However, some public schools may not have the same prestige as some of the better private schools. They may also suffer from a lack of the breadth of programs you're looking for. They will offer you correspondingly smaller aid packages as well. You'll need to take factors other than just price into account when evaluating the bottom line and making a decision. This is a subjective decision that only you can make.

Financial Planning

If you're smart enough to plan for college far enough in advance, you can significantly ease the burden of paying for college.

For example, a long-range saving plan spreads the costs of college over many years. If you had saved about $4,000 per year ($334/month) in an interest-bearing account or mutual funds from birth through college matriculation, you'd have accumulated the total cost of a college education today at a private institution.[4] A successful savings plan need not meet the student's full college bill. A plan which pays part of the cost will significantly reduce the pain of paying for college. The sooner you start saving, the better.

If you find saving money difficult, many banks can set up a forced-savings plan, in which a sum of money is automatically transferred each month from a checking account into a savings account. The money then doesn't appear in your checking account, so

---

financial aid office, because it lets them boost their figures for the total amount of aid granted to students at the school.

[4]For a child born today, you'll have to save nearly twice this amount per year to pay for his or her college education, which will run to a total of over $200,000 in the year 2010.

you're less likely to be tempted to spend it.

You can also put money into term deposit certificates. CDs get higher interest rates but lock it in for longer periods of time. Be sure to stagger the maturation dates of the CDs so that money will be available each year the child is in school, as there are substantial penalties for early withdrawal of money from CDs.

Investments such as mutual funds, stocks, bonds, and real estate have the greatest growth potential but also the greatest risk. If the parents invest in certain types of U.S. savings bonds (e.g., U.S. Series EE Savings Bonds), the income is sometimes tax exempt if it is used to pay for college tuition. If you do buy bonds, buy them at the end of the month, so that you'll get an extra month's float on your money (bonds pay interest from the first of the current month, regardless of which day you buy them).

You should also look into baccalaureate bonds if offered by your state. Interest on these bonds is exempt from federal income tax and state income tax in the state of issue. Depending on the state, baccalaureate bonds may also have a variety of extra features that make them attractive vehicles for investing money for college. For example, some states pay extra interest if the bonds are redeemed to pay tuition. Some state schools may also exclude a portion of the money invested in baccalaureate bonds from the financial need calculation. But these bonds sometimes have a long maturity, which means you have to buy them when your child is very young.

Some states have prepaid tuition plans, where the parents contribute money to a state-run trust fund when the child is young. When the child matriculates at a public university in that state, his or her tuition costs are covered by the trust. Such plans can be a good hedge against the high inflation rate for college tuition. On the other hand, the child might not choose to attend a state school, negating the benefits of the plan. Also, the tax implications of a prepaid tuition plan are extremely complicated, so be sure consult an accountant if you're thinking of pursuing this option. Finally, contributions to a prepaid tuition plan can have a negative impact on the child's eligibility for Pell Grants and other federal aid, because the amounts invested in the plan may be considered assets of the child.

The wage-earner of the household should also invest in life insurance, especially if offered by his or her employer. This protects the dependents against the early unexpected death of a parent and provides enough money to let them finish their education.

If you are going to take out loans to finance your educational costs, you should carefully analyze your career goals and other future plans, such as marriage, children, and other family matters. Financial planning can help you figure out how you'll pay back your loans and over what period of time.

Financial planning sessions for college and university study are sponsored by universities and by organizations which discuss government grants, loans, and school financial aid packages. Many schools have a variety of creative methods for financing your college education. It is incumbent upon you and your parents to take the time to procure the necessary personal financial information relevant to the preparation of financial aid forms and governmental aid applications.

Whatever you do, don't procrastinate on completing your financial aid applications. Failure to submit an application on time could lead to a disaster later — admission without an aid package.

Chapter 5

Scholarships

The programs listed in this chapter are primarily directed toward high school students and undergraduate students. Graduate fellowship programs are listed in the next chapter. Some of the scholarship programs in this chapter, however, also allow graduate students to apply.

AID ASSOCIATION FOR LUTHERANS (AAL) · 1

Type:	Scholarships
Focus:	General
Eligibility:	High school seniors holding an AAL certificate of membership and insurance or annuity in their own name. AAL associate members are not eligible. High school juniors who will be entering college early are also eligible.
Description:	For any field of study. Selection is on the basis of an application, transcripts, and SAT scores. Financial need is not a consideration.
Awards:	(25) $2,000, (50) $1,000, and (200) $500 awards, all renewable for up to three additional years. (500) $500 one-year nonrenewable awards.
Deadline:	November 30. Notification in April.
Address:	Aid Association for Lutherans (AAL) Church and Education Benefits 4321 North Ballard Road Appleton, WI 54919-0001
Telephone:	(414) 734-5721 x 3010

AIIM JOHN P. EAGER SCHOLARSHIP   2

Type:	Scholarships
Focus:	Computer Science, Engineering, Physical Sciences, and Mathematics
Eligibility:	High school seniors or undergraduate students. Must have B average or better.
Description:	Winners are selected on the basis of a 2,500-word essay on a specific topic and three recommendations. For more information, contact your local AIIM chapter.
Awards:	$5,000 scholarship.
Deadline:	March 30. Notification in early June.
Address:	Association for Information and Image Management 1100 Wayne Avenue, Suite 1100 Silver Spring, MD 20910
Telephone:	(301) 587-8202

ALEXANDER GRAHAM BELL ASSOCIATION FOR THE DEAF   3

Type:	Scholarships
Focus:	Science and Engineering
Eligibility:	Must be oral deaf.
Description:	The Association also has a variety of other awards for the deaf, not restricted to science and engineering.
Awards:	(2) $750 David J. von Hagen Scholarships and (2) $750 Robert H. Weitbrecht Scholarships.
Deadline:	April 15
Address:	Alexander Graham Bell Association for the Deaf 3417 Volta Place, NW Washington, DC 20007-2778
Telephone:	(202) 337-5220

| AMERICAN FOUNDATION FOR AGING RESEARCH (AFAR) | 4 |

Type: Scholarships and Fellowships

Focus: Aging Research

Eligibility: Undergraduate and graduate students at colleges or universities in the United States.

Description: Applicants must be actively involved or be planning active involvement in a specific biomedical or biochemical research project in the field of aging. The individuals most often chosen utilize modern and innovative approaches and technologies. Molecular and cellular biology, immunobiology, cancer, neurobiology, biochemistry, and molecular biophysics are all approaches of interest to AFAR. Selection is based on a description of proposed research, letters of reference from the research advisor and two other instructors, and official transcripts. Write to the address given below for an application.

Address: American Foundation for Aging Research
North Carolina State University
Biochemistry Department
128 Polk Hall
Raleigh, NC 27695-7622

Telephone: (919) 515-5679

AMERICAN GEOLOGICAL INSTITUTE (AGI)   5

Type:	Scholarships
Focus:	Geosciences, including Geology, Geophysics, Hydrology, Meteorology, Physical Oceanography, Planetary Geology, and Earth Sciences
Eligibility:	High school seniors, undergraduate and graduate students. Must be a member of one of the ethnic minority groups that are underrepresented in the geosciences — Black Americans, Hispanic Americans, and Native Americans. U.S. citizenship required.
Description:	Recipients are selected on the basis of academic excellence and financial need. An application consists of a financial profile, essay, transcripts, standardized test scores (SAT, ACT, GRE), and three letters of recommendation.
Awards:	(35+) scholarships and fellowships. Scholarship awards are up to $10,000/year; fellowship awards are up to $4,000/year. Scholarships and fellowships are renewable if performance is satisfactory.
Deadline:	February 1
Address:	AGI Minority Geoscience Scholarships American Geological Institute 4220 King Street Alexandria, VA 22302-1507
Telephone:	(703) 379-2480, FAX (703) 379-7563

AMERICAN INDIAN SCIENCE & ENGINEERING SOCIETY (AISES) | 6

Type:	Scholarships
Focus:	Science and Engineering
Eligibility:	Native American Indians who are student members of AISES.
Description:	The A.T. Anderson Memorial Award is for engineering, health sciences, business, and related fields. The CERT Scholars program is for energy management. The Santa Fe Pacific Foundation Scholarships require that the recipient reside in Arizona, Colorado, Kansas, New Mexico, Oklahoma, or San Bernardino County in California.
Awards:	Range from $1,000–$2,500 per year, depending on the program.
Deadline:	A.T. Anderson, June 15; CERT, August 1; Santa Fe, March 15.
Address:	American Indian Science & Engineering Society, Inc. 1085 14th Street, Suite 1506 Boulder, CO 80302-7309
Telephone:	(303) 492-8658

AMERICAN INSTITUTE OF AERONAUTICS AND ASTRONAUTICS | 7

Type:	Scholarships
Focus:	Aeronautics and Astronautics
Eligibility:	Undergraduate students. Students do not need to be an AIAA student member to apply, but must become one before receiving a scholarship award. Students must intend to major in a field of science or engineering encompassed by the technical activities of AIAA. U.S. citizenship or permanent residency required.
Description:	Recipients are selected on the basis of transcripts, an essay describing career goals, three letters of recommendation, and an application.
Awards:	$1,000 each to one or more college sophomores, juniors, and seniors. Awards to sophomores and juniors are renewable.
Deadline:	February 1. Notification May 15.
Address:	American Institute of Aeronautics and Astronautics Mr. Patrick Gouhin AIAA/Industry Scholarship Program 370 L'Enfant Promenade, SW Washington, DC 20024-2518
Telephone:	(202) 646-7458, FAX (202) 646-7508

AMERICAN INSTITUTE OF ARCHITECTS   8

Type:	Scholarship
Focus:	Architecture
Eligibility:	Undergraduate and graduate students
Description:	Undergraduate applications through office of the head of an accredited school or its scholarship committee.
Awards:	$500 to $2,000 scholarships (undergrad); $1,000 to $2,500 scholarships (grad).
Deadline:	February 1
Address:	Scholarship Programs American Institute of Architects 1735 New York Avenue, NW Washington, DC 20006
Telephone:	(202) 626-7300

AMERICAN MEDICAL TECHNOLOGISTS   9

Type:	Scholarships
Focus:	Medical Technology
Eligibility:	Undergraduate students
Description:	For students who are training to work in clinical laboratories and doctors' offices.
Awards:	(5) $250 awards
Deadline:	April 1
Address:	American Medical Technologists 710 Higgins Road Park Ridge, IL 60068
Telephone:	(708) 823-5169, FAX (708) 823-0458

AMERICAN MENSA SCHOLARSHIP | 10

Type:	Awards
Focus:	General
Eligibility:	12th grade students, undergraduate and graduate students
Description:	Entries are judged on the basis of a 500 word essay describing student's academic, vocational, or career goals. Some scholarships require a score in the top 2% of some standardized IQ test accepted by Mensa (ACT, SAT, GRE are good examples). Send a stamped self-addressed envelope for an application.
Awards:	Regional cash awards of (9) $1,000, (9) $500, and (18) $200. Two special awards of $1,000 and $600 will also be made. Total of 67 nonrenewable scholarships. Local cash awards total more than $100,000.
Deadline:	January 31, (late January, early February), with notification around June 1.
Address:	American Mensa Education and Research Foundation American Mensa Scholarship 2626 East 14th Street Brooklyn, NY 11235-3992
Telephone:	(718) 934-3700

AMERICAN METEOROLOGICAL SOCIETY	11

Type: Scholarships

Focus: Meteorology and Atmospheric Science

Eligibility: College seniors majoring in meteorology, atmospheric science, or related oceanic and hydrologic sciences. Must intend to make atmospheric or related sciences their career. U.S. citizenship or permanent residency required.

Description: Entries are judged on the basis of a letter of application, 500 word statement describing candidate's future goals and aspirations, letter of recommendation from a faculty member in the department, and official college transcripts.

Awards: $5,000 Paul H. Kutschenreuter Scholarship, $2,000 Howard T. Orville Scholarship, $700 Howard H. Hanks Scholarship. The Orville and Hanks scholarships are awarded on the basis of academic excellence and achievement. The Kutschenreuter scholarship is awarded on the basis of academic excellence, achievement, and financial need.

Deadline: June 15. Notification in October.

Address: American Meteorological Society
                 45 Beacon Street
                 Boston, MA 02108-3693

Telephone: (617) 227-2425

AMERICAN NUCLEAR SOCIETY | 12 |

Type:	Scholarships
Focus:	Nuclear Science, Nuclear Engineering, and Radioanalytical Chemistry
Eligibility:	College sophomores, juniors or seniors, graduate students. U.S. citizenship or permanent residency required.
Description:	Scholarship award to recognize an outstanding undergraduate or graduate student pursuing a career in radioanalytical chemistry or nuclear science. Academic accomplishments must be substantiated by transcript.
Awards:	(4) $1,000 scholarships for students who will be sophomores, (11) $2,000 scholarships for students who will be juniors or seniors, and seven additional scholarships ranging from $1,000 to $3,000. There are also (7) $3,000 graduate scholarships and three additional graduate scholarships ranging from $1,000 to $4,000. Also, there are eight $3,500 scholarships which take financial need into account (high school seniors and college freshmen may apply for this scholarship) and one $3,500 scholarship for a female student. Some scholarships require that the applicant be sponsored by an ANS member or section.
Deadline:	March 1
Address:	American Nuclear Society 555 North Kensington Avenue LaGrange Park, IL 60525
Telephone:	(708) 352-6611, 1-800-323-3044, (708) 579-8202, FAX (708) 352-0499

AMERICAN PHYSICAL SOCIETY   13

Type:	Scholarships
Focus:	Physics
Eligibility:	High school seniors and college freshmen or sophomores who plan to major in physics or are majoring in physics. Must be African American, Hispanic American, or Native American.
Description:	An application consists of an application form and personal statement, three recommendations, transcripts, and SAT/ACT test scores.
Awards:	(15-20) $2,000 scholarships for tuition, room, or board, plus $500 awarded to the student's physics department. Scholarships are renewable for one additional year. Each scholarship recipient is also assigned an accomplished physicist as a mentor.
Deadline:	Last Friday in February.
Address:	APS Minorities Scholarship Program The American Physical Society 335 East 45th Street New York, NY 10017-3483
Telephone:	(212) 682-7341

AMERICAN RESPIRATORY CARE FOUNDATION   14

Type:	Scholarship
Focus:	Respiratory Therapy
Description:	Write to the address below for more information.
Awards:	Various scholarships and awards ranging from $500 to $1,300.
Deadline:	June 1
Address:	American Respiratory Care Foundation 11030 Ables Lane Dallas, TX 75229

AMERICAN SOCIETY FOR ENGINEERING EDUCATION	15

Type:	Awards
Focus:	Engineering education programs, scientific research in government and industry
Eligibility:	Third-year undergraduates majoring in engineering
Description:	The purpose is to learn how the engineer can contribute to public-policy decision-making and to learn more about the relationship between government and the technical community.
Awards:	(15) awards of $2,400
Deadline:	December 1, with notification by March 1
Address:	American Society for Engineering Education 11 Dupont Circle, Suite 200 Washington, DC 20036
Telephone:	(202) 745-3616, (202) 293-7080, FAX (202) 265-8504

AMERICAN SOCIETY FOR ENOLOGY & VITICULTURE	16

Type:	Scholarships
Focus:	Enology, Viticulture, and Agriculture
Eligibility:	Undergraduate juniors or seniors and graduate students enrolled in an enology or viticulture program, or in a science basis to the wine and grape industry, such as agriculture. Students should intend to pursue a career in research or the wine and grape industry.
Description:	Recipients are selected on the basis of scholastic achievement and financial need.
Deadline:	March 1
Address:	American Society for Enology & Viticulture P.O. Box 1855 Davis, CA 95617
Telephone:	(916) 753-3142

AMERICAN SOCIETY FOR MEDICAL TECHNOLOGY   17

Type:	Scholarships
Focus:	Medical Technology
Eligibility:	College sophomores. U.S. citizenship or permanent residency required.
Description:	For students who are training to work in clinical laboratories and doctors offices.
Awards:	(2) $1,500 awards and (2) $1,000 awards. Other awards also available.
Deadline:	February 1
Address:	American Society for Medical Technology Education and Research Fund, Inc. Attn: Pamela Majors 7910 Woodmont Avenue, Suite 1301 Bethesda, MD 20814
Telephone:	(301) 657-2768

AMERICAN SOCIETY FOR METALS SCHOLARSHIP   18

Type:	Scholarships
Focus:	Metallurgy, Materials Science, and Engineering
Eligibility:	Undergraduate sophomores, juniors, and seniors. Must be a citizen of the U.S., Canada, or Mexico. Must be majoring in metallurgy or materials science.
Description:	Entries are judged on the basis of a transcript, application, essay, and three letters of recommendation.
Awards:	(1) full tuition, (3) $2,000, and (34) $500 scholarships.
Deadline:	June 1, with notification shortly after August 1.
Address:	American Society for Metals Scholarship 9639 Kinsman Metals Park, OH 44073-0002
Telephone:	(216) 338-5151 x 506, FAX (216) 338-4634

AMERICAN SOCIETY OF CIVIL ENGINEERS 19

Type:	Scholarships, Fellowships, and Research Grants
Focus:	Civil Engineering
Eligibility:	Undergraduate and graduate students majoring in civil engineering
Description:	Students must be enrolled at an ABET accredited university, be a member of an ASCE Student Chapter, and also be a National Student Member. Membership applications may be submitted along with scholarship applications.
Awards:	Awards vary in amount with a maximum of $15,000 per year. Undergraduate scholarships, $1,500 each; research grants, $3,000 to $15,000. Graduate fellowships, $3,000; research grants, $3,000 to $15,000.
Address:	American Society of Civil Engineers 345 East 47th Street New York, NY 10017-2398
Telephone:	(212) 705-7496

AMERICAN SOCIETY OF MECHANICAL ENGINEERS AUXILIARY 20

Type:	Scholarships
Focus:	Mechanical Engineering
Eligibility:	Undergraduate and graduate mechanical engineering students. U.S. citizenship required.
Description:	Several programs, including the Sylvia W. Farny Scholarship, the Elizabeth M. and Winchell M. Parsons Scholarship, and the Marjorie Roy Rothermel Memorial Scholarship.
Awards:	Scholarships and fellowships ranging from $1,000 to $1,500.
Deadline:	February 15
Address:	American Society of Mechanical Engineers Auxiliary, Inc. United Engineering Center 345 East 47th Street New York, NY 10017
Telephone:	(212) 705-7722

AMVETS National Scholarship Program   21

Type:	Scholarships
Focus:	General
Eligibility:	High school seniors who are sons or daughters of American veterans. U.S. citizenship required.
Description:	Recipients are selected on the basis of scholastic aptitude and demonstration of financial need.
Awards:	(15) $1,000 scholarships, renewable for a total of four years.
Deadline:	July 15
Address:	AMVETS National Scholarship Program AMVETS National Headquarters 4747 Forbes Boulevard Lanham, Maryland 20706
Telephone:	(301) 459-6181

AOT Foundation, Inc.   22

Type:	Awards
Focus:	Occupational Therapy
Description:	Write to the address below for more information.
Awards:	Several awards are available.
Deadline:	December 15
Address:	AOT Foundation, Inc. 1383 Piccard Drive Rockville, MD 20850
Telephone:	(301) 753-5600

ARTS RECOGNITION AND TALENT SEARCH

23

Type:	Scholarships and Awards
Focus:	Arts (Dance, Music, Theater, Visual Arts, and Writing)
Eligibility:	High school seniors
Description:	Scholarships, cash awards, apprenticeships, identification of talented students to colleges who may offer additional awards to prospects. Requires $35 application fee.
Awards:	(1) $3,000 scholarship, (1) $1,500 scholarship, (1) $500 scholarship, and (1) $100 scholarship.
Deadline:	October 1
Address:	Arts Recognition and Talent Search National Foundation for the Advancement in Arts 300 NE 2nd Avenue Miami, FL 33132
Telephone:	(305) 347-3416

ASSOCIATED GENERAL CONTRACTORS (AGC) 24

Type:	Scholarships
Focus:	Construction and/or Civil Engineering
Eligibility:	High school seniors and undergraduate students (scholarship); graduate students (fellowship)
Description:	Participants are selected on basis of academic performance, extracurricular activities, employment experience, financial need, and a demonstrated interest in a construction industry career. Finalists are selected by an application, transcripts, three recommendations, financial need, and an essay. Finalists are then interviewed to select the winners.
Awards:	(25-30) $1,500/year renewable for four years for undergraduate education. (25-30) $7,500/year renewable for four years for graduate education.
Deadline:	November 15, finalists selected in January for interviews. Award recipients announced in March.
Address:	Director of Programs Associated General Contractors Scholarships AGC Education and Research Foundation 1957 E Street, NW Washington, DC 20006
Telephone:	(202) 393-2040

ASSOCIATION FOR COMPUTING MACHINERY (ACM) | 25

Type:	Scholarships and Fellowships
Focus:	Computer Science
Eligibility:	Undergraduate and graduate students. The scholarships are available to students in any college or university in the District of Columbia, Maryland, and Virginia. This eligibility is based on the location of your school and not on your place of residence.
Description:	The DC Chapter of the ACM awards three scholarships for undergraduate and graduate students whose studies involve computers or computer science, regardless of academic department or specific area of study.
Awards:	One $1,500 undergraduate scholarship for students who are sophomores at time of application, one $1,500 master's degree fellowship, and one $3,000 Samuel N. Alexander ACM Fellowship Award.
Deadline:	April 15. Notification June 1.
Address:	Contact the financial aid office of colleges and universities throughout the District of Columbia, Maryland, and Virginia.

ASSOCIATION OF SURGICAL TECHNOLOGISTS | 26

Focus:	Surgical Technology
Description:	Write to the address below for more information.
Deadline:	March 1
Address:	Association of Surgical Technologists
8307 Shaffer Parkway
Littleton, CO 80127

AT&T DUAL DEGREE SCHOLARSHIP PROGRAM 27

Type:	Scholarships and Summer Employment
Focus:	Mathematics, Physics, Electrical Engineering, Computer Science, Computer Engineering, Mechanical Engineering, and System Engineering
Eligibility:	Outstanding minority and female high school seniors.
Description:	Participants are selected on the basis of scholastic amplitude, academic performance, rank in class, strength of high school curriculum, and demonstration of motivation and ability. Each year AT&T awards 3 scholarships and maintains 15 students in the program.
Awards:	(3) full tuition and mandatory fees, textbook allowance, room and board, ten weeks of summer employment, reimbursement for summer round-trip travel, summer housing, and the guidance of a mentor.
Deadline:	December 31, with selection by February 1.
Address:	Dual Degree Scholarship Program (DDSP) DDSP Administrator AT&T Bell Laboratories 101 Crawfords Corner Road Holmdel, NJ 07733-1988
Telephone:	(908) 949-4301, FAX (908) 949-6800

AT&T ENGINEERING SCHOLARSHIP PROGRAM   28

Type:	Scholarships
Focus:	Electical Engineering, Computer Science, Computer Engineering, Mechanical Engineering, and System Engineering
Eligibility:	Outstanding female and minority high school seniors applying full time to college with strong curricula.
Description:	Entries are judged on the basis of application, HS transcript, SAT and/or ACT scores, three letters of recommendation from teachers, counselors, or principal. Send a self-addressed stamped envelope for an application.
Awards:	(15) full tuition and mandatory fees, textbook allowance, room and board, ten weeks of summer employment, reimbursement for summer round-trip travel, summer housing, and the guidance of a mentor.
Deadline:	January 15, with notification by March 15.
Address:	Engineering Scholarship Program (ESP) ESP Administrator AT&T Bell Laboratories 101 Crawfords Corner Road Holmdel, NJ 07733-1988
Telephone:	(908) 949-4301, FAX (908) 949-6800

BARRY M. GOLDWATER SCHOLARSHIP FOUNDATION   29

Type:	Scholarships
Focus:	General, with an emphasis on Science and Mathematics
Eligibility:	College juniors and seniors. Must have a "B" average and be in the upper one-fourth of his/her class. Must be a U.S. citizen.
Description:	This is a new scholarship program sponsored by the federal government. The emphasis is on academic excellence.
Awards:	Up to 250 scholarships per year with a maximum of $7,000/year for two years.
Deadline:	February 7
Address:	Barry M. Goldwater Scholarship and Excellence in Education Foundation 499 South Capital Street, SW, Suite 405 Washington, DC 20003-4013
Telephone:	(202) 755-2312, FAX (202) 755-2948

BAUSCH & LOMB SCIENCE AWARD AND SCHOLARSHIP 30

Type:	Scholarships and Awards
Focus:	Recognition of scholastic achievement in the sciences
Eligibility:	High school juniors and seniors
Description:	The medal is awarded to the top members of the junior class at participating schools. To be eligible for the scholarship, a student must have been designated a medalist during his/her junior year. Students are nominated by their schools.
Awards:	The scholarship is based on merit, with the amount of the scholarship based on need. The minimum scholarship stipend is $1,000 per year for four years. The scholarship is tenable only at the University of Rochester.
Deadline:	February 15 for the scholarship, with notification for the medals by April 15.
Address:	Ms. Debra B. Jansen Senior Administrator, Public Affairs Bausch & Lomb Bausch & Lomb Science Award & Scholarship One Lincoln First Square, P.O. Box 54 Rochester, NY 14601-0054
Telephone:	(716) 338-5174

BELL & HOWELL SCIENCE AND ENGINEERING SCHOLARSHIP 31

Type:	Scholarships
Focus:	Electronics Engineering Technology, Computer Science, and Business
Eligibility:	High school graduates
Description:	SAT/ACT score, Achievement Test scores and high school transcript
Awards:	(60) $11,000 scholarships ($2,750 per year for four years).
Deadline:	March 25
Address:	Ms. Brenda Allen Scholarship Coordinator Devry Inc. 2201 West Howard Street Evanston, IL 60202-3698

BOY SCOUTS OF AMERICA 32

Type:	Scholarships
Focus:	General
Eligibility:	Must be a former Boy Scout.
Awards:	Several scholarships ranging from $1,000 to $3,000, some renewable.
Deadline:	Late February and early March.
Address:	Boy Scouts of America P.O. Box 152079 1325 Walnut Hill Lane Irving, TX 75015-2079
Telephone:	(214) 580-2431/2438, FAX (214) 580-2502

CHASMAN SCHOLARSHIPS FOR WOMEN 33

Type:	Scholarships
Focus:	Any technical or scientific field
Eligibility:	Women who are residents of Nassau or Suffolk County in Long Island, New York. U.S. citizenship or permanent residency required.
Description:	The purpose of the Renate W. Chasman Scholarships is to encourage women to resume their formal education in a technical field. The candidate must be returning to a minimum of a half-time academic program in a technical field at the junior or senior undergraduate or at the graduate level. Selection is on the basis of academic and career record, letters of recommendation, and a short essay on the applicant's career goals. Finalists are chosen according to merit, but financial need may be a consideration in the selection of winners.
Awards:	(2) $1,000 awards.
Deadline:	June 1. Notification August 1–15.
Address:	Brookhaven Women in Science P.O. Box 183 Upton, NY 11973
Telephone:	(516) 282-7226

THE CHEMISTS' CLUB   34

Type:	Scholarships
Focus:	Chemistry
Eligibility:	Undergraduate and graduate students majoring in Chemistry
Description:	Recipients are selected on the basis of two letters of recommendation (one from the department chair and one from a chemistry faculty member), financial aid form, transcripts, and a personal letter describing the student's background.
Awards:	$3,000/year renewable.
Deadline:	May 1
Address:	The Chemists' Club 295 Madison Avenue, 27th Floor New York, NY 10017
Telephone:	(212) 532-7649, FAX (212) 779-0349

CLAIROL LOVING CARE SCHOLARSHIP PROGRAM   35

Type:	Scholarships
Focus:	General
Eligibility:	Female undergraduate and graduate (master's) students age 30 and older
Awards:	$1,000 scholarships.
Deadline:	May 1 for fall semester and October 1 for spring semester.
Address:	Scholarship Director Business and Professional Women's (BPW) Foundation 2012 Massachusetts Avenue, NW Washington, DC 20036
Telephone:	(202) 293-1200

COCA-COLA SCHOLARS FOUNDATION, INC.	36

Type: Scholarships

Focus: Merit-based scholarship emphasizing leadership, extracurricular activities, and academic merit.

Eligibility: High school seniors attending schools in participating bottler territories. Must plan to pursue a degree at an accredited U.S. postsecondary university.

Description: Semifinalists are notified and sent the supporting application (biographical data, essay, high school transcript, recommendations). In the spring, scholars attend the national competition in Atlanta to determine recipients of the one-year and four-year awards.

Awards: The top 50 candidates are named National Coca-Cola Scholars and receive four-year, renewable $5,000/year scholarships. The remaining 100 candidates are designated Regional Coca-Cola Scholars and receive four-year $1,000/year scholarships.

Deadline: Postmarked on or before October 31.

Address: Coca-Cola Scholars Foundation, Inc.
1 Buckhead Place, Suite 1000
3060 Peachtree Road NW
Atlanta, GA 30305

Telephone: (404) 237-1300

COMMISSION ON PRESIDENTIAL SCHOLARS	37

Type: Awards

Focus: To recognize and honor the "most distinguished" graduating high school seniors.

Eligibility: Graduating seniors from U.S. high schools.

Description: Students may not apply individually to the program, nor may their schools nominate them. Instead, all high school seniors are automatically identified for the program if they have scored well on either the SAT or the ACT.

Awards: Of the 1,500 semifinalists, 500 become finalists. From this group 141 Presidential Scholars are selected. This is a recognition program. There are no awards, other than certificates, plaques, and the trip to Washington DC.

Address: Commission on Presidential Scholars
U.S. Department of Education
400 Maryland Avenue, SW
Washington, DC 20202

Telephone: (202) 245-7793

COOPER UNION	38

Type: Scholarships

Focus: Art, Architecture, and Engineering

Eligibility: Undergraduate students

Description: All admitted students receive a full scholarship for the duration of their study.

Address: Dean of Admissions
Cooper Union
41 Cooper Square
New York, NY 10003

COTE EQUAL OPPORTUNITY PUBLICATIONS   39

Focus:	Engineering
Eligibility:	Undergraduate and graduate students. Women, minorities, and disabled college students interested in engineering.
Description:	Preliminary entries are judged according to GPA (minimum 3.5).
Awards:	Vary.
Deadline:	February 15
Address:	Awards Directory Equal Opportunity Publications COTE P.O. Box 2810 Cherry Hill, NJ 08034
Telephone:	(609) 573-9400

DC MAYORAL AND CITY COUNCIL SCHOLARSHIPS   40

Type:	Scholarships and Fellowships
Focus:	Mathematics, Computer Science, Engineering, Physical Sciences, and Business
Eligibility:	Undergraduate and graduate students who are residents of the District of Columbia. Must have a B or better average.
Description:	Recipients are selected on the basis of an application, an essay of career and academic goals, four letters of recommendations, transcripts, and PSAT/SAT scores.
Awards:	(15) $1,500 scholarships.
Deadline:	February 26 or the following Monday if the 26th is on a weekend. Notification in May.
Address:	District of Columbia National Gas 1100 H Street, NW Washington, DC 20080
Telephone:	(202) 624-6758

DOG WRITERS' EDUCATIONAL TRUST   41

Type:	Scholarships
Focus:	Veterinary Medicine and Animal Behavior
Eligibility:	High school seniors, undergraduate students, and graduate students who are or have been active in dog shows (including junior showmanship, obedience training, field trials, 4-H, and raising guide dogs) or work for a veterinarian or humane group.
Description:	Recipients are selected on the basis of an application, transcripts, letters of recommendation, financial data, and a letter summarizing the applicant's dog activities and plans for the future.
Awards:	10–15 awards of $500–$1,000.
Deadline:	December 31. Notification June 15.
Address:	Dog Writers' Educational Trust 47 Kielwasser Road Washington Depot, CT 06794
Telephone:	(203) 868-2863

DOLLARS FOR SCHOLARS   42

Type:	Scholarships
Focus:	Local funds for local students
Description:	All funds raised locally are distributed by a local awards committee. Contact your local chapter for more information. Recipients are selected on the basis of an application, financial need analysis, transcripts, and a letter of recommendation. (Write to the address below for general information.)
Awards:	More than 23,000 awards totaling over $19.8 million annually.
Address:	Volunteer Services Coordinator Dollars for Scholars P.O. Box 297 1505 Riverview Road St. Peter, MN 56082
Telephone:	1-800-248-8080, (507) 931-1682, FAX (507) 931-9168

DOW CHEMICAL COMPANY 43

Type:	Scholarships
Focus:	Artistic interpretation of a scientific concept.
Eligibility:	Full-time high school students in grades 10-12.
Description:	Students must submit two copies of the official entry form, which includes a 150-word statement about the art, and the art itself. Entries must be original; the teacher sponsoring the entry must certify it as such.
Awards:	50 finalists for one first place scholarship of $1,000, four certificates of special merit and honorable mention with a prize of $500 each.
Deadline:	Usually in December or January, with notification in February.
Address:	Mr. Talbert B. Spence, Director Education Program Department New York Academy of Science 2 East 63rd Street New York, NY 10021
Telephone:	(212) 838-0230

DOW CHEMICAL PREMIER SCHOLARSHIP PROGRAM 44

Type:	Scholarships
Focus:	Chemical, Mechanical, or Electrical Engineering, Chemistry, or other disciplines of interest to Dow.
Eligibility:	Minority high school seniors. Must have a 2.7 or higher GPA.
Description:	Recipients are required to accept at least two summer work assignments from Dow.
Awards:	(45) $3,000/year four-year scholarships, plus summer internships.
Deadline:	April 30
Address:	Dow Chemical USA Attn: Rita J. Shellenberger 2020 Willard H. Dow Center Midland, MI 48674
Telephone:	(517) 636-3451

DURACELL/NATIONAL URBAN LEAGUE SCHOLARSHIPS   45

Type: Scholarships

Focus: Engineering, Sales, Marketing, Manufacturing, Finance, and Business Administration

Eligibility: Undergraduate students

Awards: (5) $10,000 and (5) $1,000.

Deadline: April 15

Address: National Urban League, Inc.
                 500 E 62nd Street, 11th Floor
                 New York, NY 10021

Telephone: (212) 310-9000

DURACELL NSTA SCHOLARSHIP COMPETITION   46

Type: Scholarships

Focus: Create and build a "working device" powered by one or more Duracell batteries.

Eligibility: High school students (grades 9-12). Must be a U.S. citizen.

Description: Device must be entrant's original creation and be built by the entrant. Entries consist of an official entry form and a photograph, two page description, and wiring diagram of the device.

Awards: There are (1) $10,000, (5) $3,000, and (10) $500 scholarships and 25 cash awards of $100. Teachers of winner receive computers and NSTA publications. All students and teachers who enter receive a Duracell Designer T-shirt.

Deadline: Mid to late January. Finalists notified by the end of February.

Address: Duracell Scholarship Competition
                 National Science Teachers Association
                 1742 Connecticut Avenue, NW
                 Washington, DC 20009-1171

Telephone: (202) 328-5800

EDUCATIONAL COMMUNICATIONS SCHOLARSHIP FOUNDATION   47

Type:	Scholarships
Focus:	General, Leadership
Eligibility:	High school seniors
Description:	Entries are judged on the basis of application ($2.50 application fee), SAT/ACT test scores, and grade point average. *Note: This is the same organization that publishes "Who's Who Among American High School Students."
Awards:	(100+) $1,000 scholarships
Deadline:	June 1. Applications received after June 1st will automatically be processed and evaluated for the following year's program.
Address:	Educational Communications Scholarship Foundation Educational Communications, Inc. 721 North McKinley Road P.O. Box 5002 Lake Forest, IL 60045-5002
Telephone:	(708) 295-6650, FAX (708) 295-3972

EIF SCHOLARSHIPS   48

Type:	Scholarships and Fellowships
Focus:	Technical and Scientific Fields, including Mathematics, Science, Computer Engineering, Computer Science, Electromechanical Technology, and Medical Technology
Eligibility:	Undergraduate and Graduate Students. Must be handicapped. U.S. citizenship required.
Description:	Selected on the basis of career goals, academic achievements, transcripts, two letters of recommendation, and financial need.
Awards:	(6) $2,000.
Deadline:	February 1.
Address:	Electronic Industries Foundation 1901 Pennsylvania Avenue, NW, Suite 700 Washington, DC 20006
Telephone:	(202) 955-5810, FAX (202) 955-5837

| ELKS MOST VALUABLE STUDENT SCHOLARSHIP | 49 |

Type:	Scholarships
Focus:	General — Scholarship and Leadership
Eligibility:	High school seniors. Must be a U.S. citizen.
Description:	Entries are judged on the basis of application, transcript, 300 word essay about the student's vocational/professional goals, recommendation and letters of endorsement and supporting documents. Financial need is taken into account. There are identical awards for boys and girls, competing separately. Write to the address given below or to your local Elks Lodge.
Awards:	National: (2) $24,000, (2) $20,000, (4) $14,000, (6) $12,000, (6) $10,000, (6) $8,000, (10) $7,000, (10) $6,000, (50) $1,400, (100) $1,200, and (300) $1,100 scholarships. State: (999) $1,000 scholarships. 1,736 awards totaling more than $2,500,000.
Deadline:	February 1
Address:	Elks Most Valuable Student Scholarship ELKS National Foundation 2750 Lake View Avenue Chicago, IL 60614

| EMSA UNDERGRADUATE SCHOLARSHIPS | 50 |

Type:	Research Grants
Focus:	Electron Microscopy
Eligibility:	Undergraduate students. U.S. citizenship or permanent residency required.
Description:	Selection on the basis of a three-page research proposal, itemized budget, two recommendations, resume, statement of career goals, and a letter from the lab supervisor where the research will be performed.
Awards:	(4) scholarships of up to $3,000.
Deadline:	November 15
Address:	Electron-Microscopy Society of America P.O. Box EMSA Woods Hole, MA 02543
Telephone:	(508) 540-7639, FAX (508) 540-5594

ESA EDUCATION AND TRAINING COMMITTEE	51

Type:	Scholarships
Focus:	Entomology
Eligibility:	Undergraduate students
Description:	Major in entomology, zoology, biology, or related science at recognized school in the U.S., Canada, or Mexico. Minimum of 30 hours must be accumulated. Candidates submit an application, statement of interest in entomology, an essay describing their career goals, three letters of recommendation, and transcripts. They are evaluated on the basis of their academic credentials and their enthusiasm, interest, and achievement in biology.
Awards:	(1) $1,000 and (1) $500 scholarship
Deadline:	May 31
Address:	Executive Director Education and Training Committee Entomological Society of America 9301 Annapolis Road, Suite 300 Lanham, MD 20706-3115
Telephone:	(301) 731-4535, FAX (301) 731-4538

FBLA NATIONAL STUDENT AWARDS PROGRAM	52

Focus:	Business
Address:	National Student Awards Program, FBLA Future Business Leaders of America Phi Beta Lambda P.O. Box 17417 – Dulles Washington, DC 22041
Telephone:	(703) 860-3334

FEEA Fund Scholarships | 53

Type:	Scholarships
Focus:	General
Eligibility:	High school, undergraduate and graduate students. For civilian federal and postal employees and members of their families. Minimum of 3 years of federal service required.
Description:	Entries are judged on the basis of an essay, transcript (minimum 3.0 GPA), recommendations, SAT scores, and community service. Write to the address below for more information.
Awards:	(200) awards ranging from $500 to $2,500
Deadline:	May 1
Address:	Federal Employee Education and Assistance Fund P.O. Box 2811 Washington, DC 20013
	Federal Employee Education and Assistance Fund 8441 West Bowles Avenue, Suite 200 Littleton, CO 80123-3245
Telephone:	1-800-323-4140, (303) 933-7580

General Motors Engineering Scholarship Program | 54

Type:	Scholarships
Focus:	Engineering
Eligibility:	Undergraduate sophomores at selected schools. Must maintain a 3.2 GPA.
Awards:	(125–150) full tuition scholarships, include all fees and a book allowance. Awards also include a summer internship with a GM unit.
Address:	General Motors Attn: Jenny Machak 3044 West Grand Boulevard Detroit, MI 48202
Telephone:	(313) 556-3565

GRANDMET/NATIONAL URBAN LEAGUE SCHOLARSHIPS 55

Type: Scholarships

Focus: Engineering, Sales, Marketing, Manufacturing, Finance, and Business Administration

Eligibility: High school seniors and undergraduate students

Awards: (15) $1,000.

Deadline: April 26

Address: National Urban League, Inc.
500 E 62nd Street, 11th Floor
New York, NY 10021

Telephone: (212) 310-9000

HARRY S TRUMAN SCHOLARSHIP FOUNDATION 56

Type: Scholarships

Focus: Leadership in Public Service

Eligibility: Undergraduate students who will be juniors or seniors in the fall and graduate students. Must be a U.S. citizen.

Description: Students are nominated by a selection committee and may not apply directly to the program. Candidates must pursue baccalaureate or graduate degree programs that will prepare them for some aspect of government employment, and intend to pursue a degree in public service.

Awards: Up to (92) $30,000 scholarships covering tuition, books, fees, room, and board. Scholarships are run for the senior year ($3,000) and two ($13,500/year) or three ($9,000/year) years of graduate study.

Deadline: December 1. Notification in March.

Address: Harry S Truman Scholarship Foundation
712 Jackson Place, NW
Washington, DC 20006

Telephone: (202) 395-4831

HARVEY W. WILEY SCHOLARSHIP 57

Type:	Scholarships
Focus:	Analytical Chemistry, Chemistry, Microbiology, Food Technology, Environmental Sciences, and related fields
Eligibility:	Undergraduate juniors
Description:	Award for an undergraduate junior (for the senior year) majoring in a subject of concern to the AOAC, including chemistry, microbiology, food technology, environmental sciences, and related fields. Must have career goals of research, regulatory work, quality control, or teaching in an area of interest to the AOAC. Must have a B or better average during the first three years of undergraduate school, and demonstrate some financial need.
Awards:	(1) $1,000.
Deadline:	May 1
Address:	Association of Official Analytical Chemists 2200 Wilson Boulevard, Suite 400 Arlington, VA 22201-3301
Telephone:	(703) 522-3032, FAX (703) 522-5468

HAZARDOUS MATERIALS MANAGEMENT TRAINING PROGRAM 58

Type:	Scholarships
Focus:	Health Physics, Environmental Health, and Hazardous Waste Management
Eligibility:	Full-time minority undergraduate students. U.S. citizenship required.
Description:	Provides competitive scholarship support and internship appointments to students interested in pursuing a career in hazardous waste management or environmental restoration. Students may be majoring in a variety of science and engineering fields related to waste management. Participants will be required to complete a three-month internship at a DOE facility engaged in environmental restoration or waste management activities.
Awards:	(25) scholarships consisting of full tuition and fees and a $600 monthly stipend while enrolled in school; $900 stipend per month during the summer internship; renewable for up to two years.
Deadline:	February
Address:	Ms. Regina V. Clark Program Manager Minority Students Hazardous Materials Management Training Program Oak Ridge Associated Universities P.O. Box 117 Oak Ridge, TN 37831-0117
Telephone:	(615) 576-9278

HERB SOCIETY OF AMERICA	59

Type: Research Grants

Focus: Herbs

Eligibility: Individuals with a proposed program of scientific, academic, or artistic investigation of herbal plants.

Description: Applications consist of a 500 word research proposal and a proposed itemized budget. A complete copy of the finished work must be furnished to the Herb Society Library, a summary of the work provided for publication in the Society's publication, *The Herbarist*, and the recipient must present the work at the annual meeting of the society or one of the regional meetings.

Awards: Grants of up to $5,000.

Deadline: January 31. Notification May 1.

Address: Research and Education Grant Program
The Herb Society of America, Inc.
9019 Kirtland Chardon Road
Mentor, OH 44060

Telephone: (216) 256-0514

HERFF JONES PRINCIPAL'S LEADERSHIP AWARD	60

Type: Awards

Focus: General, Leadership

Eligibility: High school seniors nominated by their school.

Description: Entries are judged on the basis of an application, transcripts, GPA, and an essay on leadership.

Awards: (150) $1,000 awards.

Deadline: December 20

Address: Principal's Leadership Award Scholarship Program
P.O. Box 6317
Princeton, NJ 08541-6317

HUGHES AIRCRAFT COMPANY SCHOLARSHIPS 61

Type: Scholarships

Focus: Electrical, Mechanical, Aerospace or Systems Engineering, Computer Science, or Physics

Eligibility: High school seniors for undergraduate study. Must be a U.S. citizen.

Description: Undergraduate scholarships for study at any ABET-accredited university, but usually at selected universities near major Hughes facilities. GPA must be 3.0/4.0. Most are awarded on a work-study basis. Entries are judged on the basis of application, references, and transcripts. Recipients spend the summer working at Hughes.

Awards: Scholarships include tuition, academic fees, parking fees, books, materials, stipend, travel and relocation expenses, and full salary for summer work and any other periods of full-time work.

Deadline: March 15

Address: Hughes Aircraft Company
Corporate Fellowship and Rotation Programs
Technical Education Center
Hughes Aircraft Company Fellowships
P.O. Box 45066, Building C1/B168
Los Angeles, CA 90045-0066

Telephone: (213) 568-6711

IEEE COMPUTER SOCIETY MERWIN SCHOLARSHIP 62

Type: Scholarships

Focus: Electrical Engineering, Computer Engineering, Computer Science, or other well-defined computer-related engineering fields

Eligibility: Undergraduate juniors and seniors and graduate students

Description: Students must be active in their IEEE Computer Society branch chapter to be eligible.

Awards: (4) $3,000 scholarships for one academic year.

Deadline: May 15

Address: The Computer Society of the IEEE
1730 Massachusetts Avenue, NW
Washington, DC 20036-1903

Telephone: (202) 371-0101

INSTITUTE OF FOOD TECHNOLOGISTS   63

Type:	Scholarships
Focus:	Food Science and Technology
Eligibility:	Undergraduate and graduate students
Description:	Write to the address below for more information.
Awards:	(85) scholarships ranging from $750 to $2,500 and (25) graduate fellowships ranging from $1,000 to $10,000. All are renewable.
Deadline:	February 1 for juniors, seniors, and graduate students, February 15 for freshmen, and March 1 for sophomores.
Address:	Scholarship Department Institute of Food Technologists 221 N. LaSalle Street, Suite 2120 Chicago, IL 60601
Telephone:	(312) 782-8424, FAX (312) 782-8348

INTERLOCHEN ARTS ACADEMY   64

Type:	Scholarships
Focus:	Music
Eligibility:	Financial aid applicants must complete all requirements for admission before consideration for financial aid.
Description:	Scholarships are given in the following categories: Arts, Music, Visual Arts, Dance, Creative Writing, Theater, and Design and Production. Audition required. Interested persons should request financial aid when applying for admissions.
Awards:	The Academy grants need-based assistance to students with superior talent who cannot pay the full tuition fee. Award amounts vary up to half tuition. No full tuition scholarships are given.
Deadline:	Rolling basis for admission.
Address:	Interlochen Arts Academy Admissions Office P.O. Box 199 Interlochen, MI 49643
Telephone:	(616) 276-9221

INTERNATIONAL SCIENCE AND ENGINEERING FAIR (ISEF)	65

Type: Scholarships and Awards

Focus: Science, Mathematics, Computers, and Engineering

Eligibility: Students in the 9th-12th grades who are under 21 years old as of May 1. Also open to students in Puerto Rico, U.S. territories, and foreign countries.

Description: At most two students per regional/state science fair may be certified as finalists to the ISEF. Science Service publishes a booklet listing the finalists' research projects and a book of of their abstracts.

Awards: General Motors ISEF Grand Awards: Up to 200 $50 to $250 cash awards. Science Service sponsors first, second, third, and fourth place cash Grand Awards in each of the research categories ($100-$500) and sends two finalists to the Nobel Prize ceremonies in Sweden. The U.S. Navy sponsors four $10,000 scholarships. Many other organizations sponsor awards and scholarships.

Deadline: Affiliate fairs must be held in mid-April; Science Service must receive finalists' paperwork by late April. The fair is held in a different city each year in the second week of May.

Address: International Science and Engineering Fair
Science Service
1719 N Street, NW
Washington, DC 20036

Telephone: (202) 785-2255

INTERNATIONAL SOC. FOR CLINICAL LAB. TECHNOLOGY	66

Type: Scholarships

Focus: Laboratory Technology

Eligibility: Limited to International Society for Clinical Laboratory Technology members or their children.

Description: Several scholarships to help obtain an education in medical lab technology.

Address: ISCLT Scholarship Committee
818 Olive Street, #918
St. Louis, MO 63101

JAPANESE AMERICAN CITIZENS LEAGUE | 67

Type:	Scholarships and Fellowships
Focus:	General
Eligibility:	High school seniors, undergraduate students, and graduate students of Japanese ancestry. U.S. citizenship required.
Description:	Selection is on the basis of test scores, transcripts, honors and awards, extracurricular activities, community involvement, a personal statement, and a letter of recommendation. Preference may be given to JACL members. Student membership is available.
Awards:	Several nonrenewable scholarship awards.
Deadline:	March 1 for graduating high school seniors, April 1 for all other applications. Notification in August.
Address:	JACL National Headquarters 1765 Sutter Street San Francisco, CA 94115
Telephone:	(415) 921-5225

JOSTEN'S FOUNDATION NATIONAL SCHOLARSHIP | 68

Type:	Scholarships
Focus:	General, Leadership
Eligibility:	High school seniors in the U.S. and U.S. territories
Description:	Entries are merit-based and judged on the basis of the application. Announcement and guidelines are sent to high schools in September. Write to the Josten's Foundation for more information.
Awards:	(300+) $1,000 scholarships
Deadline:	December 10
Address:	Jostens Foundation 5501 Norman Center Drive Minneapolis, MN 55437 Josten's Foundation National Scholarship Citizen's Scholarship Foundation of America P.O. Box 297 St. Peter, MN 56082
Telephone:	(507) 931-1682

KAPPA DELTA SCHOLARSHIPS 69

Type:	Scholarships
Focus:	General — Communications, Journalism, Education, and Business
Eligibility:	Must be female. Collegiate members of the Kappa Delta Sorority.
Awards:	18 awards of varying amounts, around $750.
Deadline:	March 1
Address:	Kappa Delta Scholarships
Kappa Delta Sorority, National Headquarters
2211 South Josephine Street
Denver, CO 80210

KAPPA KAPPA GAMMA 70

Type:	Scholarships
Focus:	Therapy
Eligibility:	Completed minimum two years of undergraduate study. Must be a U.S. or Canadian resident.
Description:	Write to the address below for more information.
Awards:	Several $750/$1,000 undergraduate and graduate awards
Address:	Kappa Kappa Gamma
P.O. Box 2079
Columbus, OH 43216

KNIGHTS OF COLUMBUS   71

Type:	Scholarships
Focus:	General
Eligibility:	High school seniors. Must be a member in good standing of the Knights of Columbus, or the son or daughter of such a member, or the son or daughter of a deceased member who was in good standing at the time of his death.
Description:	For study at the Catholic college or university of the student's choice in the United States. Selection is on the basis of transcripts, class rank, SAT scores, and an autobiographical essay.
Awards:	(5) $1,000 scholarships renewable for a total of up to four years.
Deadline:	March 1
Address:	Director of Scholarship Aid Knights of Columbus P.O. Drawer 1670 New Haven, CT 06507

KOREAN-AMERICAN SCHOLARSHIP FOUNDATION   72

Type:	Scholarships
Focus:	General Scholarship
Eligibility:	Korean-American high school seniors and undergraduate students
Description:	Entries are judged on the basis of a resume.
Awards:	Varied number, $500–$1,000.
Deadline:	August 1
Address:	Korean-American Scholarship Foundation P.O. Box 9751 McLean, VA 22102-0751

LANDSCAPE ARCHITECTURE FOUNDATION 73

Type:	Scholarships
Focus:	Landscape Architecture and Horticulture
Eligibility:	Undergraduate and graduate students
Description:	Although the primary focus is on landscape architecture and ornamental horticulture, there are some awards for horticultural research. There are also some awards earmarked for female and minority students.
Awards:	A variety of awards, ranging from $500 to $5,000.
Deadline:	Early May. Notification in early August.
Address:	Landscape Architecture Foundation 4401 Connecticut Avenue, NW, Suite 500 Washington, DC 20008
Telephone:	(202) 686-0068, FAX (202) 686-1001

MARC PROGRAM 74

Type:	Scholarships
Focus:	Minority access to research careers in the Biomedical Sciences. Fields supported include Biology, Chemistry, Physics, Psychology, Computer Science, and Mathematics (with Biology or Chemistry).
Eligibility:	Must be a third-year undergraduate student. U.S. citizenship or permanent residency required. MARC also runs a graduate fellowship program for selected graduates of the MARC undergraduate research training program.
Description:	Funded through schools with substantial minority student bodies.
Awards:	Provides full tuition.
Deadline:	September 10, January 10, and May 10
Address:	MARC Program National Institute of General Medical Sciences National Institutes of Health Westwood Building, Room 9A-18 Bethesda, MD 20205
Telephone:	(301) 496-7941

MARY JANE & JEROME A. STRAKA SCHOLARSHIP   75

Type:	Scholarships
Focus:	Science, Mathematics, and Economics
Eligibility:	High school seniors
Description:	Entries are judged on the basis of application, essay, recommendation, and transcript.
Awards:	Renewable scholarships (number and amounts vary from year to year).
Deadline:	May 31
Address:	Mary Jane & Jerome A. Straka Scholarship American Association for Gifted Children 15 Gramercy Park New York, NY 10003
Telephone:	(212) 473-4266

MINORITY CHALLENGE PROGRAM IN SCIENCE AND ENGINEERING   76

Type:	Scholarships and Awards
Focus:	Sciences, Mathematics, and Engineering
Eligibility:	High school juniors and seniors
Description:	Selected high school juniors and seniors with interest and aptitude in science and engineering participate in a structured program of summer and academic-year activities.
Awards:	(30) awards each year. There are stipends for summer camps and internships with potential scholarships.
Deadline:	Early spring
Address:	Ms. Regina Clark Program Manager Oak Ridge Associated Universities P.O. Box 117 Oak Ridge, TN 37831-0117
Telephone:	(615) 576-8158

| NASA UNDERGRADUATE STUDENT RESEARCHERS PROGRAM (USRP) | 77 |

Type: Scholarships

Focus: Science, Mathematics, Engineering, and Computer Science

Eligibility: High school seniors for undergraduate study. U.S. citizenship required. Must be an underrepresented minorty (African Americans, Hispanic Americans, Native American Indians, and Native Pacific Islanders) or an individual with a disability. Minimum GPA of 3.2/4.0 and combined SAT scores of 1100.

Description: The program is administered through the cooperation of universities. Grants will be awarded to the universities in the name of the students selected to receive awards. Students are required to conduct summer research relevant to their field of study. The institutions will provide paid summer research experiences for the students or ensure that the students have appropriate technical experiences during the four years of the scholarship. When possible, each student will be assigned to a NASA Center which is conducting research relevant to the student's planned career and assigned a mentor at that center. Students must be willing to spend their summers in a research experience. Students must submit an application through the university he/she plans to attend. Applications include two letters of recommendation, transcripts, a one-page statement of accomplishments, and a proposal outlining the student's educational and career goals and research interests. Students receiving support under this program do not incur any formal obligation to the government of the United States.

Awards: (75) scholarships of $8,000 per year for tuition, room and board, books and fees. NASA also provides the university with $4,000 per academic year which may be used for summer stipend, mentorship, and NASA-related travel.

Deadline: Institutions must submit completed applications by April 26, with student deadlines earlier. Notification on or about July 1.

Address: National Aeronautics and Space Administration (NASA)
Attn: Ms. Deborah Russell
NASA Headquarters – Code EU
300 E Street, SW
Washington, DC 20546

Telephone: (202) 358-0970

NATIONAL ACTION COUNCIL OF MINORITIES IN ENGINEERING | 78

Type:	Scholarships
Focus:	Engineering
Eligibility:	Minority undergraduate students. Must maintain a 2.5 GPA.
Description:	Schools select scholarship recipients. Obtain list of funded schools from address below.
Awards:	$2 million plus awarded through schools. Participating schools distribute renewable awards ranging from $500 to $3,000 to eligible students.
Address:	National Action Council of Minorities in Engineering 3 West 35th Street, Third Floor New York, NY 10001-2281
Telephone:	(212) 279-2626

NATIONAL AMBUCS SCHOLARSHIPS FOR THERAPISTS | 79

Type:	Scholarship
Focus:	Therapy (All kinds)
Eligibility:	Undergraduate and graduate students
Description:	(Write to the address below for more information.)
Awards:	(400) awards per year, $500 to $15,000 undergraduate and graduate grants, fellowships, and scholarships.
Deadline:	Various deadlines
Address:	National AMBUCS Scholarships for Therapists P.O. Box 5127 High Point, NC 27262

NATIONAL BASKETBALL ASSOCIATION SCHOLARSHIP 80

Type:	Scholarships
Focus:	High school seniors located near an NBA Professional Basketball Team
Eligibility:	High school seniors
Description:	Scholarships awarded on the basis of academic excellence, based on application, essay, and scholastic scores (ACT or SAT). Athletic ability is not needed.
Awards:	(2) $1,000 scholarships to two applicants living within 75 miles of each NBA team's home city. An additional (4) $1,000 scholarships are awarded nationally.
Deadline:	Near the end of the basketball season (usually about March 1).
Address:	Write to the Team's Public Relations Department, or to: NBA Scholarships 645 Fifth Avenue New York, NY 10022

NATIONAL FEDERATION OF MUSIC CLUBS 81

Type:	Music
Focus:	Professional careers in music
Eligibility:	Junior age — must not have reached the 19th birthday by March 1. Student age — must not have reached the 26th birthday by March 1. Entrants of 16, 17, and 18 years may enter either Junior or Student competitions but not both at the same time.
Description:	Scholarships provide opportunities for students interested in professional music careers. Request student audition booklet at the address below (price $1.75).
Awards:	Various amounts varying from $35 to $5,000 per category (instrument).
Deadline:	December 1
Address:	National Federation of Music Clubs 1336 N. Delaware Street Indianapolis, IN 46202
Telephone:	(317) 638-4003

| NATIONAL 4-H COUNCIL | 82 |

Type:	Scholarships
Focus:	Agriculture, Animal Science, and Food Technology
Eligibility:	High school seniors and undergraduate students
Description:	There are a variety of programs. Contact your state's 4-H officer for details.
Awards:	Several ranging from $750 to $1,000.
Address:	National 4-H Council 7100 Connecticut Avenue Chevy Chase, MD 20815

| NATIONAL FUTURE FARMERS OF AMERICA (FFA) | 83 |

Type:	Scholarships
Focus:	Agricultural Research Projects
Eligibility:	High school juniors or seniors, college freshmen enrolled in an agriculture program.
Description:	Students are encouraged to conduct agricultural research projects related to their classroom or lab instruction. Awards are based on originality, creative ability, scientific goals, academic achievement, and school and community activities.
Awards:	At the state level, (50) $1,000 scholarships are awarded; at the regional level there are (8) $2,500 scholarships. The national winner receives a $5,000 scholarship and the national runner-up receives a $3,000 scholarships.
Deadline:	Mid-July at the state level, and regional finalists travel to Kansas City, Missouri in early November.
Address:	Ms. Carol Duval, Program Coordinator National Future Farmers of America Agriscience Student Recognition Program National Future Farmers of America Organization National Future Farmers of America Center 5632 Mt. Vernon Memorial Highway P.O. Box 15160 Alexandria, VA 22309-0160
Telephone:	(703) 360-3600

NATIONAL FUTURE FARMERS OF AMERICA (FFA)	84

Type:	Scholarships
Focus:	Agriculture, Animal Science, and Food Science and Technology
Eligibility:	High school seniors and undergraduate students.
Description:	There are a variety of programs with different restrictions.
Awards:	Several ranging from $1,000 to $25,000.
Deadline:	March 1
Address:	National FFA Foundation P.O. Box 5117 310 N. Midvale Boulevard Madison, WI 53705-0117
Telephone:	(608) 238-4222, FAX (608) 238-6350

NATIONAL HISPANIC SCHOLARSHIP FUND	85

Type:	Scholarships
Focus:	Engineering, Science, Medicine, Business, and Law
Eligibility:	Undergraduate and graduate students. Only U.S. citizens or permanent residents who come from a Mexican American, Puerto Rican, Cuban, Caribbean, Central American, or South American heritage are eligible to apply.
Description:	The program focuses on fields in which Hispanic Americans are underrepresented, such as those listed above. Recipients are selected on the basis of academic achievement, personal strengths, leadership, and financial need. Candidates submit an application, transcripts, documentation of financial need, a typed personal statement, and letters of recommendation, one of which should be from a school official.
Awards:	More than 2,000 renewable awards of $1,000 and over.
Deadline:	June 15. Notification after February 1.
Address:	National Hispanic Scholarship Fund P.O. Box 728 Novato, CA 94948
Telephone:	(415) 892-9971

NATIONAL HONOR SOCIETY SCHOLARSHIPS 86

Type:	Scholarships
Focus:	Academic Excellence
Eligibility:	High school seniors. Must be nominated by local chapter and be a member of NHS.
Description:	Must be a member of a local chapter of the National Honor Society. Each local chapter may nominate two seniors. Contact your local National Honor Society group or write to the address below.
Awards:	(1,250) $1,000 scholarships
Deadline:	High school principal should receive nomination forms by early November. Forms are due by February 7, with notification on May 1.
Address:	National Honor Society Scholarships National Association of Secondary School Principals 1904 Association Drive Reston, VA 22091
Telephone:	(703) 860-0200

NATIONAL SCIENCE SCHOLARS 87

Type:	Scholarships
Focus:	Science
Eligibility:	High school seniors admitted to an accredited college or university
Description:	Sponsored by the U.S. Department of Education and administered by the State Departments of Education, students must submit an application, high school transcript, three letters of recommendation, and an essay.
Awards:	(2) renewable awards of varying amounts (between $1,000 and $5,000, depending on the state) for one male student and one female student from each Congressional district.
Deadline:	November 1 (fall) of senior year. Notification January 1. States may set earlier deadlines.
Address:	Contact your local State Department of Education or Congressional representative, or write to the following address: National Science Scholars Program U.S. Department of Education Office of Student Financial Assistance Room 4621-ROB#3 400 Maryland Avenue, SW Washington DC 20202-5453

NATIONAL SOCIETY OF BLACK ENGINEERS 88

Type:	Scholarships
Focus:	Engineering
Eligibility:	Undergraduate and graduate student members of NSBE
Description:	Selection is based on academic achievement, NSBE service, and extracurricular activities. Applications must be endorsed by the student's NSBE advisor or department head.
Awards:	(1) $2,500 cash award and (39) $1,500 cash awards.
Deadline:	January 1
Address:	NSBE Scholars Program 1454 Duke Street Alexandria, VA 22314
Telephone:	(703) 549-2307, FAX: (703) 683-5312

NATIONAL SOCIETY OF PROFESSIONAL ENGINEERS (NSPE) | 89

Type:	Scholarships
Focus:	Engineering
Eligibility:	High school seniors. Must be a U.S. citizen. Some scholarships are reserved for minorities and women.
Description:	Must be in top 25% of high school graduating class, have minimum 3.0 GPA, and have minimum scores of V-500 and M-600 on the SAT. Entries are judged on the basis of application, transcript, test scores, financial need, and interview.
Awards:	150 scholarships ranging from $1,000 to $25,000
Deadline:	November 15, with notification in May.
Address:	National Society of Professional Engineers NSPE Scholarships, Education Foundation 1420 King Street Alexandria, VA 22314
Telephone:	(703) 684-2800

NAVY SCIENCE AWARDS PROGRAM | 90

Type:	Scholarships
Focus:	Science Fair Projects
Eligibility:	High school sophomores, juniors, and seniors. U.S. citizenship required.
Description:	Students who are top winners of their state science fairs or designated as Navy first or second place winners are eligible to submit an abstract of their projects to the National Naval Science Awards Program Competition.
Awards:	From among the competitors, 25 winners are selected to receive an all expenses paid trip to San Diego, California, with the top five winners also receiving college scholarships of (3) $8,000 and (2) $3,000.
Deadline:	April/May
Address:	Ms. Barbara M. Thurman, Project Officer Navy Science Awards Program Office of the Chief of Naval Research (Code 11SP) 800 North Quincy Street Arlington, VA 22217-5000
Telephone:	(703) 696-5787

NEH YOUNGER SCHOLARS PROGRAM 91

Type: Summer Grants

Focus: Humanities

Eligibility: High school students and undergraduate students

Description: Entries are judged on the basis of a project proposal detailing project in the humanities (history, philosophy, languages, linguistics, literature, archaeology, jurisprudence, ethics, comparative religion, anthropology, sociology, political theory, etc.) and a letter from the project advisor.

Awards: (200) grants of up to $2,500. Grants are for nine weeks of full-time summer study/research commencing June 1.

Deadline: November 1, with notification during mid-March.

Address: National Endowment for the Humanities
Office of Youth Programs
NEH Younger Scholars Program
1100 Pennsylvania Avenue, NW, Room 316
Washington, DC 20506

Telephone: (202) 786-0438, (202) 786-0361

NSA Undergraduate Training Program   92

Type: Scholarships

Focus: Electrical Engineering, Computer Engineering, Computer Science, Mathematics, or Asian, Middle Eastern, or Slavic languages

Eligibility: High school seniors. Minorities are encouraged to apply. Students must maintain at least a 3.0 GPA on a 4.0 scale after their freshman year in college. U.S. citizenship required for applicant and immediate family members.

Description: During the academic year students attend classes full-time, and work at NSA during summers in jobs tailored to their course of study. Housing assistance is available during summer work tours. If selected for the program, students are required to work for NSA after college graduation for at least one and a half times the length of study — usually five or six years. All NSA jobs are located at the NSA headquarters midway between Baltimore, Maryland, and Washington, DC. Recipients are selected on the basis of letters of recommendation, transcripts, SAT/ACT results (1,000/24 minimum total), lists of extracurricular activities, completed Application for Federal Employment (SF-171), completed Background Survey Questionnaire (OPM 1386), and a personal summary sheet.

Awards: Full tuition, stipend, summer employment, and a guaranteed job after graduation.

Deadline: Early November.

Address: National Security Agency
                Manager, Undergraduate Training Program
                Attn: M322 (UTP)
                Ft. Meade, MD 20755-6000

Telephone: 1-800-962-9398

NUCLEAR ENGINEERING EDUCATION PROGRAM   93

Type:	Employment
Focus:	Nuclear Engineering
Eligibility:	Undergraduate students
Description:	Provides opportunities and support for research and training and advanced nuclear-related technologies and procedures as well as access to modern and extensive energy research facilities.
Awards:	$200 per week; plus travel reimbursement.
Deadline:	January 16
Address:	Mr. Richard Wiesehuegel Program Manager Nuclear Engineering Education Program Oak Ridge Associated Universities P.O. Box 117 Oak Ridge, TN 37831-0117
Telephone:	(615) 576-3383

OAK RIDGE SCIENCE AND ENGINEERING RESEARCH SEMESTER   94

Type:	Scholarships
Focus:	Computer Science, Engineering, Environmental and Life Sciences, Mathematics, and Physical Sciences
Eligibility:	Undergraduate juniors and seniors
Description:	Offers challenging energy-related research opportunities in collaboration with laboratory scientists.
Awards:	Weekly stipends of $200; travel reimbursement; complimentary housing
Deadline:	October 20 and March 15
Address:	Ms. Ernestine Friedman Program Manager Oak Ridge Associated Universities P.O. Box 117 Oak Ridge, TN 37831-0117
Telephone:	(615) 576-2358

OCCUPATIONAL SAFETY & HEALTH TRAINING GRANTS   95

Type:	Grants
Focus:	Occupational Safety and Health Training
Eligibility:	Undergraduate and graduate students
Description:	Write to the address below for more information.
Address:	Public Health Service 5600 Fishers Lane Rockville, MD 20857
Telephone:	(301) 468-2600

ORACLE CORP. SCHOLARSHIP FOR THE BLIND   96

Type:	Scholarships
Focus:	Computer Science and Engineering
Eligibility:	Blind students
Description:	Recipients are selected on the basis of an application, personal letter of goals and aspirations, two letters of recommendation, transcripts, and a letter from the state officer of the NFB. Contact the NFB for more information, including the name of your local NFB state officer. The NFB also has a variety of other field-restricted and unrestricted scholarships for blind students.
Awards:	$2,500
Deadline:	March 31. Notification June 1.
Address:	National Federation of the Blind (NFB) Grinnell State Bank Building, 2nd Floor 814 4th Avenue Grinnell, IA 50112
Telephone:	(515) 236-3366

PHARMACEUTICAL MANUFACTURERS ASSOC. FOUNDATION 97

Type: Scholarships and Fellowships

Focus: Pharmacy, Pharmacology, Pharmaceutics, Chemistry, and Biology

Eligibility: Undergraduate and graduate students

Awards: $5,000 stipend for undergraduate students. Graduate students receive a $12,000 stipend plus $500 for expenses associated with their thesis research.

Deadline: October 1

Address: Maurice Q. Bectel, D.Sc.
President
Pharmaceutical Manufacturers Association Foundation Inc.
1100 Fifteenth Street, NW
Washington, DC 20005

Telephone: (202) 835-3470

PHI DELTA KAPPA SCHOLARSHIP GRANTS 98

Type: Scholarships

Focus: Students interested in pursuing a career in elementary and high school education.

Eligibility: High school seniors from the U.S.

Description: Entries are judged on the basis of an application, national test scores, transcripts, two references, and an essay. Two grants are reserved for dependents of Kappans and four for minority students. Students should request applications from the chapter nearest their homes.

Awards: (1) $2,000 grant and (41) $1,000 grants will be awarded. Some chapters will award additional scholarships.

Deadline: February 1, (late January, early February), with notification in April.

Address: Phi Delta Kappa Scholarship Grants
Phi Delta Kappa
The Professional Fraternity in Education
Eighth Street & Union Avenue, P.O. Box 789
Bloomington, IN 47402-0789

Telephone: (812) 339-1156, (800) 766-1156, FAX (812) 339-0018

PRINCIPAL'S LEADERSHIP AWARD   99

Type:	Scholarships
Focus:	Leadership
Eligibility:	High school seniors
Description:	Each high school principal may nominate one student leader from the senior class.
Awards:	(150) $1,000 scholarships
Deadline:	December 20. Each high school principal receives a scholarship nomination packet in mid-October. Winners announced April 19-25.
Address:	Principal's Leadership Award National Association of Secondary School Principals 1904 Association Drive Reston, VA 22091
Telephone:	(703) 860-0200

PRIVATE COLLEGES AND UNIVERSITIES SCHOLARSHIP   100

Type:	Scholarships
Focus:	General Scholarship
Eligibility:	Minority (including Asian) high school seniors planning to attend a private college or university (including Harvard, MIT, Wellesley, and CMU).
Description:	Entries are judged at the preliminary level by SAT/ACT scores. Finalists are judged by essays and high school transcripts.
Awards:	Varied number, $1,000.
Deadline:	November 1
Address:	Carnegie Communications, Inc. PC&U Scholarship Program 750 Third Avenue, 31st Floor New York, NY 10017

PROFESSIONAL PLANT GROWERS SCHOLARSHIP 101

Type:	Scholarships
Focus:	Horticulture
Eligibility:	Undergraduate and graduate students studying horticulture. U.S. or Canadian citizenship required.
Description:	Emphasis on academic excellence in the field of horticulture and good citizenship.
Awards:	Up to (14) scholarships ranging from $750 to $2,000 each year. Some are renewable for up to four years.
Deadline:	May 1, with notification in July.
Address:	Ms. Sue Goepp Executive Director Professional Plant Growers Scholarship Foundation P.O. Box 27517 Lansing, MI 48909
Telephone:	(517) 694-7700

PUBLIC EMPLOYEES ROUNDTABLE SCHOLARSHIP 102

Type:	Scholarships
Focus:	Public Service
Eligibility:	Undergraduate and graduate students
Description:	Must be working toward degree, 3.5 GPA. Must plan to pursue a career in government at the federal, state, or local levels. Contact congressional representative.
Awards:	$500 and $1,000 awards
Deadline:	May 15
Address:	Public Employees Roundtable P.O. Box 6184 Ben Franklin Station Washington, DC 20044-6184
Telephone:	(202) 535-4324

RC EASLEY SCHOLARSHIP PROGRAM   103

Type:	Scholarships and Awards
Focus:	Scholastic excellence, intellectual potential, personal integrity.
Eligibility:	High school seniors accepted to an accredited four-year academic institution. U.S. citizenship required.
Description:	Entries are judged on the basis of SAT/ACT scores, high school transcripts (minimum C GPA), essay, and recommendations. Send SASE and $1 handling fee to obtain information packet and applications. Note: This program requires a $4 application fee per program ($12 total) when you submit the application.
Awards:	Gold award wins $25,000 scholarship, Silver $10,000, and Bronze $5,000. All 10 finalists receive a $250 cash award.
Deadline:	February 1. Finalists interviewed in April. Notification June 1.
Address:	National Academy of American Scholars RC Easley Scholarship Program P.O. Box 7640 La Verne, CA 91750-7640
Telephone:	(714) 621-6856

ROBERT C. BYRD HONORS SCHOLARSHIP   104

Type:	Scholarships
Focus:	General Scholarship
Eligibility:	High school seniors accepted to an institution of higher education.
Description:	Entries are judged on the basis of an application, high school transcripts, standardized test results, three letters of recommendation, an essay, and the school's official written evaluation (must be nominated by the school).
Awards:	125 awards of $1,500.
Deadline:	May 21
Address:	Contact your local State Department of Education.

ROBERT H. GODDARD SCHOLARSHIP 105

Type:	Scholarships
Focus:	Science and Engineering related to space research and exploration.
Eligibility:	Undergraduate juniors or seniors and graduate students. U.S. citizenship required.
Description:	Recipients are selected on the basis of transcripts, letters of recommendation, academic/career plans that would lead to participation in aerospace science and technology, and past research and involvement in space-related science and engineering. Financial need is considered but not controlling.
Awards:	(1) $10,000 scholarship plus travel and lodging to attend the Goddard Memorial Dinner in March.
Deadline:	Early January. Notification in March.
Address:	Goddard Scholarship National Space Club 655 15th Street, NW, Suite 300 Washington, DC 20005
Telephone:	(202) 639-4210

RUST INTERNATIONAL CORPORATION SCHOLARSHIP 106

Type:	Scholarships
Focus:	Engineering
Eligibility:	High school seniors. Must be a U.S. citizen and plan to major in engineering.
Description:	Entrants will be judged on the basis of application and transcript.
Awards:	(1) $1,000 per year scholarship renewable for up to four years.
Deadline:	November 15
Address:	Rust International Scholarship Rust International Corporation P.O. Box 101 Birmingham, AL 35201

SEDS SPACE SCHOLARSHIP   107

Type:	Scholarships
Focus:	Space and space-related disciplines
Eligibility:	High school students and undergraduate students
Description:	Selection is on the basis of resume, transcripts, letters of recommendation, and an essay of career goals related to space.
Awards:	(2) $1,000 scholarships, one to a high school student and one to a undergraduate student.
Deadline:	June 1
Address:	Students for the Exploration and Development of Space (SEDS) MIT Building W20-445 77 Massachusetts Avenue Cambridge, MA 02139
Telephone:	(617) 253-8897

SHELL CENTURY III LEADERS PROGRAM   108

Type:	Scholarships
Focus:	Leadership and Current Events
Eligibility:	High school seniors from the U.S.
Description:	Entries are judged on the basis of application, projection for innovative leadership, and current events examination. Contact your high school principal.
Awards:	National winner: $11,500; (9) $2,000 runner-ups. Also two primary winners of $1,500 per state including DC and two state alternates of $500 each. Each state winner also receives an all-expense-paid trip to Virginia for a three-day national meeting.
Deadline:	Mid-October: Application and current events exam deadline. Winners announced by mid-January.
Address:	Shell Century III Leaders Program National Association of Secondary School Principals 1904 Association Drive Reston, VA 22091
Telephone:	(703) 860-0200

SIGMA PI SIGMA	109

Type:	Scholarships
Focus:	Physics
Eligibility:	Undergraduate physics majors during the junior year. Must be an active member of Sigma Pi Sigma (Society of Physics Students).
Description:	Recipients are selected on the basis of an application, transcripts, and two letters of recommendation.
Awards:	(6) $1,000 nonrenewable grants to help fund the final year of undergraduate study.
Deadline:	January 31. Notification April 30.
Address:	Society of Physics Students American Institute of Physics 1825 Connecticut Avenue, NW, Suite 213 Washington, DC 20009
Telephone:	(202) 232-6688, FAX (202) 328-3729

SIGMA XI GRANTS-IN-AID OF RESEARCH	110

Type:	Research Grants
Focus:	Scientific Research
Eligibility:	Undergraduate and graduate students
Description:	Two letters of recommendation and endorsement from specialists in the student's field, including the research advisor, and a project proposal.
Awards:	$100 to $1,000 to pay for research costs. Awards normally do not exceed $600.
Deadline:	The committee meets three times per year with closing dates for application on February 1, May 1, and November 1.
Address:	Committee on Grants-in-Aid of Research Sigma Xi Headquarters 99 Alexander Drive, Box 13975 Research Triangle Park, NC 27709
Telephone:	1-800-243-6534, (919) 549-4691

SIMON'S ROCK ACCELERATION TO EXCELLENCE PROGRAM   111

Type:	Scholarships
Focus:	Academic and extracurricular excellence in the arts and sciences
Eligibility:	High school sophomores. Candidates should have a cumulative GPA of 3.3 or above. Candidates must also demonstrate sustained effort and achievement in one or more extracurricular activities in the arts, science, community service, athletics, or another area of interest.
Description:	The Acceleration to Excellence Program offers outstanding tenth-graders full scholarships to enroll as freshmen at Simon's Rock College of Bard. Simon's Rock is a highly rated college of the liberal arts and sciences, specifically designed for students of high school age. The school is located in western Massachusetts. Applications consist of student essays, a parental statement, two academic recommendations, and one extracurricular recommendation.
Awards:	(30) full tuition scholarships, including fees, room, and board, for two full years of attendance at Simon's Rock. Upon successful completion of the college's two-year Associate in Arts degree program, students will be eligible to complete their B.A. at Simon's Rock or Bard College at tuition equal to the tuition of their state college. Students also receive a $1,500 stipend during the summer to pay for registration for a summer study program at Simon's Rock, Bard, or another college or university of their choice during the summer between their freshman and sophomore years.
Deadline:	May 1. Finalists notified May 15. Finalists and their families will be interviewed by May 30, and award winners announced in early June.
Address:	The Acceleration to Excellence Program Office of Academic Affairs Simon's Rock College of Bard 84 Alford Road Great Barrington, MA 01230-9702
Telephone:	(413) 528-0771

SOCIETY OF ACTUARIES 112

Type:	Scholarships
Focus:	Actuarial Science
Eligibility:	Minority undergraduate students who are interested in pursuing actuarial careers. Eligible minorities include Black/African Americans, Hispanic Americans, Asian Americans, and Native American Indians. U.S. citizenship or permanent residency required.
Description:	Applicants should have taken Exam 100 of the Actuarial Examinations, the SAT, or the ACT, and must have demonstrated mathematical ability. Applicants must submit a Financial Aid Form (FAF) and two nomination forms. Scholarships are awarded on the basis of academic merit and financial need. The SOA scholarship committee also administers the CIGNA Actuarial Science Fellowships for Minorities scholarship program.
Awards:	The amount of the scholarship is determined by a committee of members of the Society of Actuaries and the Casualty Actuarial Society.
Deadline:	May 1
Address:	Society of Actuaries 475 N. Martingale Road, Suite 800 Schaumburg, IL 60173-2226
Telephone:	(708) 706-3500

SOCIETY OF AUTOMOTIVE ENGINEERS 113

Type:	Scholarships
Focus:	Engineering
Eligibility:	High school seniors and undergraduate students
Description:	Selection is on the basis of transcripts and SATs.
Awards:	Amounts range from $500 to $6,000.
Deadline:	January 1
Address:	Society of Automotive Engineers Scholarship Program 400 Commonwealth Drive Warrendale, PA 15096
Telephone:	(412) 776-4841

SOCIETY OF EXPLORATION GEOPHYSICISTS   114

Type:	Scholarships
Focus:	Geophysics or a closely related field
Eligibility:	High school seniors, undergraduate students, and graduate students
Description:	Entries are judged on the basis of application, transcripts, and letters of recommendation. Students should intend to pursue a major in geophysics. Results of aptitude test, college entrance exams, etc., are not required but should be included if taken.
Awards:	(112+) awards. Renewable scholarships ranging from $750 to $3,000.
Deadline:	March 1
Address:	Scholarship Committee Society of Exploration Geophysicists Foundation P.O. Box 702740 Tulsa, OK 74170-2740
Telephone:	(918) 493-3516, FAX (918) 493-2074

SOCIETY OF HISPANIC PROFESSIONAL ENGINEERS   115

Type:	Scholarships
Focus:	Engineering and Science
Eligibility:	Minorities enrolled or about to be enrolled full time in an engineering or science program.
Description:	Preference is given to SHPE members and to students with high academic achievement and high community involvement. Must demonstrate financial need.
Awards:	(100+) grants ranging from $300 to $1,500.
Deadline:	April 1
Address:	The Society of Hispanic Professional Engineers 5400 East Olympic Boulevard, Suite 225 Los Angeles, CA 90022
Telephone:	(213) 725-3970/3988

SOCIETY OF MANUFACTURING ENGINEERS	116

Type:	Scholarships
Focus:	Manufacturing Engineering or Robotics
Eligibility:	Undergraduate students. U.S. citizenship required.
Awards:	$1,000
Deadline:	March 1
Address:	Society of Manufacturing Engineers Educational Foundation P.O. Box 930 One SME Drive Dearborn, MI 48121
Telephone:	(313) 271-1500

SOCIETY OF MINING ENGINEERS	117

Type:	Scholarships
Focus:	Mining Engineering
Eligibility:	Undergraduate students
Description:	The SME publishes a detailed guide to their scholarships. Write to the address below for a copy.
Awards:	(100+) scholarships of up to $2,000.
Address:	Society of Mining Engineers P.O. Box 625002 Littleton, CO 80162-5002

SOCIETY OF NAVAL ARCHITECTS AND MARINE ENGINEERS	118

Type:	Scholarships and Fellowships
Focus:	Naval Engineering, including Naval Architecture, Marine Engineering, Ocean Engineering, Mechanical Engineering, Civil Engineering, Electrical Engineering, and the Physical Sciences
Eligibility:	Undergraduate and graduate students. U.S. or Canadian citizenship required.
Description:	The undergraduate scholarship program is limited to MIT, University of Michigan, University of California at Berkeley, State University of New York Maritime College, and Florida Atlantic University. Scholarship recipients are selected by the schools. Thus applications for SNAME's undergraduate scholarships should be made directly to the schools. In addition, the Webb Institute of Naval Architecture, Crescent Beach Road, Glen Cove, NY 11542, charges no tuition to any of its undergraduate students, and is supported in part by SNAME.
Awards:	Graduate fellowships are usually made for one year of study leading to a master's degree.
Deadline:	February 1
Address:	Society of Naval Architects and Marine Engineers (SNAME) 601 Pavonia Avenue, Suite 400 Jersey City, NJ 07306
Telephone:	(201) 798-4800, FAX (201) 798-4975

SOCIETY OF PETROLEUM ENGINEERS (SPE)	119

Type:	Scholarships
Focus:	Petroleum Engineering
Eligibility:	High school seniors
Description:	Contact the section officer nearest you or nearest the school you plan on attending. For a list of section officers, write to the address below.
Awards:	The Gus Archie Memorial Scholarship provides $3,000 per year for four years. SPE sections also run their own scholarship programs.
Deadline:	April 30
Address:	Society of Petroleum Engineers P.O. Box 833836 Richardson, TX 75083-3836
Telephone:	(214) 669-3377, FAX (214) 669-0135

SOCIETY OF WOMEN ENGINEERS SCHOLARSHIP · 120

Type:	Scholarships
Focus:	Engineering
Eligibility:	Must be a female undergraduate majoring (or a female high school senior planning to major) in engineering in a school, college, or university with an accredited engineering program.
Description:	Entries are judged on the basis of application, transcript, recommendations, and essay.
Awards:	(38) scholarships ranging from $500 to $3,000
Deadline:	Postmarked no later than May 15, with notification by September 15.
Address:	Society of Women Engineers United Engineering Center, Room 305 345 East 47th Street New York, NY 10017
Telephone:	(212) 705-7855

SOIL & WATER CONSERVATION SCHOLARSHIPS · 121

Type:	Scholarships
Focus:	Conservation
Eligibility:	Undergraduate juniors and seniors
Description:	Students majoring in an agricultural or natural resource conservation program.
Awards:	(9) $1,000 awards.
Deadline:	April 1. Notification in August.
Address:	Soil and Water Conservation Society 7515 NE Ankeny Road Ankeny, IA 50021
Telephone:	(515) 289-2331, FAX (515) 289-1227

SOROPTIMIST TRAINING AWARDS PROGRAM (TAP)   122

Type:	Awards
Eligibility:	Female high school seniors. Must be a U.S. citizen.
Description:	Recipients are chosen on the basis of financial need as well as the statement of clear career goals, with primary consideration given to women completing undergraduate degrees.
Awards:	(54) $3,000 cash awards. One finalist is chosen from among these 54 regional recipients to receive an additional cach award of $10,000.
Deadline:	December 15, with notification in April
Address:	Soroptimist Training Awards Program Soroptimist International of the Americas 1616 Walnut Street Philadelphia, PA 19103

SOROPTIMIST YOUTH CITIZENSHIP AWARD (YCA)   123

Type:	Awards
Focus:	Good Citizenship
Eligibility:	High school seniors. Must be a U.S. citizen.
Description:	Entries are judged on the basis of the application. The student must have demonstrated service in the home, school, and community; dependability and leadership throughout his/her high school years.
Awards:	(54) $1,250 cash awards. One finalist is chosen from among these 54 regional recipients to receive an additional cash award of $2,500.
Deadline:	December 15, with notification in April
Address:	Soroptimist Youth Citizenship Award Soroptimist International of the Americas 1616 Walnut Street Philadelphia, PA 19103

Space Shuttle Student Involvement Project (SSIP) | 124

Type:	Scholarships and Awards
Focus:	Space Experiments
Eligibility:	High school students in all U.S. public, private, parochial, and overseas schools, including Puerto Rico, Guam, and U.S. territories.
Description:	The NSTA/NASA Space Shuttle Student Involvement Program provides an opportunity for high school students to propose experiments which might be suitable for possible flight aboard the Space Shuttle. Entries judged on 1,000 word project and recommendations.
Awards:	Awards ranging from certificates of recognition and plaques to space center trips, cash awards, and scholarships.
Deadline:	March 15
Address:	Space Shuttle Student Involvement Project National Science Teachers Association 1742 Connecticut Avenue, NW Washington, DC 20009-1171
Telephone:	(202) 328-5800

State Farm Companies Foundation | 125

Type:	Scholarships
Focus:	Business-related fields, including Accounting, Business Administration, Actuarial Science, Computer Science, Economics, Finance, Insurance, Investments, Management, Marketing, Mathematics, and Statistics
Eligibility:	College juniors and seniors. Must have a 3.4 or higher GPA. U.S. citizenship required.
Description:	Students must be nominated by an academic officer of their current institution.
Awards:	(50) $3,000 nonrenewable scholarships. A $250 grant is made to the nominating institution, and a $500 grant will be made to the college or university the student will be attending if it is not tax-supported.
Deadline:	February 15
Address:	State Farm Companies Foundation One State Farm Plaza, SC-3 Bloomington, IL 61710-0001

TAILHOOK ASSOCIATION SCHOLARSHIPS   126

Type:	Scholarships
Focus:	Aerospace Technology
Eligibility:	High school seniors. Must be sponsored by an Association member or be the dependent of an Association member.
Description:	Entries are judged on the basis of application, 300 word statement of educational goals, high school transcript, and national test scores (SAT/ACT).
Awards:	(4) $1,000 scholarships
Deadline:	July 15, with notification on or about August 1.
Address:	Tailhook Association Scholarships P.O. Box 40 Bonita, CA 92002

TANDY TECHNOLOGY SCHOLARS   127

Type:	Scholarships
Focus:	Mathematics, Science, and Computer Science
Eligibility:	High school seniors
Description:	The high schools must register so that their students may compete for scholarships. Awards are based on GPA, standardized test scores (PSAT, SAT, ACT), high school transcript, and recommendations. Students must also be in the top 2% of graduating class.
Awards:	(100) $1,000 scholarships awarded nationally.
Deadline:	November 1
Address:	Tandy Technology Scholars P.O. Box 32897 TCU Station Fort Worth, TX 76129
Telephone:	(817) 924-4087, FAX (817) 927-1942

TECHNICAL COMMUNICATION SCHOLARSHIPS 128

Type: Scholarships and Fellowships

Focus: Technical Communication

Eligibility: Upperclass undergraduates and graduate students majoring in established degree programs in technical communication.

Description: Selection is on the basis of academic record and financial need. Write for an application.

Awards: (12) $1,500 awards, 6 to undergraduates and 6 to graduate students.

Deadline: February 15

Address: Society for Technical Communication
901 N. Stuart Street, Suite 304
Arlington, VA 22203

Telephone: (703) 522-4144, FAX (703) 522-2075

TELLURIDE ASSOCIATION SCHOLARSHIPS 129

Type: Scholarships

Focus: Leadership

Description: For students demonstrating intellectual capacity, idealism, leadership ability, and common sense in practical situations.

Awards: (20-30) full room and board scholarships at Cornell University.

Deadline: May/June

Address: Telluride Association Scholarships
217 West Avenue
Ithaca, NY 14850

Telephone: (607) 273-5011

| THOMAS EDISON/MAX MCGRAW SCHOLARSHIP PROGRAM | 130 |

Type: Scholarships

Focus: Science and Engineering Projects

Eligibility: All students in grades 7–12 in public, private, and parochial schools in the U.S., Canada, or other participating nations.

Description: Entries consist of: (1) A double-spaced five-page proposal (1,000 words max) of a completed experiment or a project that deals with a practical application in science or engineering; (2) A single letter of recommendation from student's teacher/sponsor; and (3) a coversheet with the title, the student's name, address, phone, and grade, and the teacher's name, school address, and school phone number.

Awards: $6,000 and $3,000 for Junior (7–9) and Senior Division (10–12) Grand Scholars respectively. The four remaining finalists in each of the Junior and Senior Divisions will receive $750 and $1,500 respectively.

Deadline: December 1, with notification by February 1.

Address: Dr. Kenneth R. Roy
NSSA LISE Executive Director
Thomas Edison/Max McGraw Scholarship Program
Copernicus Hall, Suite 227
Central Connecticut State University
New Britain, CT 06050

TOSHIBA NSTA EXPLORAVISION AWARDS | 131

Type: Scholarships

Focus: Future of Science and Technology

Eligibility: Students in kindergarten through grade 12

Description: Students work in teams of four with a teacher advisor (and an optional community advisor). Each team selects a form of technology currently used in the home, school, or community, and projects it 20 years into the future. Teams are judged by their project description, storyboard, and application form.

Awards: The forty-eight student teams selected as regional winners will receive funding for the production of a video presentation of their ExploraVision project. Twelve teams will be selected as finalists. The finalists, their parents, and their teacher advisors will receive an all-expense paid trip to the awards ceremony in Washington, DC in June. Student members of the four winning teams in the national competition will each receive $10,000 U.S. savings bonds; members of the eight runner-up teams will receive $5,000 U.S. savings bonds. Teacher advisors and the schools of winning teams will receive Toshiba products.

Deadline: February 1

Address: Toshiba NSTA ExploraVision Awards
National Science Teachers Association
1742 Connecticut Avenue, NW
Washington, DC 20009-1171

Telephone: (202) 328-5800, FAX (202) 328-0974

UNDERGRADUATE RESEARCH PARTICIPATION PROGRAM/ORNL — 132

Type:	Research Grants
Focus:	Behavioral Sciences, Computer Science, and Engineering
Eligibility:	Undergraduate students
Description:	Provides opportunities and support for research participation in advanced simulation and systems training technology.
Awards:	Stipend based on research areas and academic classification.
Deadline:	Ongoing
Address:	Mr. Jim Wright Program Manager Oak Ridge Associated Universities P.O. Box 117 Oak Ridge, TN 37831-0117
Telephone:	(615) 576-1716

USA TODAY ALL-USA ACADEMIC TEAM — 133

Type:	Scholarships
Focus:	General — Scholarship and Leadership
Eligibility:	High school students
Description:	Entries are judged on the basis of a nomination and a description of the student's outstanding original academic or intellectual product in the student's own words.
Awards:	(25) $2,500 scholarships
Deadline:	March 6
Address:	USA Today All-USA Academic Team 1000 Wilson Blvd. Arlington, VA 22229
Telephone:	(703) 276-3400

U.S. DEPARTMENT OF EDUCATION 134

Type:	Scholarships and Fellowships
Focus:	Undergraduate and graduate programs in Education, Law, Medicine, Psychology, Natural Resources, Business, and Engineering
Eligibility:	Native American Indians
Awards:	Full tuition and stipends.
Deadline:	February
Address:	U.S. Department of Education Indian Fellowship Program 400 Maryland Avenue, SW Room 2177, Mail Stop 6267 Washington, DC 20202

U.S. SENATE YOUTH PROGRAM 135

Type:	Scholarships
Focus:	Student Government Officers
Eligibility:	High school students
Description:	Selections are done by state.
Awards:	(104) $2,000 scholarships to elected student government officers.
Address:	William Randolph Hearst Foundation U.S. Senate Youth Program 90 New Montgomery Street, #1212 San Francisco, CA 94105

VA HEALTH PROFESSIONAL SCHOLARSHIP PROGRAM   136

Type:	Scholarships
Focus:	Physical Therapy
Eligibility:	Third and fourth year students in bachelor's or master's programs.
Description:	Must serve one-year as a full-time RN or physical therapist in a VA medical center for each year of scholarship support. Contact Chief of Nursing Service or the Chief of Rehabilitation Medicine at any VA medical center.
Awards:	Tuition, expenses, and a monthly stipend of $621. Maximum length of award is two years.
Deadline:	May 29
Address:	Veterans Administration Health Professional Scholarship Program Office of Academic Affairs (14N) 810 Vermont Avenue, NW Washington, DC 20420
Telephone:	1-800-368-5896

VERTICAL FLIGHT FOUNDATION   137

Type:	Scholarships
Focus:	Vertical Flight
Eligibility:	Undergraduate and graduate students
Description:	For a career in vertical flight technology.
Awards:	$2,000 scholarship.
Deadline:	February 1
Address:	Vertical Flight Foundation 217 N. Washington Street Alexandria, VA 22314
Telephone:	(703) 684-6777, FAX (703) 739-9279

WASHINGTON CROSSING NATIONAL SCHOLARSHIP 138

Type:	Scholarships
Focus:	Government
Eligibility:	High school seniors. Must be a U.S. citizen and plan a carrer of service to U.S. local, state, or federal government.
Description:	Entries are judged on the basis of application, high school transcript, recommendations, national test scores (SAT/ACT), and a one-page essay stating why the student has chosen a career in government service.
Awards:	$5,000 scholarship ($2,000 for the first year and $1,000 per year for the remaining three). There are also scholarships for students from specific states (PA, NJ, 13 original colonies) and additional awards as well.
Deadline:	January 15, with notification by telephone by April 15.
Address:	Mr. Eugene C. Fish, Esquire President Washington Crossing Foundation Washington Crossing National Crossing 1280 General DeFermoy Road, P.O. Box 1976 Washington Crossing, PA 18977
Telephone:	(215) 493-6577

WEBB INSTITUTE OF NAVAL ARCHITECTURE 139

Type:	Scholarships
Focus:	Naval Architecture
Eligibility:	Top high school students with high SAT scores
Description:	Ship design.
Awards:	Full tuition.
Address:	Webb Institute of Naval Architecture Cresent Beach Road Glen Cove, NY 11542-1398

WESTINGHOUSE SCIENCE TALENT SEARCH	140

Type: Scholarships and Awards

Focus: All scientific and mathematical fields

Eligibility: High school seniors from the U.S. and its territories

Description: Entries are judged on the basis of 1,000 word report on an independent research project in mathematics or science (excluding live vertebrae experimentation), personal data given out by the student, his/her teachers, and principal, and high school transcript.

Awards: The top 300 entries are named to the Honors Group and are provided with recommendations to their colleges. The top 40 finalists from this group will compete for one $40,000 and nine other scholarships. The rest of the top 40 receive a $1,000 cash award.

Deadline: Early December

Address: Science Service, Inc.
               Ms. Carol Luszcz, Program Director
               Westinghouse Science Talent Search
               1719 N Street, NW
               Washington, DC 20036

Telephone: (202) 785-2255

WESTON, INC.	141

Type: Scholarships

Focus: Geosciences

Eligibility: Undergraduate students

Description: Some information on private assistance for minorities in the geosciences is available from the address below.

Address: Dr. D.D. Gonzales
               c/o Roy F. Weston, Inc.
               5301 Central Avenue, NE
               Albuquerque, NM 87108

WILSON ORNITHOLOGICAL SOCIETY RESEARCH | 142

Type:	Awards
Focus:	Ornithology
Eligibility:	High school students and undergraduate students
Awards:	March 1
Deadline:	(3) $200 awards
Address:	Museum of Zoology Wilson Ornithological Society Research Awards University of Michigan Ann Arbor, MI 48109-1079
Telephone:	(313) 764-0457

YOUNG WOMAN OF THE YEAR | 143

Type:	Scholarships
Focus:	General, Scholarship
Eligibility:	Female high school seniors. Must be U.S. citizens and must never have been married.
Description:	Formerly *America's Junior Miss*, this program is not so much a pageant as a scholarship competition. Finalists and winners are selected on the basis of a panel evaluation (30%), scholastic achievement (20%), creative and performing arts (20%), fitness (15%), and poise (15%).
Awards:	The national winner receives a $30,000 scholarship to the college of her choice. Scholarships presented at the local, state, and national levels now exceed $3.5 million annually.
Address:	Young Woman of the Year Program P.O. Box 2786 Mobile, AL 36652-2786

Chapter 6

Fellowships

This chapter lists graduate fellowship programs. Some of the programs in the previous chapter, however, also allow graduate students to apply.

AABB SCHOLARSHIP PROGRAM	144

Type: Scholarships

Focus: Blood Technology

Eligibility: Graduate students accepted or enrolled in an accredited program.

Description: Studying in a program leading to specialist in blood banking certification.

Awards: (5) $1,500 awards

Deadline: April 1

Address: AABB
Suite 600
1117 N. 19th Street
Arlington, VA 22209

AACSB/GMAC Fellowship Program   145

Type:	Fellowships
Focus:	Computer Science, Economics, History, Mathematics, Psychology, Political Science, Sociology, Systems Engineering, Industrial Engineering, and Business Administration
Eligibility:	Students who will enroll in doctoral programs in business and management. U.S. or Canadian citizenship required. Women and ethnic minorities are encouraged to apply.
Awards:	(100+) fellowships providing tuition and fees and a $10,000 stipend.
Deadline:	January 5
Address:	National Doctoral Fellowship Program c/o AACSB P.O. Box 78185 St. Louis, MO 63178

ADHA Institute of Oral Health   146

Type:	Scholarships
Focus:	Dental Hygiene
Eligibility:	Students enrolled in at least the second year of dental hygiene program.
Description:	Also has a minority program.
Awards:	Up to $1,500 awards.
Deadline:	May 1
Address:	ADHA Institute for Oral Health 444 N. Michigan, #3400 Chicago, IL 60611

AEROSPACE EDUCATION FOUNDATION 147

Type: Fellowships

Focus: Science, Mathematics, Physics, and Engineering

Eligibility: Senior Air Force ROTC cadets who plan to pursue a master's degree.

Awards: (10) $5,000 Dr. Theodore von Kármán graduate scholarships.

Address: Aerospace Education Foundation
1501 Lee Highway
Arlington, VA 22209-1198

Telephone: (703) 247-5839

AIR FORCE LABORATORY GRADUATE FELLOWSHIP PROGRAM 148

Type: Fellowships

Focus: Science, Mathematics, and Engineering

Eligibility: Students must be at or near the beginning of their graduate studies. Preference is given to graduating college seniors and first year graduate students. Must be a U.S. citizen. Fellowship tenable only at approved U.S. institutions.

Description: Fellowships support study and research leading to a doctoral degree. Recipients are required to spend one summer research period at their sponsoring Air Force laboratory during the first two years of the program. Recipients selected on the basis of an application, transcripts, three letters of recommendation, and GRE scores (General Test only). Write to the address below or to the American Society for Engineering Education, 11 Dupont Circle, Suite 200, Washington, DC 20036. Fellows do *not* incur any military or other service obligation.

Awards: (25) 36-month fellowships. Stipend is $17,000 per year (with a $1,000 annual increase each subsequent year), plus full tuition, fees, and $2,000 per year to the Fellow's department.

Deadline: Mid to late January. Notification mid-April.

Address: Air Force Laboratory Graduate Fellowship Program (AFLGFP)
Southeastern Center for Electrical Engineering Education
11th & Massachusetts
St. Cloud, FL 34769

Telephone: (407) 892-6146, FAX (407) 957-4535

ALEXANDER HOLLAENDER FELLOWSHIP PROGRAM   149

Type:	Postdoctoral Fellowships
Focus:	Biomedical Sciences, Life Sciences, Environmental Sciences, and other related scientific disciplines
Eligibility:	Must have completed doctoral degree within the last two years.
Description:	Provides opportunities and support for research and training in energy-related life, biomedical, and environmental sciences.
Awards:	Annual stipend of $35,000; reimbursement for inbound travel and moving.
Deadline:	January 16
Address:	Ms. Linda McCamant Program Manager Alexander Hollaender Distinguished Postdoctoral Fellowship Program Oak Ridge Associated Universities P.O. Box 117 Oak Ridge, TN 37831-0117
Telephone:	(615) 576-1089

| AMERICAN ASSOCIATION FOR DENTAL RESEARCH | 150 |

Type: Fellowships

Focus: Dental and Oral Health Research

Eligibility: Students must be enrolled in an accredited DDS/DMD or hygiene program in dental health institution within the U.S. and must be sponsored by a faculty member at that institution.

Description: Students submit proposals for basic and clinical research related to oral health, along with recommendations, curriculum vitae, and a biographical sketch of the sponsor. If human subjects or vertebrate animals will be used, copies of the institutional review boards approval must be included. Proposals are evaluated on their scientific merits, and awards are made on the basis of the creativity of the project, its feasibility, and its potential significance to oral health research.

Awards: Approximately 26 fellowships consisting of a $1,600 stipend and $300 for supplies. Upon completion of the research, winners will also receive travel and accommodation funds to attend the AADR annual meeting to present their research.

Deadline: Early January. Winners are announced at the AADR annual meeting in mid-March.

Address: American Association for Dental Research
Attn: Patricia J. Lewis, Administrative Coord.
1111 Fourteenth Street, NW, Suite 1000
Washington, DC 20005

Telephone: (202) 898-1050, FAX (202) 789-1033

AMERICAN ASSOCIATION OF UNIVERSITY WOMEN   151

Type:	Grants and Fellowships
Focus:	Grants for advanced research, graduate study, and community service. Some eligible fields include Computer Science, Engineering, Mathematics, Statistics, and Architecture.
Eligibility:	Must be female and a U.S. citizen. Some fellowships are available for foreign citizens; write to the AAUW for more information.
Description:	Requires application.
Awards:	Fellowships and grants are available, including: dissertation $10,000, postdoctoral (1) $20,000, (7) $16,500, career-related study within five years of receipt of bachelor's degree $500-$5,000, grants for nonacademic projects $500-$2,500. The dissertation fellowship is for women who expect to receive the doctorate degree at the end of the fellowship year.
Deadline:	November 15 for dissertation/postdoctoral and February 1 for research and project grants
Address:	American Association of University Women 1111 16th Street, NW Washington, DC 20036
Telephone:	(202) 728-7603, FAX (202) 872-1425

| AMERICAN FOUNDATION FOR PHARMACEUTICAL EDUCATION | 152 |

Type: Fellowships

Focus: Pharmaceutical Sciences

Eligibility: Graduate students enrolled in a Ph.D. program in the pharmaceutical sciences. Students must have completed at least one semester in their program, and must be U.S. citizens or permanent residents.

Description: Selection is on the basis of an application, transcripts, references, and a description of the proposed research.

Awards: (70) regular fellowships of $6,000, renewable twice for a total coverage of three years. Several special fellowships are also available with stipends ranging from $7,500 to $10,000. Some $5,000 scholarships for first-year support are also available.

Deadline: March 1, with notification in mid-April.

Address: American Foundation for Pharmaceutical Education
618 Somerset Street, P.O. Box 7126
North Plainfield, NJ 07060

Telephone: (201) 561-8077

| AMERICAN FUND FOR DENTAL HEALTH | 153 |

Type: Scholarships

Focus: Dental Lab Technology

Eligibility: Students enrolled or planning to enroll in accredited Dental Administration or DLT program.

Description: Also has a minority program.

Awards: (30) scholarships each year ranging from $500 to $600.

Deadline: June 1

Address: American Fund for Dental Health
211 East Chicago Avenue, Suite 820
Chicago, IL 60611

Telephone: (312) 787-6270, FAX (312) 787-9114

AMERICAN FUND FOR DENTAL HEALTH   154

Type:	Scholarships
Focus:	Dentistry
Eligibility:	Students enrolled or planning to enroll in accredited Dental Administration or DLT program.
Description:	Scholarships for each of first two years of dental school.
Awards:	$2,000 scholarships
Deadline:	May 1
Address:	American Fund for Dental Health 211 East Chicago Avenue, Suite 820 Chicago, IL 60611
Telephone:	(312) 787-6270, FAX (312) 787-9114

AMERICAN GEOPHYSICAL UNION   155

Type:	Fellowship Research Grants
Focus:	Hydrology (including its physical, chemical or biological aspects) and Water Resources Policy Sciences (including Economics, Systems Analysis, Sociology, and Law).
Eligibility:	Graduate students
Description:	The Hydrology Section of the AGU awards 2 Horton Research Grants per year for support of research in hydrology and/or water resources by Ph.D. candidates.
Deadline:	March 1
Address:	American Geophysical Union Attn: Kathy Cooper 2000 Florida Avenue, NW Washington, DC 20009
Telephone:	(202) 462-6900 x310

AMERICAN MUSICOLOGICAL SOCIETY 156

Type:	Fellowships
Focus:	Music
Eligibility:	Graduate students
Awards:	(3) dissertation fellowships/year, twelve-month stipend (nonrenewable) of $10,000.
Deadline:	October 1
Address:	Secretary
	AMS Fellowship Committee
	Department of Music
	New York University, 268 Waverly Building
	Washington Square
	New York, NY 10003

AMERICAN SOCIETY OF NAVAL ENGINEERS (ASNE) 157

Type:	Scholarships
Focus:	Naval Engineering, including Naval Architecture, Marine Engineering, Mechanical Engineering, Civil Engineering, Electrical Engineering, and the Physical Sciences
Eligibility:	College seniors and first-year graduate students. U.S. citizenship required. Must demonstrate or express a genuine interest in a career in naval engineering.
Description:	Recipients are selected on the basis of the candidate's academic record, work history, professional promise and interest in naval engineering, extracurricular activities, and recommendations from college faculty and employers. Financial need may also be considered.
Awards:	$2,000 scholarship. Successful applicants also receive honorary student membership in ASNE.
Deadline:	February 15. Notification in early May.
Address:	The American Society of Naval Engineers
	1452 Duke Street
	Alexandria, VA 22314-3458
Telephone:	(703) 836-6727

AMERICAN VACUUM SOCIETY   158

Type:	Fellowships
Focus:	Vacuum Science and Technology, including Vacuum Metallurgy, Surface Physics, Thin Film Research, and Electronic Materials and Processing
Eligibility:	Graduate students in North American schools.
Description:	Russell and Sigurd Varian Fellowship Award recipients are selected on the basis of their academic record, advisor's recommendation, research plans, and accomplishments. Finalists receive up to $500 to cover the costs of attending the Vacuum Society National Symposium, where they are interviewed by the scholarship committee to select the winner.
Awards:	$1,500 fellowship
Deadline:	March 31
Address:	American Vacuum Society 335 East 45th Street New York, NY 10017
Telephone:	(212) 661-9404

AMOCO PH.D. FELLOWSHIPS   159

Type:	Fellowships
Focus:	Science and Engineering
Eligibility:	Graduate students who have a B.S. or M.S. in engineering or earth and physical sciences (e.g., geology, geophysics).
Description:	Candidates apply directly through participating universities. Write to the foundation for a list of participating universities.
Awards:	Engineering fellowships consist of a $11,000 stipend which is renewable for up to 2 additional years. Science fellowships consist of a nonrenewable $9,000 stipend.
Address:	Amoco Foundation Inc. 200 East Randolph Drive Chicago, IL 60601
Telephone:	(312) 856-6306

ARTHUR ANDERSON DISSERTATION FELLOWSHIPS	160

Type:	Fellowships
Focus:	Computer Science, Accounting, Business Administration, MIS
Eligibility:	Graduate students close to finishing the dissertation.
Description:	Recipients agree to teach at the university level in one of the above fields for at least three years or to repay the fellowship. Recipients are selected on the basis of transcripts, GREs, 2500-word dissertation description statement, and five recommendations, including one from the thesis advisor.
Awards:	(3) $1,500/month stipend plus in-state dissertation tuition.
Deadline:	March 1 (October 1). Notification April 1 (November 1).
Address:	Arthur Anderson & Co. Foundation 69 West Washington Street Chicago, IL 60602
Telephone:	(312) 507-3402, FAX (312) 507-2548

ASA COX STATISTICS SCHOLARSHIP	161

Type:	Fellowships
Focus:	Statistics
Eligibility:	Female graduate students. U.S. or Canadian citizenship or permanent residency required.
Awards:	(3) $1,000
Deadline:	April 30. Notification in August at the annual ASA meeting.
Address:	Gertrude M. Cox Scholarship American Statistical Association 1429 Duke Street Alexandria, VA 22314
Telephone:	(703) 684-1221

ASA MINORITY SOCIOLOGY FELLOWSHIP PROGRAM   162

Type:	Fellowships
Focus:	Sociological aspects of Mental Health
Eligibility:	Minority graduate students, including Black Americans, Hispanic Americans, Native American Indians, Asian Americans, and Native Pacific Islanders. U.S. citizenship required.
Description:	Recipients must demonstrate an interest in a teaching, research, or service career in the sociological aspects of mental health. Students are selected on the basis of potential for academic success and financial need, using an application, transcripts, letters of recommendation, and a statement of career goals. Upon receipt of their degree, ASA fellows are required to engage in behavioral research for a period equal to the length of support beyond 12 months. Program continuation is subject to the renewal of federal funding.
Awards:	(10) fellowships with a stipend of $8,500 per year plus tuition, books, and supplies. Fellowships are renewable for two additional years. There are also dissertation awards of $5,000 (nonrenewable).
Deadline:	December 31. Notification April 15.
Address:	American Sociological Association 1722 N Street, NW Washington, DC 20036-2981
Telephone:	(202) 833-3410 x326

ASM MINORITY FELLOWSHIPS   163

Type:	Fellowships
Focus:	Microbiology
Eligibility:	Graduate students. U.S. citizenship or permanent residency required. Must be a member of one of the following minority groups: African American, Hispanic American, Native Alaskan, Native American, or Native Pacific Islander.
Description:	Applicant must have been formally admitted as a candidate for a Ph.D. in microbiology in an accredited U.S. institution at the time of application.
Awards:	$10,000 stipend, a portion of which must be used for tuition and fees.
Deadline:	May 1
Address:	Christina M. Johnson Office of Public and Scientific Affairs American Society for Microbiology 1325 Massachusetts Avenue, NW Washington, DC 20005-4171
Telephone:	(202) 737-3600 x295, FAX (202) 737-0233

ASSOCIATION OF WOMEN IN SCIENCE   164

Type:	Awards
Focus:	Any field of Science — including the Physical Sciences, Natural Sciences, Social Sciences, and Behavioral Sciences — Mathematics, and Engineering.
Eligibility:	Must be a female graduate student majoring in science, mathematics, or engineering. If not a U.S. citizen, must be studying in a U.S. institution. If a U.S. citizen, may be used in the U.S. or abroad.
Awards:	(5) $500 fellowships
Deadline:	January 15. Notification after June 15.
Address:	Association for Women in Science (AWIS) Educational Foundation Predoctoral Awards Program 1522 K Street, NW, Suite 820 Washington, DC 20005
Telephone:	(202) 408-0742, FAX (202) 408-8321

AT&T COOPERATIVE RESEARCH FELLOWSHIP PROGRAM   165

Type:	Fellowships
Focus:	Chemistry, Chemical Engineering, Communications Science, Computer Science & Engineering, Electrical Engineering, Information Science, Materials Science, Mathematics, Mechanical Engineering, Operations Research, Physics, and Statistics
Eligibility:	Outstanding minority seniors applying to graduate school for Ph.D.
Description:	The objective of the CRFP is to develop scientific and engineering ability among members of those minority groups underrepresented in science. During the summer preceding graduate work, fellowship recipients are employed at AT&T Bell Laboratories.
Awards:	(9–12) fellowships, providing all tuition, university fees, books, an annual living stipend of $13,200, and related travel expenses.
Deadline:	January 15, with selection by March 29.
Address:	Cooperative Research Fellowship Program (CRFP) CRFP Administrator AT&T Bell Laboratories 101 Crawfords Corner Road Holmdel, NJ 07733-1988
Telephone:	(908) 949-2943

AT&T GRADUATE RESEARCH PROGRAM FOR WOMEN | 166

Type:	Fellowships and Grants
Focus:	Chemistry, Chemical Engineering, Communications Science, Computer Science & Engineering, Electrical Engineering, Information Science, Materials Science, Mathematics, Mechanical Engineering, Operations Research, Physics, and Statistics
Eligibility:	Outstanding female seniors applying to graduate school for Ph.D.
Description:	The program provides support for outstanding students pursuing full-time doctoral studies in the disciplines listed.
Awards:	(4) fellowships with a $13,200 stipend, full tuition and fees, textbook allowance, summer employment at AT&T, and guidance of a mentor. (6) grants of $1,500, eligibility for summer employment at AT&T, and guidance of a mentor.
Deadline:	January 15, with notification by March 29.
Address:	Graduate Research Program for Women (GRPW) GRPW Administrator AT&T Bell Laboratories 101 Crawfords Corner Road Holmdel, NJ 07733-1988
Telephone:	(908) 949-2943

AT&T PH.D. SCHOLARSHIP PROGRAM   167

Type:	Fellowships
Focus:	Chemistry, Electrical Engineering, Computer Science, Physics, Materials Science, and Manufacturing Engineering
Eligibility:	Outstanding Ph.D. students nominated by graduate department chairperson.
Description:	The purpose of the program is to increase the number of highly trained doctorates in selected technical fields important to AT&T and the nation.
Awards:	(25) fellowships, providing an annual stipend of $13,200, $500 for books, full tuition, recurring fees, up to $1,000 for travel to conferences and optional research assignments at AT&T Bell Laboratories.
Deadline:	January 15, with notification by March 15.
Address:	Ph.D. Scholarship Program (Ph.D.) Ph.D. Administrator AT&T Bell Laboratories 101 Crawfords Corner Road Holmdel, NJ 07733-1988
Telephone:	(908) 949-3728

CALIFORNIA STATE GRADUATE FELLOWSHIPS   168

Type:	Fellowships
Focus:	Graduate study in California
Eligibility:	California residents
Description:	Fellowships covering tuition and fees only for residents of California who attend accredited graduate or professional schools located in California with the intent to become college or university faculty members.
Awards:	Awards ranging from $700 to $6,490.
Deadline:	March 2
Address:	California Student Aid Commission California State Graduate Fellowships P.O. Box 510621 1410 Fifth Street Sacramento, CA 94245-0621

CANADIAN FEDERATION OF UNIVERSITY WOMEN 169

Type:	Fellowships
Focus:	General, science and technology
Eligibility:	College graduates. Canadian citizenship required.
Awards:	A variety of programs are available, with awards ranging from $1,000 to $9,000.
Deadline:	November 30. Notification of awards on May 31.
Address:	Canadian Federation of University Women 55 Parkdale Avenue Ottawa, Ontario K1Y 1E5
Telephone:	(613) 722-8732

CHARLES BABBAGE INSTITUTE GRADUATE FELLOWSHIP 170

Type:	Fellowships
Focus:	History of Information Processing
Eligibility:	Graduate students who are near completion of the Ph.D.
Description:	For a graduate student whose dissertation deals with a historical aspect of information processing.
Awards:	$7,000 stipend for one year, plus up to $7,000 to be used for tuition, fees, travel, and other research expenses.
Deadline:	January 15
Address:	Charles Babbage Institute University of Minnesota 104 Walter Library 117 Pleasant Street, SE Minneapolis, MN 55455
Telephone:	(612) 624-5050

CHARLES LEGEYT FORTESCUE FELLOWSHIP   171

Type:	Fellowships
Focus:	Electrical Engineering
Eligibility:	First year graduate students
Description:	GRE scores are required.
Awards:	$24,000 stipend for one year.
Deadline:	January 31
Address:	Fellowship Committee IEEE Awards Board 345 East 47th Street New York, NY 10017-2394
Telephone:	(212) 705-7882

CIC PREDOCTORAL FELLOWSHIPS PROGRAM   172

Type:	Fellowships
Focus:	Science, Mathematics, Engineering, Humanities, and Social Sciences
Eligibility:	Fellowships are offered to Native American Indians, Black Americans, Mexican Americans, and Puerto Ricans for graduate study leading to Ph.D.
Description:	Fellowships may be used at any of the following universities: Univ. of Chicago, Univ. of Illinois, Indiana Univ., Univ. of Michigan, Michigan State Univ., Univ. of Minnesota, Northwestern Univ., Ohio State Univ., Purdue Univ., or Univ. of Wisconsin.
Awards:	Fellowships provide full-tuition plus an annual stipend of $9,000 or $10,000 each year for five years.
Deadline:	January 5
Address:	Committee on Institutional Cooperation (CIC) CIC Predoctoral Fellowships Program Kirkwood Hall, Room 111 Indiana University Bloomington, IN 47405
Telephone:	1-800-457-4420, (812) 855-0823, FAX (812) 855-9943

CLEO PROGRAM 173

Focus:	Legal training for the disadvantaged.
Eligibility:	All minorities. U.S. citizenship required.
Description:	Program prepares students for entry into law school.
Awards:	Stipend ($2,200 for the first year of law school, less for subsequent years).
Deadline:	March 1
Address:	Council on Legal Education Opportunity (CLEO) 1800 M Street, NW Suite 290, North Lobby Washington, DC 20036
Telephone:	(202) 785-4840

DANIEL AND FLORENCE GUGGENHEIM FOUNDATION 174

Type:	Fellowships
Focus:	Jet Propulsion, Energy Conversion, Fluid Mechanics, and Flight Structures
Eligibility:	U.S. and Canadian residents
Description:	For information on flight structures, write to the Department of Civil Engineering at Columbia University. For information on applied physics, dynamics and control systems, energy conversion, propulsion, combustion, energy and environmental policy, flight science and technology, or fluid mechanics, write to the address below.
Address:	Director of Graduate Studies Department of Mechanical and Aerospace Engineering Princeton University Princeton, NJ 08544

ELECTRICAL WOMEN'S ROUND TABLE   175

Type: Fellowships

Focus: Fields related to Electrical Living and Energy Conservation

Eligibility: Female graduate students

Awards: $2,000 Julia Kiene Fellowship and $1,000 Lyle Mamer Fellowship

Deadline: March 1

Address: Electrical Women's Round Table, Inc.
                 P.O. Box 292793
                 Nashville, TN 37229-2793

Telephone: (615) 890-1272, FAX (615) 890-5679

EPILEPSY FOUNDATION OF AMERICA   176

Type: Fellowships

Focus: Epilepsy

Eligibility: Medical and health science students or students in the behavioral
                 sciences (sociology, social work, psychology, anthropology, nursing,
                 and political science) studying epilepsy. Applications from women
                 and minorities are encouraged.

Description: The Epilepsy Foundation sponsors two fellowship programs, the
                 Health Sciences Student Fellowships and the Mary Litty Memorial
                 Behavioral Sciences Student Fellowships.

Awards: Several three-month fellowships of $2,000 are awarded. The number
                 varies; in 1992, nine fellowships were awarded.

Deadline: March 1

Address: Epilepsy Foundation of America
                 Research Administration
                 4351 Garden City Drive
                 Landover, MD 20785

Telephone: (301) 459-3700

ESA LaFage Graduate Research Award   177

Type:	Awards
Focus:	Entomology
Eligibility:	Graduate students
Description:	The Jeffrey P. LaFage Graduate Student Research Award is given to a graduate student for research on the biology and control of urban insect pests, especially termites and other wood-destroying organisms. Recipients are selected on the basis of a research proposal, itemized budget, and two references.
Awards:	(1) $2,000 award and a plaque.
Deadline:	August 1
Address:	Executive Director Entomological Society of America 9301 Annapolis Road, Suite 300 Lanham, MD 20706-3115
Telephone:	(301) 731-4535, FAX (301) 731-4538

The Exploration Fund   178

Type:	Grants
Focus:	Exploration and Field Research
Eligibility:	Graduate students and members of expeditions
Description:	Obtain application from address listed below.
Awards:	Grants in amounts up to $1,200 are made to support exploration and field research.
Deadline:	January 31
Address:	The Exploration Fund Committee The Explorers Club 46 East 70th Street New York, NY 10021
Telephone:	(212) 628-8383

FANNIE & JOHN HERTZ FOUNDATION FELLOWSHIPS   179

Type:	Fellowships
Focus:	Applied Physical Sciences, including Mathematics, Computer Science, and Engineering.
Eligibility:	Awards are made only to students who have completed less than one year of graduate study.
Description:	Offered on the basis of academic (undergraduate GPA) and research performance, recommendations, and personal technical interview. Tenable at only twenty-three universities. Write to the address below for more information.
Awards:	Stipend of $15,000 per year plus $8,000 cost of education allowance per nine-month year, renewable for up to four years. Honorable mentions receive a $500 research fellowship grant.
Deadline:	November 1
Address:	Hertz Foundation Fannie & John Hertz Foundation Fellowships P.O. Box 2230 Livermore, CA 94550-0130
Telephone:	(415) 373-1642

FLORIDA ENDOWMENT FOR HIGHER EDUCATION	180

Type: Fellowships

Focus: McKnight Doctoral Fellowships. Available for all disciplines except Law, Medicine and Education, with the exception of Science and Mathematics Education. Study in Agriculture, Biology, Business, Computer Science, Engineering, Mathematics, Marine Biology, Physics, and Psychology is especially encouraged.

Eligibility: Afro-American students. U.S. citizenship required. Applicants must hold a bachelor's degree and may hold a master's degree.

Description: Graduate fellowships tenable at five Florida universities. Upon completion of the program, applicants are encouraged to remain in Florida.

Awards: (25) awards consisting of a stipend of $11,000 per year (plus up to $5,000 to the institution in lieu of tuition) for three years. If a fourth year is necessary, the institution will fund it.

Deadline: January 15

Address: The Florida Endowment Fund for Higher Education
201 E. Kennedy Boulevard, Suite 1525
Tampa, FL 33602

Telephone: (813) 221-2772

FORD FNDTN. PREDOCTORAL FELLOWSHIPS FOR MINORITIES   181

Type:	Fellowships
Focus:	Research in Mathematics, Engineering, Physical and Biological Sciences, Behavioral and Social Sciences, Humanities, and other fields.
Eligibility:	Minority college seniors and first and second year graduate students. Native Alaskans, Native American Indians, Black/African Americans, Hispanic Americans, Puerto Ricans, and Native Pacific Islanders.
Description:	For support of graduate study and dissertation research to minorities enrolled in research based doctoral programs.
Awards:	Stipends of $10,350 (graduate study) and $18,000 (dissertation), plus an allowance to awardee's university in lieu of tuition and fees.
Deadline:	November 14, with notification in early April.
Address:	Ford Foundation Predoctoral Fellowships for Minorities The Fellowship Office National Research Council 2101 Constitution Avenue Washington, DC 20418
Telephone:	(202) 334-2872/2860

FORD FNDTN. POSTDOCTORAL FELLOWSHIPS FOR MINORITIES 182

Type:	Postgraduate Fellowships
Focus:	Research in Mathematics, Engineering, Physical and Biological Sciences, Behavioral and Social Sciences, Humanities and other fields.
Eligibility:	Native Alaskans, Native American Indians, Black Americans, Hispanic Americans, and Native Pacific Islanders.
Description:	For support of graduate study and dissertation research to minorities enrolled in research based doctoral programs.
Awards:	The stipend for Fellows is $25,000 and the travel and relocation allowance is $3,000.
Deadline:	November 14, with notification in early April.
Address:	Ford Foundation Postdoctoral Fellowships for Minorities The Fellowship Office National Research Council 2101 Constitution Avenue Washington, DC 20418
Telephone:	(202) 334-2872/2860

FOUNDATION FOR SCIENCE & THE HANDICAPPED   183

Type:	Scholarships
Focus:	Science, Mathematics, Engineering, Computer Science, and Medicine
Eligibility:	Handicapped graduate students
Description:	To enable students with a physical or sensory disability to obtain a graduate degree in a technical field. College seniors who have been accepted to graduate school may also apply. Selection is based on financial need, sincerity of purpose, scholarship, and research ability. Candidates submit transcripts, two letters of recommendation, and a 250-word essay describing the applicant's educational goals (including a summary of what the funds will be used for). Funds may be used for assistive devices or instruments or as financial support to work with a professor on an individual research project.
Awards:	(5) $1,000 awards
Deadline:	December 1
Address:	Foundation for Science & the Handicapped 115 South Brainard Avenue LaGrange, IL 60525
Telephone:	(708) 352-1091

FRANK M. CHAPMAN MEMORIAL FUND   184

Type:	Research Grants
Focus:	Ornithological research, including Neontology and Paleontology
Eligibility:	Graduate students
Description:	Grants support consumable supplies or expendable equipment, living expenses in the field or at a research station, and travel expenses. Proposals are selected on the basis of an application, research proposal, itemized budget, and two letters of recommendation.
Awards:	Average award $700, with most grants ranging from $200 to $1,000.
Deadline:	January 15. Notification April 15.
Address:	Frank M. Chapman Memorial Fund American Museum of Natural History Central Park West at 79th Street New York, NY 10024-5192
Telephone:	(212) 769-5000

GEM MINORITIES FELLOWSHIPS | 185

Type:	Fellowships
Focus:	Science and Engineering
Eligibility:	Must be a U.S. citizen. Fellowships are offered to Native American Indians, Black Americans, and Hispanic Americans.
Description:	GEM Fellows are not allowed to earn monies for services rendered, in any form, while attending graduate school. Fellows are expected to carry a full academic load toward a master's degree and must intern at a member employer location during the summer.
Awards:	Fellowships include tuition, fees, stipend of $12,000 (Ph.D.) and $6,000 (M.S.) per academic year, and travel to and from summer work site (M.S. only).
Deadline:	December 1. Notification February 1.
Address:	National Consortium for Graduate Degrees for Minorities in Engineering Executive Director GEM Minorities Fellowships P.O. Box 537 Notre Dame, IN 46556
Telephone:	(219) 287-1097, (219) 239-7183, FAX (219) 287-1486

GEOLOGICAL SOCIETY OF AMERICA | 186

Type:	Fellowships
Focus:	Geology and Earth Sciences
Eligibility:	Graduate students at universities in the U.S., Canada, Mexico, and Central America. Membership in GSA not required.
Description:	Master's and doctoral thesis research.
Awards:	Up to $1,000
Address:	Grants Research Administrator Geological Society of America P.O. Box 9140 Boulder, CO 80301
Telephone:	(303) 447-2020, FAX (303) 477-1133

| THE GRASS FOUNDATION | 187 |

Type: Fellowships

Focus: Neurophysiology, including Electrophysiology, Experimental Neuroanatomy, Neurochemistry, Cellular Neurobiology, Developmental Neurobiology, Tissue Culture, and Behavioral Analysis.

Eligibility: Graduate students in neurophysiology who are close to receiving the Ph.D. or M.D. Preference is given to those who have demonstrated a commitment to a research career.

Description: Funds approximately 10 young researchers in neurophysiology for one summer (14 weeks) at the Marine Biological Laboratory (MBL) in Woods Hole, Massachusetts. Candidates are evaluated on the basis of an application consisting of a research proposal, itemized budget, and a letter of recommendation from a senior investigator familiar with the candidate's work.

Awards: Provides laboratory research space, housing and board, travel expenses to and from MBL, and a modest budget for laboratory research expenses and personal expenses.

Deadline: December 2. Notification March 1.

Address: The Grass Foundation
                 77 Reservoir Road
                 Quincy, MA 02170

HASELTINE FELLOWSHIPS IN SCIENCE WRITING | 188

Type:	Fellowships
Focus:	Science Journalism — writing about Science, Medicine, Health, Technology, and the Environment for the general public via the mass media.
Eligibility:	Journalists and journalism students. Students must have undergraduate degrees in science or journalism. Priority will be given to journalists with two years of experience who wish to learn science writing. Fellows may attend school full or part time. Fellowships are not available for those who are pursuing, or plan to pursue, careers in public relations.
Description:	Selection is on the basis of a resume, transcripts (if students), three faculty or employer recommendations, three writing samples, and a short statement of career goals.
Awards:	(5–7) $2,000/year
Deadline:	June 1
Address:	Council for the Advancement of Science Writing, Inc. Attn: Ben Patrusky, Executive Director P.O. Box 404 Greenlawn, NY 11740
Telephone:	(516) 757-5664, FAX (516) 757-0069

HOWARD HUGHES DOCTORAL FELLOWSHIP

Type:	Fellowships
Focus:	Electrical, Mechanical, Aerospace or Systems Engineering, Computer Science, or Physics
Eligibility:	College seniors for graduate study. Must be a U.S. citizen.
Description:	Graduate fellowships for study at any ABET-accredited university (e.g., MIT, Stanford, UC/Berkeley), but usually at selected universities near major Hughes facilities (Los Angeles or Orange Counties of Southern California, or in Tucson, Arizona). GPA must be 3.0/4.0. Most are awarded on a work-study basis. Entries are judged on the basis of application, references, and transcripts. Fellows spend the summer working at Hughes. Fellows are expected to stay with the company for at least one year following completion of the degree.
Awards:	Fellowships include tuition, academic fees, parking fees, books, materials, cost of thesis preparation and reproduction, stipend of $5,000, travel and relocation expenses, and full salary for summer work and any other periods of full-time work.
Deadline:	January 10. Notification in April.
Address:	Hughes Aircraft Company Corporate Fellowship and Rotation Programs Technical Education Center Hughes Aircraft Company Fellowships P.O. Box 45066, Building C1/B168 Los Angeles, CA 90045-0066
Telephone:	(213) 568-6711

HOWARD HUGHES MEDICAL INSTITUTE FELLOWSHIPS	190

Type: Fellowships

Focus: Medical and Biological Sciences, including Cell Biology and Regulation, Genetics, Immunology, Neuroscience, Structural Biology, Biostatistics, Epidemiology, and Mathematical Biology

Eligibility: Graduate students with less than one year of postbaccalaureate graduate study in biology. No citizenship requirements. U.S. citizens may study abroad; others may study in the United States.

Description: Selection is by the National Research Council of the National Academy of Sciences. Selection is on the basis of academic record, letters of recommendation, GRE scores, and proposed plan of research. HHMI also awards grants/fellowships for other programs, including a minority fellowship program in the biological sciences.

Awards: (66) awards of $25,700 annually which consist of $14,000 stipend and $11,700 cost-of-education allowance. Renewable for up to five years.

Deadline: Mid-November, with notification in April.

Address: Office of Grants and Special Programs
Howard Hughes Medical Institute
6701 Rockledge Drive
Bethesda, MD 20817

Hughes Predoctoral Fellowships
National Research Council Fellowship Office
2101 Constitution Avenue
Washington, DC 20418

Telephone: HHMI: (301) 571-0335/0200, NRC: (202) 334-2872

HOWARD M. SOULE GRADUATE FELLOWSHIPS   191

Type:	Fellowships
Focus:	To promote the advancement of education through development of leadership.
Eligibility:	Full-time graduate students
Description:	Applicants must be good standing members of Phi Delta Kappa. Activity in Phi Delta Kappa will also be considered.
Awards:	(2) $1,500 fellowships toward tuition for doctoral students, (1) $750 fellowship toward tuition for a master's student, (2) $500 fellowships for research on thesis or dissertation preparation.
Deadline:	May 1, with notification by July 1
Address:	Howard M. Soule Graduate Fellowships Phi Delta Kappa Educational Foundation Eighth Street & Union Avenue, P.O. Box 789 Bloomington, IN 47402

HUBERT H. HUMPHREY DOCTORAL FELLOWSHIPS   192

Type:	Fellowships
Focus:	Arms Control
Eligibility:	Applicants must be U.S. citizens or nationals and have completed all requirements for the doctorate except the dissertation at a U.S. university. (Law students are also eligible.)
Description:	Supports unclassified doctoral dissertation research in the field of arms control. Recipients are selected on the basis of an application, thesis proposal and bibliography, transcripts, and three recommendations.
Awards:	(3) fellowships with a stipend of $5,000 for a 12-month period, plus applicable tuition and fees of up to $3,400 for one year.
Deadline:	March 15
Address:	U.S. Arms Control and Disarmament Agency Hubert H. Humphrey Doctoral Fellowships 320 21st Street, NW Washington, DC 20451
Telephone:	(202) 647-4695

| IBM GRADUATE FELLOWSHIPS | 193 |

Type: Scholarships and Fellowships

Focus: Computer Science, Electrical Engineering, Mechanical Engineering, Mathematics, Physics, Manufacturing Engineering, Materials Science, Chemistry, and Chemical Engineering

Eligibility: Graduate students

Description: Students may not apply directly, but instead are selected by the department or dean of the graduate school. IBM also has a minority and women fellowship program.

Awards: 200–300 fellowships which provide full tuition (excluding summer) and a stipend. Departments also receive a $2,000 unrestricted grant.

Deadline: February 1

Address: International Business Machines
T.J. Watson Research Center
P.O. Box 218
Yorktown Heights, New York 10598

| IEEE FELLOWSHIP IN ELECTRICAL ENGINEERING HISTORY | 194 |

Type: Fellowships

Focus: History of Electrical Engineering

Eligibility: Graduate students

Description: For one year of full-time graduate work in the history of electrical engineering and technology at a college or university of recognized standing. Candidates are selected on the basis of the proposed research project.

Awards: $8,500 stipend, plus an additional $2,000 for tuition and fees.

Deadline: February 1

Address: Director
IEEE Center for the History of Electrical Engineering
345 East 47th Street
New York, NY 10017

Telephone: (212) 705-7501

| JAVITS FELLOWSHIPS | 195 |

Type:	Fellowships
Focus:	Humanities, Arts, and Social Sciences
Eligibility:	Graduate students
Awards:	(400) fellowships of up to $14,500 per year
Address:	Graduate Programs Branch Department of Education 400 Maryland Avenue, SW Washington, DC 20202
Telephone:	(202) 357-6187

| JOHN CLARKE SLATER FELLOWSHIP | 196 |

Type:	Dissertation Fellowship
Focus:	History of Modern Physical Sciences
Eligibility:	Graduate students who are near the Ph.D. The fellowship is open to doctoral candidates who have passed their preliminary examinations and are writing dissertations on a topic in the history of the physical sciences in the twentieth century.
Description:	Fellows are selected on the basis of an application form, summary of project, dissertation proposal, writing sample, two letters of recommendation, and official graduate and undergraduate transcripts.
Awards:	Stipend of $12,000.
Deadline:	December 15. Notification March 1.
Address:	Slater Fellowship Executive Office American Philosophical Society 104 South Fifth Street Philadelphia, PA 19106-3386
Telephone:	(215) 440-3400

JULIETT A. SOUTHARD SCHOLARSHIP TRUST FUND 197

Type: Scholarships

Focus: Dentistry

Eligibility: Graduate students

Description: Teaching scholarship.

Awards: $100 to $1,000 awards.

Address: Juliett A. Southard Scholarship Trust Fund
American Dental Assistants Association
919 N. Michigan Avenue, Suite 3400
Chicago, IL 60611

LERNER-GRAY FUND FOR MARINE RESEARCH 198

Type: Research Grants

Focus: Marine Zoology (Neontology or Paleontology) with an emphasis on Systematics, Evolution, Ecology, and field-oriented behavior, with the exclusion of Botany

Eligibility: Graduate students

Description: Grants support consumable supplies or expendable equipment, living expenses in the field or at a research station, and travel expenses. Proposals are selected on the basis of an application, research proposal, itemized budget, and two letters of recommendation.

Awards: Average award $700, with most grants ranging from $200 to $1,000.

Deadline: March 15. Notification May 15.

Address: Lerner-Gray Fund for Marine Research
American Museum of Natural History
Central Park West at 79th Street
New York, NY 10024-5192

Telephone: (212) 769-5000

LINK FOUNDATION

Type:	Fellowships
Focus:	Simulation and Training Research
Eligibility:	Graduate students (Ph.D. only). U.S. citizenship (or green card residency) required.
Description:	To foster advanced level study in simulation and training research and to enhance and expand the theoretical and practical knowledge of creating artificial environments which simulate real life events. Recipients are selected on the basis of an application to the foundation in the form of a research proposal.
Awards:	The award consists of a grant totaling $17,000. This includes a stipend of $13,500. $2,500 is available for expenses associated with the research and the remaining $1,000 is to help defray publication costs of the student's research results.
Deadline:	December 2. Awards announced in March.
Address:	The Link Foundation Fellowship Program in Simulation and Training c/o The Institute for Simulation and Training ATTN: Ms Debbie Goff University of Central Florida 12424 Research Parkway, Suite 300 Orlando, FL 32826
Telephone:	(407) 658-5000

| MARCH OF DIMES BIRTH DEFECTS FOUNDATION | 200 |

Type:	Fellowship
Focus:	Birth Defects
Eligibility:	Graduate students (Ph.D. candidates), preferably in the early stages of their training.
Description:	Predoctoral Graduate Research Training Fellowships are available to doctoral students with potential for successful research careers in the area of birth defects prevention. Students must be recommended by their deans or the chair of their department. Application forms are sent after a 300-word abstract of the proposed research has been submitted to and evaluated by the March of Dimes.
Deadline:	February 28 for the following September 1.
Address:	March of Dimes Birth Defects Foundation 1275 Mamaroneck Avenue White Plains, NY 10605
Telephone:	(914) 428-7100, FAX (914) 428-8203

| MELLON FELLOWSHIPS IN THE HUMANITIES | 201 |

Type:	Fellowships
Focus:	Humanities
Eligibility:	Graduate students. U.S. or Canadian citizens.
Description:	Graduate studies in the humanities. Must agree to pursue a career of teaching and scholarship in a humanities field.
Awards:	(100-125) awards, tuition plus $12,500 stipend. Renewable for a second year.
Deadline:	Must be nominated by early November and must apply by early December.
Address:	Mellon Fellowships Woodrow Wilson National Fellowship Foundation P.O. Box 642 Princeton, NJ 08542
Telephone:	(609) 924-4666/4713, FAX (609) 497-2939/9064

NASA Global Change Research Fellowship Program	202

Type: Fellowships

Focus: Global Change Research, including Climate and Hydrologic Systems, Ecological Systems, Biogeochemical Dynamics, Solid Earth Processes, Solar Influences, Human Interactions, Atmospheric Chemistry and Physics, Ocean Biology and Physics, Ecosystem Dynamics, Hydrology, Cryospheric Processes, Geology, and Geophysics

Eligibility: Ph.D. Students at U.S. universities. U.S. citizens and resident aliens are given preference, although the program isn't restricted to them. Students may enter the program at any time during their graduate work. Students may also apply in their senior year of undergraduate school, provided that they are enrolled in a Ph.D. program at a U.S. university at the time of the award.

Description: Applicants may not receive other federal fellowships concurrently. Recipients are selected on the basis of an application, transcripts, a letter of recommendation from the student's advisor, research plan, and the relevance of the proposed research to NASA's role in the U.S. Global Change Research Program (Mission to Planet Earth). Students receiving support under this program do not incur any formal obligation to the government of the United States.

Awards: (50) awards of up to $20,000, renewable for a total of three years. In addition, a $2,000 allowance may be requested by the faculty advisor for use in support of the student's research.

Deadline: April 1, with notification June 30.

Address: National Aeronautics and Space Administration (NASA)
Global Change Fellowship Program
NASA Headquarters – Code SE-44
300 E Street, SW
Washington, DC 20546

NASA GRADUATE STUDENT RESEARCH FELLOWSHIPS 203

Type:	Fellowships
Focus:	Space Science and Engineering
Eligibility:	Graduate students. U.S. citizenship required.
Description:	Applicants may not receive other federal fellowships concurrently. Recipients are selected on the basis of an application, transcripts, research plan, and proposed utilization of NASA facilities. Must be sponsored by the department chair or faculty advisor.
Awards:	(80) awards of up to $18,000, renewable for a total of three years. School receives $6,000 in lieu of tuition.
Deadline:	February 1
Address:	National Aeronautics and Space Administration (NASA) Mail Code: XEU NASA Headquarters - R802 University Programs Branch Washington, DC 20546
Telephone:	(202) 453-8344/8396, FAX (202) 755-2977

NASA GRADUATE STUDENT RESEARCH PROGRAM (GSRP)   204

Type:	Fellowships
Focus:	Space Science and Aerospace Technology, including Astrophysics, Solar System Exploration, Space Physics, Earth Science, Microgravity Science and Applications, Life Sciences, and Information Systems
Eligibility:	Graduate students. U.S. citizenship required. Students may enter the program at any time during their graduate work or may apply prior to receiving their baccalaureate degrees.
Description:	Applicants may not receive other federal fellowships concurrently. Recipients are selected on the basis of an application, transcripts, and research plan. Some programs also consider proposed utilization of NASA facilities. Must be sponsored by the department chair or faculty advisor. Students receiving support under this program do not incur any formal obligation to the government of the United States. NASA also runs an Underrepresented Minority Focus Component of the GSRP for Black Americans, Hispanic Americans, Native American Indians, Native Pacific Islanders, and individuals with a disability. Applicants for the GSRP/UMF may study engineering, physics, mathematics, computer science, biology, aeronautics, space sciences, life sciences, or other disciplines of interest to NASA.
Awards:	(100) student stipends of up to $16,000, renewable for a total of three years. In addition, a $6,000 allowance may be requested (half to the school and half to the university) to defray tuition and travel costs. Half the awards require the recipient to spend a period of time in residence at a NASA field center. Five additional awards will be granted as part of the Federal High Performance Computing and Communications Program (HPCC).
Deadline:	February 1, with notification in April.
Address:	National Aeronautics and Space Administration (NASA) Higher Education Branch Education Division NASA Headquarters – Code FEH 300 E Street, SW Washington, DC 20546
Telephone:	(202) 358-1531/0734, FAX (202) 358-3048

NATIONAL DEFENSE SCIENCE & ENGINEERING FELLOWSHIP 205

Type: Fellowships

Focus: Science, Mathematics, and Engineering

Eligibility: Must be a U.S. citizen or national. Fellowship tenable only at approved U.S. institutions. Students must be at or near the beginning of their graduate studies in science, mathematics, or engineering. Fellows are selected on the basis of an application form, college transcripts, three references, and GRE scores (general test only).

Description: Write to the address below or to the American Society for Engineering Education, 11 Dupont Circle, Suite 200, Washington, DC 20036. NDSEG Fellows do *not* incur any military or other service obligation.

Awards: (120) 36-month fellowships awarded each year. Stipend is $15,000 per 12-month year (with a $1,000 annual increase each subsequent year), plus full tuition, fees, and $2,000 per year to the Fellow's department.

Deadline: Mid to late January. Notification mid-April.

Address: National Defense Science and Engineering Fellowship Program (NDSEG)
Battelle Columbus Division
Attn: Dr. George Outterson
200 Park Drive, Suite 211
P.O. Box 13444
Research Triangle Park, NC 27709-3444

Telephone: (919) 549-8505

NATIONAL HEALTH SERVICE CORPS SCHOLARSHIP PROGRAM   206

Type:	Medical Scholarships
Focus:	Medicine, Osteopathy, and other selected health care disciplines
Eligibility:	U.S. citizens or nationals who are enrolled in medical school.
Description:	Recipients owe one year of professional clinical service in a health manpower shortage area for each year of support, with a 2-year service minimum. Recipients will perform the required service obligation as either officers in the commissioned corps of the Public Health Service or as civilian members of the U.S. Civil Service. Recipients are selected on the basis of an application and must sign a contract agreeing to the terms of the scholarship award.
Awards:	Approximately 72 new awards per year. Awards include a monthly stipend (12 month year), tuition, and fees.
Address:	U.S. Department of Health and Human Services Bureau of Health Care Delivery & Assistance Parklawn Building, Room 7-18 5600 Fishers Lane Rockville, MD 20857
Telephone:	(301) 443-1650, FAX (301) 443-8338

NATIONAL MEDICAL FELLOWSHIPS 207

Type:	Medical Fellowships
Focus:	Allopathic and Osteopathic Medicine
Eligibility:	Minority medical students. Eligible minorities include Black Americans, Puerto Ricans, Mexican Americans, and Native American Indians. U.S. citizenship required.
Description:	Recipients are selected on the basis of academic merit and financial need. Applicants submit a financial aid application, personal statement, and letters of recommendation.
Awards:	Amount varies, but typically $1,000 to $2,000. A variety of special awards and fellowships are also available, with amounts ranging from $2,000 to $6,000, some renewable.
Deadline:	August 31 (May 31 for previous scholarship applicants).
Address:	Scholarship Program National Medical Fellowships, Inc. 254 West 31st Street, 7th Floor New York, NY 10001
Telephone:	(212) 714-1007

| National Physical Science Consortium | 208 |

Type:	Fellowships
Focus:	Physical Sciences, including Astronomy, Chemistry, Computer Science, Geology, Materials Science, Mathematics, and Physics
Eligibility:	Women and minority undergraduate seniors. Must be African American, Hispanic American, Native American Indian and/or female. U.S. citizenship required. Minimum 3.0 GPA.
Description:	Students must pursue graduate study at a participating NPSC member university. Each student is assigned a mentor from a major research laboratory.
Awards:	(40) fellowships, providing full tuition and fees plus a substantial monthly stipend for up to 6 years of support. Paid summer employment and technical experience for at least two years from leading national employers in the U.S.
Deadline:	November 15
Address:	L. Nan Snow, Executive Director National Physical Science Consortium New Mexico State University Box 30001, Dept. 3NPS Las Cruces, New Mexico 88003-0001 NPSC Headquarters University of CA/San Diego D-016 La Jolla, CA 92093
Telephone:	1-800-952-4118, (505) 646-6038, FAX (505) 646-6097; 1-800-854-NPSC, (619) 534-7183, FAX (619) 534-7379

NATIONAL SEA GRANT COLLEGE FEDERAL FELLOWS PROGRAM | 209

Type:	Fellowships
Focus:	Marine Sciences
Eligibility:	Graduate students
Description:	For students who are in a graduate or professional degree program at an accredited institution of higher education.
Address:	Fellowship Director National Sea Grant College Program Office 1335 East West Highway Silver Spring, MD 20910

NATIONAL WILDLIFE FEDERATION FELLOWSHIP | 210

Type:	Graduate Fellowships
Focus:	Natural Resources, Environmental Sciences, and Resource Conservation Research
Eligibility:	Graduate students. U.S., Canadian, and Mexican Citizens.
Awards:	$10,000 fellowship.
Deadline:	November 30
Address:	National Wildlife Federation 1412 16th Street, NW Washington, DC 20036-2266
Telephone:	(202) 797-6800, FAX (202) 797-6646

NORTHRUP FELLOWSHIPS   211

Type:	Fellowships
Focus:	Aerospace Engineering, Applied Mathematics, Computer Science, Electrical Engineering, Manufacturing, Systems Engineering, and Materials Technology
Eligibility:	Graduate students pursuing a master's or doctorate at California State University, CalTech, MIT, UCLA, UC/Irvine, or the University of Southern California.
Description:	Northrup Fellows receive employment in a paid position related to their field of graduate study at a sponsoring Northrup Division, and work half-time during the school year, and full-time during holidays, spring break, and the summer. Recipients are selected on the basis of an application, three letters of recommendation, and transcripts.
Awards:	Fellowships provide full tuition, fees, books, and a stipend of $15,000.
Deadline:	February 28
Address:	Northrup Corporation Fellowship Program Education and Training 137/CC 1840 Century Park East Los Angeles, CA 90067-2199
Telephone:	(213) 201-3168

NSF GRADUATE RESEARCH FELLOWSHIPS 212

Type:	Fellowships
Focus:	Science and Mathematics
Eligibility:	For citizens or nationals of the U.S. for full-time study leading to a master's or doctoral degree in science and mathematics.
Description:	Awards are made only to students who have completed less than one year of graduate study.
Awards:	Stipends of $13,500 for a 12-month tenure, plus an education allowance of $6,000 paid to the fellowship institution in lieu of tuition. Awards are for three years.
Deadline:	Mid-November, with notification in mid-March.
Address:	The Fellowship Office National Research Council 2101 Constitution Avenue Washington, DC 20418
Telephone:	(202) 357-9498, (202) 334-2872

NSF MINORITY RESEARCH FELLOWSHIPS 213

Type:	Fellowships
Focus:	Science and Mathematics
Eligibility:	Native Alaskans, Native American Indians, Black Americans, Hispanic Americans, and Native Pacific Islanders
Description:	Awards are made only to students who are members of an ethnic minority group underrepresented in the advanced levels of the U.S. science personnel pool.
Awards:	Stipends of $13,500 for a 12-month tenure, plus an education allowance of $6,000 paid to fellowship institution in lieu of tuition. Awards are for three years.
Deadline:	Mid-November, with notification in mid-March.
Address:	The Fellowship Office National Research Council 2101 Constitution Avenue Washington, DC 20418
Telephone:	(202) 357-9498, (202) 334-2872

ONR GRADUATE FELLOWSHIP PROGRAM   214

Type: Fellowships

Focus: Electrical Engineering, Computer Science, Naval Architecture, Ocean Engineering, Materials Science, Physics, Applied Physics, Aerospace/Mechanical Engineering, Oceanography, Mathematics, Chemistry, Biology/Biomedical Science, and Cognitive/Neural Science

Eligibility: College seniors. Recipients may not have attended graduate school in science or engineering since receiving their baccalaureate degree. Must be a U.S. citizen. Fellowship tenable only at approved U.S. institutions.

Description: Fellowships support study and research leading to a doctoral degree. These awards also include optional summer research appointments at various ONR laboratories. Recipients selected on the basis of an application, transcripts, three letters of recommendation, and GRE scores (General Test only). Fellows do *not* incur any military or other service obligation.

Awards: (50) 36-month fellowships. Stipend is $15,000 per year (with a $1,000 annual increase each subsequent year), plus full tuition, fees, and $2,000 per year to the Fellow's department. If the Fellow works during the summer at a Navy laboratory, ONR will raise the monthly stipend to $2,000 and pay a travel and subsistence allowance to cover relocation expenses.

Deadline: Mid to late January. Notification mid-April.

Address: American Society for Engineering Education
                 ONR Graduate Fellowship Program
                 11 Dupont Circle, Suite 200
                 Washington, DC 20036-1207

Telephone: (202) 986-8525/8500, (202) 986-8516,
                 Debbie Hughes (703) 696-4108/4111

PI GAMMA MU 215

Type:	Scholarships
Focus:	Economics, Sociology, Anthropology, History, Political Science, and International Relations
Eligibility:	Must be a member of Pi Gamma Mu. Primarily for the first year of graduate study.
Description:	Selection based on a personal statement, transcript, and three letters of recommendation.
Awards:	(10) $1,000 grants
Deadline:	January 30. Notification April 1.
Address:	Pi Gamma Mu International Honor Society in Social Science 1717 Ames Winfield, KS 67156
Telephone:	(316) 221-3128

PURINA MILLS RESEARCH FELLOWSHIP 216

Type:	Fellowships
Focus:	Animal Science (food and companion animals), with a particular emphasis on Nutrition as applied to Animal, Dairy, and Poultry Science.
Eligibility:	Graduate students for full-time graduate study.
Description:	Selection is on the basis of transcripts, grade report sheets (3 if the applicant is entering graduate study for the first time, 4 if the applicant has completed previous graduate work), three letters of recommendation, and a detailed description of the proposed research.
Awards:	(4) fellowships of $12,500. Purina Mills Research Fellows may not accept other aid in excess of $5,000 without written approval from Purina Mills.
Deadline:	February 1
Address:	Purina Research Awards Committee c/o Mary A. Timpe, 2E Purina Mills, Inc. P.O. Box 66812 St. Louis, MO 63166-6812

RTCA William E. Jackson Award   217

Type: Awards

Focus: Aviation Electronics and Telecommunications

Eligibility: Graduate students studying for an advanced degree in the field of aviation electronics or telecommunication systems.

Description: Submissions must be made in the form of a thesis, project report, or technical journal paper. Candidates must also submit a 1–2 page summary of the written material, a biographical sketch, and a letter of endorsement from the candidate's instructor, professor, or department chair.

Awards: $1,500 and a plaque.

Deadline: June 30

Address: William E. Jackson Award Committee
                 c/o RTCA
                 1140 Connecticut Avenue, NW, Suite 1020
                 Washington, DC 20036

Telephone: (202) 833-9339, FAX (202) 833-9434

SIGMA DELTA EPSILON	218

Type: Research Grants

Focus: Natural Sciences (Physical, Environmental, Mathematical, Computer, and Life Sciences)

Eligibility: Female graduate students and postdoctoral students. Appointments will be made irrespective of race, nationality, creed, or age. SDE Fellowships are open to applicants in all the natural sciences. Eloise Gerry Fellowships are restricted to applicants in the biological and chemical sciences.

Description: Applicants must hold a degree from a recognized institution of higher education in the fields specified. There are two programs: one for those currently involved in research and one for those with an approved research proposal. Fellowships are for research or research support, not for tuition or scholarship support. Travel, child care, and personal computers are not likely to be funded.

Awards: SDE Fellowships and Eloise Gerry Fellowships, with award amounts ranging from $1,500 to $4,000. Awards are nonrenewable.

Deadline: December 1. Notification by July 1.

Address: Graduate Women in Science, Inc.
Sigma Delta Epsilon
One Illinois Center, Suite 200
111 East Wacker Drive
Chicago, IL 60601-4298

Telephone: (312) 616-0800

| SIMULATION AND TRAINING SYSTEMS FELLOWSHIP | 219 |

Type: Fellowships

Focus: Aerospace Engineering, Electronics Engineering, Human Factors (Psychology or Engineering), Operations Research, Physics, Computer Science, Mathematics, and Education.

Eligibility: Graduate students enrolled in or accepted for a full-time master's or doctoral degree program. U.S. citizenship required.

Description: The fellowship is sponsored by the Interservice/Industry Training Systems and Education Conference (I/ITSEC) for students interested in pursuing careers in the simulation and training systems industry. Selection is on the basis of a personal statement and résumé, transcripts, letters of recommendation, and an endorsement by the Director of Graduate Programs at the applicant's institution.

Awards: (1) $10,000 graduate fellowship and an all-expense-paid trip to the annual November meeting of the I/ITSEC. Recipients may hold other awards simultaneously.

Deadline: March 8, with notification April 23.

Address: American Defense Preparedness Association
               I/ITSEC Scholarship Program
               Two Colonial Place, Suite 400
               Arlington, VA 22201-3061

| SLOAN DOCTORAL DISSERTATION FELLOWSHIPS | 220 |

Type: Fellowships

Focus: Economics and Mathematics

Eligibility: Graduate students near completion of Ph.D.

Description: Students may not apply directly, but instead are nominated by the department chairmen at leading departments of economics and mathematics.

Awards: (50) $12,000 stipend and full tuition fellowships, 25 in each field.

Address: Alfred P. Sloan Foundation
               630 5th Avenue, Suite 2550
               New York, NY 10111

Telephone: (212) 649-1649

| SPACE FOUNDATION EDUCATIONAL GRANT PROGRAM | 221 |

Type: Research Grants

Focus: Disciplines related to the commercialized use of space resources, including Microgravity, Remote Sensing, Biotechnology, Materials Processing, Space Robotics, Solar Power, Satellite Engineering, Heat Transfer, Artificial Intelligence, and Space Transport

Eligibility: Graduate students who intend to devote their careers to the furtherance of practical space research, engineering, or business.

Description: The Space Foundation is a nonprofit organization dedicated to promoting the private sector exploration and utilization of space. The Space Industrialization Fellowship is awarded to a graduate student whose work makes a relevant contribution to the foundation's interests in the commercial development of space. Applicants are evaluated on the basis of an abstract of the thesis project, a biographical sketch of the applicant, an essay describing personal career goals of the applicant, an itemized budget showing how the fellowship funds will be used, a research plan for the project, and two letters of recommendation. The foundation also sponsors the Space Development Strategies Award of $1,000 for the best paper by an undergraduate or graduate student describing methods of accelerating private sector involvement in space.

Awards: $4,000 stipend.

Deadline: October 1. Notification in December.

Address: Dr. David J. Norton, Chairman
                 Space Foundation Educational Grant Program
                 c/o Houston Advanced Research Center
                 4800 Research Forest Drive
                 The Woodlands, TX 77381

Telephone: (713) 363-7944, FAX (713) 363-7914

SPENCER FOUNDATION DISSERTATION FELLOWSHIPS   222

Type: Dissertation Fellowships

Focus: Education Research

Eligibility: Applicants must be candidates for the doctoral degree at a graduate
                 school in the United States, but do not need to be U.S. citizens.

Description: For completing dissertations in any field that are relevant to the im-
                 provement of education. All applicants must provide a clear and
                 specific plan for completing the dissertation within a two-year time
                 frame. Although the work must concern education, graduate study
                 may be in any academic discipline. Candidates should be interested in
                 pursuing further research in education once the doctorate is attained.
                 Recipients are selected on the basis of transcripts, letters of recom-
                 mendation, a brief personal statement, a dissertation abstract, and a
                 six-page narrative discussion of and work-plan for the dissertation.

Awards: (30) nonrenewable fellowships of $15,000 each, to be spent over a
                 period of one to two years.

Deadline: Early November. Notification in April.

Address: The Spencer Foundation
                 900 North Michigan Avenue, Suite 2800
                 Chicago, IL 60611-1542

Telephone: (312) 337-7000

TAU BETA PI FELLOWSHIPS 223

Type:	Fellowships
Focus:	Engineering
Eligibility:	Graduate students. Tau Beta Pi membership required. Preference is given to students who will be first year graduate students.
Description:	Tau Beta Pi administers many fellowship programs — the 3M Fellowship, the Fife Fellowship, the Stark Fellowship, the Hughes Fellowship, the Spencer Fellowship, the Kind Fellowship, the Sigma Tau Fellowship, the Deuchler Fellowship, the Williams Fellowship, the Centennial Fellowship, and several other fellowships. The criteria for each fellowship vary, but all related somehow to engineering and Tau Beta Pi. Fellows are selected on the basis of an application, academic records, two letters of recommendation, and extracurricular activities.
Awards:	Approximately 35 fellowships of $7,500.
Deadline:	Mid to late January. Notification April 1.
Address:	Tau Beta Pi Fellowships P.O. Box 8840, University Station Knoxville, TN 37996-0002
Telephone:	(615) 546-4578

THEODORE ROOSEVELT MEMORIAL FUND 224

Type:	Research Grants
Focus:	Research on North American fauna (Neontology or Paleontology) with the exception of birds.
Eligibility:	Graduate students
Description:	Grants support consumable supplies or expendable equipment, living expenses in the field or at a research station, and travel expenses. Proposals are selected on the basis of an application, research proposal, itemized budget, and two letters of recommendation.
Awards:	Average award $700, with most grants ranging from $200 to $1,000.
Deadline:	February 15. Notification April 30.
Address:	Theodore Roosevelt Memorial Fund American Museum of Natural History Central Park West at 79th Street New York, NY 10024-5192
Telephone:	(212) 769-5000

U.S. DEPARTMENT OF DEFENSE   225

Type:	Fellowships
Focus:	Engineering and Science
Eligibility:	Graduate students
Description:	Support of graduate education by the Department of Defense. No service obligation.
Awards:	Stipends and tuition
Address:	Air Force: Office of Scientific Research Bolling AFB Washington, DC 20332 Navy: ASEE 11 Dupont Circle, Suite 200 Washington, DC 20036

U.S. DEPARTMENT OF DEFENSE M.B.A. SCHOLARSHIPS   226

Type:	Fellowships
Focus:	Business Administration, Management, Science, and Engineering
Eligibility:	Graduate Students pursuing an M.B.A.
Description:	Recipients must have an undergraduate degree in one of the specified fields and a 3.5 GPA. For each year of coverage, recipients agree to work in Acquisitions for the U.S. Department of Defense.
Awards:	(10) M.B.A. scholarships consisting of a $15,000/year stipend, $500 for books, $1,000 to your department, and $13,500 to cover tuition and fees. If funds are available, all tuition and fees in excess of $13,500 will also be covered.
Deadline:	April 21
Address:	Defense Acquisition Scholarship Program Northeast Consortium for Engineering Education 1101 Massachusetts Avenue St. Cloud, FL 34769
Telephone:	(407) 892-6146

U.S. DEPARTMENT OF EDUCATION 227

Type:	Fellowships
Focus:	National need areas
Eligibility:	Graduate students
Description:	Fellowships to enhance teaching and research in academic areas. These awards go to graduate students of superior ability who demonstrate financial need. Funded through schools.
Address:	Division of Higher Educational Incentive Programs Office of Postsecondary Education Department of Education Room 3022, ROB-3, Mail Stop 3327 7th and D Streets, SW Washington, DC 20202

U.S. DEPARTMENT OF EDUCATION 228

Type:	Fellowships
Focus:	Public Service
Eligibility:	Graduate students. U.S. citizenship or permanent residency required.
Description:	Fellowships for graduate students who plan public service careers.
Awards:	$10,000 annual stipend plus $6,000 to the institution in lieu of tuition and fees.
Address:	U.S. Department of Education Division of Higher Educational Incentive Programs 400 Maryland Avenue, SW, Room 3022 Washington, DC 20202-5152
Telephone:	(202) 732-4395

U.S. DEPARTMENT OF ENERGY GRADUATE FELLOWSHIPS	229

Type: Fellowships

Focus: Computer Science

Eligibility: Graduate students. Students having an approved thesis topic prior to acceptance to the program are not eligible. Applicants must be U.S. citizens or permanent resident aliens.

Awards: Pays all tuition and required fees, and a stipend of $1,500/month during the first year (increasing to $1,600, $1,700, and $1,800 in the subsequent years). The award is for a maximum of 48 months, but it must be renewed each year.

Deadline: January 27

Address: Computational Science Graduate Fellowship
Oak Ridge Associated Universities
Science/Engineering Education Division
120 Badger Avenue, P. O. Box 117
Oak Ridge, TN 37831-0117

U.S. DEPARTMENT OF ENERGY INTEGRATED MANUF. FELLOWSHIP   230

Type:	Fellowships
Focus:	Integrated Manufacturing
Eligibility:	Graduate Students pursuing a Ph.D. in a field related to integrated manufacturing in U.S. colleges or universities. Candidates must hold a master's degree or be already admitted to a doctoral degree program. Applicants must be U.S. citizens or nationals, or permanent resident aliens.
Description:	Individuals from engineering backgrounds as well as those from other applied science fields that can be related to the multidisciplinary nature of integrated manufacturing are encouraged to apply. Recipients are selected on the basis of academic records, recommendations, and the applicant's proposed plan of study. Fellows may not accept simultaneous remuneration for another major fellowship, scholarship, or similar award. However, remuneration from a teaching or research assistantship may be accepted, as may fees from consulting and educational benefits from the Department of Veterans Affairs.
Awards:	(12) three-year fellowships. Pays a $20,000 annual stipend directly to the fellow and a cost-of-education allowance of up to $15,000 per year to the fellowship institution for tuition and fees.
Deadline:	Part 1 is due November 6. Part 2 is due January 5. Notification will be in April.
Address:	The Fellowship Office National Research Council 2101 Constitution Avenue Washington, DC 20418
Telephone:	(202) 334-2872

U.S. Department of Energy Laboratory Graduate Partic.   231

Type: Fellowships

Focus: Life Sciences, Physical Sciences, Social Sciences, Mathematics, and
                 Engineering

Eligibility: Graduate students (both master's and doctoral students). Students
                 must have completed all requirements for the degree except thesis or
                 dissertation research. Applicants must be U.S. citizens or permanent
                 resident aliens.

Awards: Supports full-time thesis and dissertation research at participating
                 DOE research facilities. The annual stipend is $12,000 to $14,400
                 plus tuition, fees, and an allowance for dependents.

Address: Science/Engineering Education Division
                 Oak Ridge Associated Universities
                 Science/Engineering Education Division
                 120 Badger Avenue, P. O. Box 117
                 Oak Ridge, TN 37831-0117

WREI CONGRESSIONAL FELLOWSHIPS 232

Type:	Fellowships
Focus:	Public Policy, Gender Differences, and other general research topics
Eligibility:	Female graduate students
Description:	The Women's Research and Education Institute's (WREI) Congressional Fellowships Program places female graduate students in Congressional offices and on strategic committee staffs. The duration of the appointment is one academic year. Fellows complete a month-long orientation on women and public policy before commencing their appointment. They spend 30 hours per week in their assigned offices and receive 6 hours of arranged credit for the legislative and academic research they perform. Fellows are selected on the basis of academic performance, experience with community groups, interest in the analysis of gender differences as they affect federal laws, and an interview. WREI also has a program of unpaid internships for undergraduate students.
Awards:	Fellows receive a tuition and living stipend for the academic year.
Deadline:	Mid-February. Regional interviews held in April. Notification by May 1.
Address:	WREI Congressional Fellowships 1700 18th Street, NW, Suite 400 Washington, DC 20009
Telephone:	(202) 328-7070, FAX (202) 328-3514

ZONTA INTERNATIONAL – AMELIA EARHART FELLOWSHIP | 233

Type:	Fellowship Grants
Focus:	Aerospace-related science and engineering
Eligibility:	Female graduate students. Must be accepted by or already enrolled in a graduate institution offering accredited courses in aerospace-related studies.
Description:	Students are selected on the basis of an application, transcripts, essay, and three recommendations. Candidates must clearly identify the relevance of their research program to aerospace-related science or engineering.
Awards:	(35–40) $6,000 grants for graduate students.
Deadline:	December 1. Notification May 15.
Address:	Zonta International Amelia Earhart Fellowship Awards 557 West Randolph Street Chicago, IL 60606-2206
Telephone:	(312) 930-5848, FAX (312) 930-0951

Chapter 7

Contests and Competitions

Mathematics Competitions

American Regional Mathematics League (ARML)
23 Garland Place
Roslyn Heights, NY 11577

Atlantic and Pacific Math Meet
P.O. Box 11242
Elkins Park, PA 19117

Continental Mathematics League
P.O. Box 306
Hauppauge, NY 11788

MAA American High School Mathematics Exam (AHSME)
Dr. Walter E. Mientka
Chairman, Committee on High School Contests
Mathematical Association of America
Department of Mathematics and Statistics
917 Oldfather Hall
University of Nebraska-Lincoln
Lincoln, NE 68588-0658
(402) 472-2257

The MAA competition is a three-level exam — American High School Mathematics Exam (AHSME), American Invitational Mathematics Exam (AIME), and U.S. Mathematical Olympiad (USAMO) — which is used to select the student members of the U.S. team to the International Mathematical Olympiad (IMO).

Mathcounts
National Council of Teachers of Mathematics
1906 Association Drive
Reston, VA 22091
(703) 620-9840

Mathcounts is a team and individual competition for middle school students.

National Mathematics League Competition
Southern Regional Office
P.O. Box 9459
Coral Springs, FL 33075

Test of Engineering Aptitude in Math and Science (TEAMS)
Junior Engineering Technical Society (JETS)
1420 King Street, Suite 405
Alexandria, VA 22314
(703) 548-JETS

TEAMS is a national competition for high school students interested in science and engineering problem solving. JETS also runs the National Engineering Design Challenge, in which students compete as five-member teams in state competitions in December and in a national competition in February. JETS also sponsors the National Engineering Aptitude Search (NEAS).

Wisconsin Mathematics Talent Search
University of Wisconsin-Madison
Department of Mathematics, Room 218 Van Vleck
480 Lincoln Drive
Madison, WI 53706

(Only students of Wisconsin schools are eligible for the awards, but students of any state are welcome to submit solutions. The problems are well-written and a good way to "keep in shape" for the AHSME and other national mathematics competitions.)

Science Competitions

ACSL Computer Science Contest
American Computer Science League
P.O. Box 40118
Providence, RI 02940
(401) 331-ACSL
E-mail: mhb@src.dec.com

Computer Science Olympiad
USA Computing Olympiad (USACO)
Attn: Prof. Donald T. Piele
Univ. of Wisconsin/Parkside, Box 2000
Kenosha, WI 53141-2000
(414) 634-0868
E-mail: piele@cs.uwp.edu

International Chemistry Olympiad
American Chemical Society
Education Department
1115 Sixteenth Street, NW
Washington, DC 20036
(202) 872-6169

International Physics Olympiad
American Assoc. of Physics Teachers
5110 Roanoke Place, Suite 101
College Park, MD 20740

Junior Science and Humanities Symposium
Academy of Applied Science
JSHS Office
4603 Western Boulevard
Raleigh, NC 27606

National Science League, Inc.
P.O. Box 9700
Coral Springs, FL 33075

National Science Olympiad
P.O. Box 306
Hauppauge, NY 11788

Physics Bowl
David Issing, Program Coordinator
5112 Berwyn Road
College Park, MD 20740
(301) 345-4200

Science Olympiad
5955 Little Pine Lane
Rochester, MN 48064

Other Competitions

National High School Chess Championship
U.S. Chess Federation
86 Route 9W
New Windsor, NY 12550

OM Association, Inc.
Olympics of the Mind
114 E. High Street, P.O. Box 27
Glassboro, NJ 08028

| AAA SCHOOL TRAFFIC SAFETY POSTER PROGRAM | 234 |

Type:	Contest
Focus:	Traffic Safety
Eligibility:	High school students
Awards:	(1) $500 savings bond. Also, savings bonds for designs selected for reproduction.
Deadline:	February 19
Address:	American Automobile Association Your Local AAA Chapter AAA School Traffic Safety Poster Program

| AADR CAULK/DENTSPLY COMPETITION | 235 |

Type:	Contest
Focus:	Dental and Oral Health Research
Eligibility:	Undergraduate dental students who have authored or coauthored no more than two publications in refereed journals. Students must be members of AADR at the time of entry into the competition, and must have an abstract accepted for the IADR/AADR annual meeting in poster format. Students may not participate simultaneously in the AADR Hatton Awards Competition.
Description:	Students submit abstracts via the normal process to the AADR. A copy of the abstract must also be sent to the president of the AADR Student Research Group. 12 finalists will be selected, and their posters judged at the IADR/AADR Annual Meeting.
Awards:	First place, $600; second place, $400; third place, $300; and fourth place, $200.
Deadline:	September 25.
Address:	American Association for Dental Research Attn: Patricia J. Lewis, Administrative Coord. 1111 Fourteenth Street, NW, Suite 1000 Washington, DC 20005
Telephone:	(202) 898-1050, FAX (202) 789-1033

AADR HATTON AWARDS COMPETITION

236

Type:	Contest
Focus:	Dental and Oral Health Research
Eligibility:	Students must be U.S. citizens, permanent residents, or noncitizen nationals of the United States, or persons of other nationalities whose research is performed in the United States. Winners will compete in the IADR Edward H. Hatton Awards Competition for Junior Investigators, which has an age limit of 36 years. Entrants may not have been published (even as an abstract) or presented at any national or international meeting. Students participating in the ADA Student Clinicians Competition or in the Caulk/Dentsply Student Research Group Award Competition are not eligible to compete in the AADR Hatton Awards Competition.
Description:	The 20 students who submit the best abstracts are asked to submit an extended abstract and prepare a poster for the AADR meeting.
Awards:	The 9 individuals selected at the AADR meeting will compete in the IADR Hatton Competition, which has a first place prize of $500 and a second place prize of $250.
Deadline:	September 25
Address:	American Association for Dental Research Attn: Patricia J. Lewis, Administrative Coord. 1111 Fourteenth Street, NW, Suite 1000 Washington, DC 20005
Telephone:	(202) 898-1050, FAX (202) 789-1033

ALICE T. SCHAFER MATHEMATICS PRIZE | 237

Type:	Contest
Focus:	Mathematics
Eligibility:	Female undergraduate students.
Description:	The Association for Women in Mathematics awards the *Alice T. Schafer Mathematics Prize* to an undergraduate woman who has demonstrated excellence in mathematics. The selection criteria include the quality of the student's performance in mathematics, evidence of a real interest in mathematics, and ability for independent work. Performance in local and national mathematics competitions will also be considered, if mentioned by the nominator. Past recipients have also participated in service projects for the undergraduate mathematics community at their schools. Students may not apply for this award, but must be nominated by a member of the mathematics community.
Awards:	The Schafer Prize carries a $1,000 cash stipend.
Deadline:	March/April. (Changes year to year.)
Address:	Alice T. Schafer Award Selection Committee c/o Jodi L. Beldotti, Executive Director Association for Women in Mathematics Box 178, Wellesley College Wellesley, MA 02181 E-mail: jbeldotti@lucy.wellesley.edu
Telephone:	(617) 237-7517

APA POETRY CONTEST 238

Type:	Contest
Focus:	Poetry
Eligibility:	All poets, especially students.
Description:	Contestants may submit up to six poems, each no more than 20 lines.
Awards:	Over $11,000 in prizes, including grand prize of $1000, first prize of $500, and 150 other prizes. Winning poems are published by the Association.
Deadline:	June 30
Address:	APA Poetry Contest American Poetry Association Department CT-22 250 A Potrero Street, P.O. Box 1803 Santa Cruz, CA 95061-1803

AYN RAND ESSAY COMPETITION 239

Type:	Contest
Focus:	Essay Contest in Philosophy
Eligibility:	High school juniors and seniors
Description:	Winners selected on the basis of a four-page essay.
Awards:	(1) $5,000 first prize, (1) $1,000 second prize, and (10) $500 third prizes.
Deadline:	April 15. Notification June 1.
Address:	Ayn Rand Institute 330 Washington Street, Suite 509 Marina del Rey, CA 90292
Telephone:	(213) 306-9232, FAX (213) 306-4925

DUPONT CHALLENGE/SCIENCE ESSAY AWARDS PROGRAM   240

Type:	Awards
Focus:	Science Essays
Eligibility:	Students in grades 7–12. Must be enrolled in a school in the U.S. or Canada or in a U.S.-sponsored school abroad.
Description:	Participants must write an essay, 600–1,000 words in length, on a scientific topic of their choice, explaining how the topic has — or will have — a dramatic effect on society.
Awards:	There will be a separate division for students in grades 7-9 and 10-12. First place winners will receive grants worth $1,500; second place, $750; and third place, $500. In addition, 24 honorable mention students receive $50 cash each.
Deadline:	January 15
Address:	Ms. Andrea Solzman Science Essay Awards Program c/o General Learning Corporation 60 Revere Drive, Suite 200 Northbrook, IL 60062-1563
Telephone:	1-800-323-5471

ELIAS LIEBERMAN STUDENT POETRY AWARD   241

Type:	Awards
Focus:	Poetry
Eligibility:	High school students grades 9-12
Description:	Send two unsigned copies of entry. Enclose name, address, and the school attended in a sealed envelope with the title of the poem sealed on the outside.
Awards:	$100 cash
Deadline:	December 31
Address:	Elias Lieberman Student Poetry Award Poetry Society of America The National Arts Club 15 Gramercy Park, South New York, NY 10003

FATHER JAMES B. MACELWANE ANNUAL AWARD   242

Type:	Awards
Focus:	Meteorology and Atmospheric Science
Eligibility:	Undergraduate students
Description:	Entries are judged on the basis of a paper dealing with some phase of atmospheric science and meteorology, and faculty recommendation/paper referral.
Awards:	First prize $300, second prize $200, and third prize $100
Deadline:	June 15
Address:	American Meteorological Society Father James B. Macelwane Annual Award 45 Beacon Street Boston, MA 02108-3693
Telephone:	(617) 227-2425

GRAVITY RESEARCH FOUNDATION   243

Type:	Awards
Focus:	Essays on the subject of gravitation, its theory, application, and effects.
Eligibility:	No restrictions. Typically graduate students, doctorates, and university professors.
Description:	1,500-word essays must be typewritten and double spaced, and in English. The essay must also include a 125-word abstract and three copies must be submitted. The five award winning essays will be published in the Journal of Relativity and Gravitation.
Awards:	First prize $2,000, second prize $750, third prize $250, fourth prize $150, and fifth prize $100
Deadline:	April 1, with notification by May 15.
Address:	Gravity Research Foundation P.O. Box 81389 Wellesley Hills, MA 02181-0004

GROLIER POETRY PRIZE	244

Type:	Awards
Focus:	Unpublished poetry
Eligibility:	Poets whose work has not been published in book-form.
Description:	For further information, send a self-addressed stamped envelope to the address below.
Awards:	$150 plus publication.
Address:	Ellen La Forge Memorial Poetry Foundation Grolier Poetry Prize 6 Plympton Street Cambridge, MA 02138

INTERNATIONAL COMPUTER GRAPHICS IMAGE CONTEST	245

Type:	Contest
Focus:	Computer Graphics
Eligibility:	Students and professionals
Description:	Entries are outstanding computer graphics images.
Awards:	Up to $20,000 in merchandise.
Deadline:	June 15
Address:	International Computer Graphics Image Contest c/o True Vision Inc. Mr. Dennis Collins 7351 Shadeland Station, Suite 100 Indianapolis, IN 46256
Telephone:	(317) 841-0332, 1-800-858-TRUE

JOHNS HOPKINS COMPUTING TO HELP PERSONS W/DISABILITIES | 246

Type:	Awards
Focus:	Computing to Assist Persons with Disabilities (CAPD)
Eligibility:	High school students and full-time undergraduate and graduate students
Description:	People interested in the field of computing are encouraged to apply their imagination to ways and means by which these powerful tools may help in education, vocational training, work, home and community environments, and leisure.
Awards:	(100) awards including $10,000 grand prize and many additional awards. Contestants submitting the 10 best entries selected for the national awards will be invited to exhibit their entry at the Smithsonian Institute in Washington, DC.
Deadline:	August 23
Address:	The Johns Hopkins National Search Computing to Assist Persons with Disabilities P.O. Box 1200 Laurel, MD 20723

KOSCIUSZKO FOUNDATION CHOPIN PIANO COMPETITION | 247

Type:	Scholarships
Focus:	Designed to encourage highly talented American students of piano to study and play works of Chopin.
Eligibility:	Applicants must be between the ages of 16 and 22, as of the opening day of the competition. Must be a U.S. citizen.
Description:	The Competition is held annually at the Foundation House for three consecutive days in the middle of May, before a team of jurors.
Awards:	First prize $2,500, second prize $1,500, and third prize $1,000
Address:	The Kosciuszko Foundation Chopin Piano Competition 15th East 65th Street New York, NY 10021-6595
Telephone:	(212) 734-2130, FAX (212) 628-4552

NATIONAL COUNCIL OF TEACHERS OF ENGLISH   248

Type: Awards

Focus: Creative Writing

Eligibility: High school juniors

Address: Achievement Awards
                   National Council of Teachers of English
                   1111 Kenyon Road
                   Urbana, IL 61801

NATIONAL FRENCH CONTEST   249

Type: Scholarships and Awards

Focus: French Language and Culture

Eligibility: High school students

Description: 60 minute exam

Awards: Medals, scholarships of varying amounts, trips to France.

Deadline: February 6

Address: Mr. Sidney L. Teitelbaum, Director
                   National French Contest
                   American Association of Teachers of French
                   P.O. Box 86
                   Plainview, NJ 11803

NATIONAL HIGH SCHOOL ORATORICAL CONTEST 250

Type:	Contest
Focus:	U.S. Constitution, and Leadership
Eligibility:	High school students in grades 9–12. U.S. citizenship required. Must be under 20 years old.
Description:	Students are judged on their ability to think and speak clearly about the U.S. Constitution and related issues. Contestants give a prepared 8-minute talk on a topic related to the U.S. Constitution, and an extemporaneous 5-minute talk on an assigned topic.
Awards:	Each state winner receives a $1,000 scholarship. Each regional winner receives a $3,000 scholarship. National winners receive $18,000, $16,000, $14,000, and $12,000 scholarships for first, second, third, and fourth places, respectively.
Deadline:	Beginning of the school year.
Address:	American Legion – National Headquarters P.O. Box 1055 Indianapolis, IN 46206

NATIONAL PEACE ESSAY CONTEST 251

Type:	Contest
Focus:	Peace
Eligibility:	High school students from the United States
Description:	Student and school must register. Winning essays will be published.
Awards:	State awards of $500, $250, and $100. National awards of $10,000, $5,000, and $3,000 scholarships.
Deadline:	February 14
Address:	U.S. Institute of Peace 1550 M Street, NW, Suite 700 Washington, DC 20005-1708
Telephone:	(202) 457-1706, FAX (202) 429-6063

NATIONAL SPANISH CONTEST   252

Type:	Scholarships and Awards
Focus:	Spanish Language and Literature
Eligibility:	High school students
Awards:	Scholarships and cash awards of varying amounts and value.
Deadline:	March 15
Address:	National Spanish Contest American Association of Teachers of Spanish Attn: Professor Joseph Schraibman 10 Pricewoods Lane Olivette, MI 63132

NEW WAYS OF COMPUTING   253

Type:	Awards
Focus:	Essays about the near future of computing and information technology
Eligibility:	Undergraduate and graduate students
Description:	Essays must be original, unpublished work on the topic: New Ways of Computing. Sponsored by Computerworld, the Computer Society of IEEE, and NCR Corporation.
Awards:	First place winner receives $10,000, second place $5,000, and third place $3,000. All winners and their professors receive a NCR notebook computer.
Deadline:	December 15. Notification mid-May.
Address:	Manning, Selvage and Lee, Public Relations New Ways of Computing 79 Madison Avenue New York, NY 10016
Telephone:	(212) 213-0909

OPTIMIST INTERNATIONAL ESSAY CONTEST | 254

Type:	Scholarships
Focus:	400-500 word essays about freedom
Eligibility:	High school sophomores, juniors, and seniors
Description:	Club winners progress to the district finals. The district winners receive a four-day all-expense-paid trip to participate in a leadership conference at the Freedoms Foundation in Valley Forge, Pennsylvania. District winning essays will be judged and the winner will receive an all-expense-paid trip to the Optimist convention.
Awards:	International winners receive a $5,000 scholarship (first place), a $3,000 scholarship (second place), and a $2,000 scholarship (third place).
Deadline:	Club contests run from November 15 through December 15.
Address:	Optimist International Activities Department 4494 Lindell Boulevard St. Louis, MO 63108
Telephone:	(314) 371-6000

PATRIOTIC ART COMPETITION | 255

Type:	Scholarships
Focus:	Art
Eligibility:	High school students
Description:	(1) Art must on paper or canvas, no smaller than 8"x10" but no larger than 18"x24". (2) Entry form must be endorsed by a member of the Ladies Auxiliary to the Veterans of Foreign Wars of the United States.
Awards:	(1) $1,500, (1) $1,000, (1) $500, (1) $300, and (1) $200 scholarships. Funds must be used toward winner's art education or art supplies.
Deadline:	May 1 (state deadline)
Address:	Ms. Brenda Hampton, Public Relations Director Patriotic Art Competition Ladies Auxiliary to the Veterans of Foreign Wars of the United States 406 West 34th Street Kansas City, MO 64111

ROBERT H. GODDARD HISTORICAL ESSAY AWARD   256

Type:	Contest
Focus:	History of Rocketry and Astronautics
Eligibility:	U.S. citizenship required.
Description:	Essay should explore aspects of the historical development of rocketry and astronautics. Essays are judged on their originality and scholarship. Essays must not have been previously published.
Awards:	$1,000 prize and plaque for the best essay.
Deadline:	Early December.
Address:	Goddard Historical Essay Contest National Space Club 655 15th Street, NW Washington, DC 20005
Telephone:	(202) 639-4210

SAUL JAKEL MEMORIAL SCHOLARSHIP   257

Type:	Scholarships
Focus:	Essays on the topic of freedom from religion
Eligibility:	High school seniors and undergraduate students
Description:	Essays are six to eight double-spaced typewritten pages. Topics change from year to year. Past topics have included: Problems relating to state-church entanglement in public schools; the problems of growing up as a free-thinker in a religion-oriented society; and the case against giving public tax dollars to church schools and tuition credits to parents who send their children to religiously segregated schools. Entries should also include a short biography.
Awards:	First prize is a $1,000 scholarship, second prize $500, third prize $200.
Deadline:	August 1
Address:	Freedom from Religion Foundation, Inc. P.O. Box 750 Madison, WI 53701
Telephone:	(608) 256-5800/8900

SCHOLASTIC ART AWARD   258

Type:	Scholarships and Awards
Focus:	Art
Eligibility:	College-bound high school seniors
Description:	Write to the address below for more information.
Awards:	Cash, scholarships, other.
Deadline:	October 1
Address:	Ms. Lori Maccione, Awards Coordinator Scholastic Magazine's Art Awards Scholastic Inc., Awards Program 730 Broadway, P.O. Box 731 New York, NY 10003
Telephone:	(212) 505-3566

SCHOLASTIC PHOTOGRAPHY AWARD   259

Type:	Scholarships
Focus:	Photography
Eligibility:	College-bound high school seniors
Description:	Portfolio of photographs, B&W or color.
Awards:	(1) $4,000, (1) $2,000, (1) $1,000, and (1) $500 scholarships. (15) $100 cash awards.
Deadline:	October 1
Address:	Ms. Lori Maccione, Awards Coordinator Scholastic Magazine's Photography Award Scholastic Inc., Awards Program 730 Broadway, P.O. Box 731 New York, NY 10003
Telephone:	(212) 505-3566

SCHOLASTIC WRITING AWARDS PROGRAM   260

Type:	Scholarships and Awards
Focus:	Creative Writing
Eligibility:	Students in grades 7–12 in schools in the U.S. and Canada.
Description:	Selected winning entries will be published in May issues of various Scholastic magazines. Categories include essays, short stories, poetry, and drama. Sponsored in part by Smith Corona.
Awards:	(3) $1,000 scholarships, and some portable electric typewriters. Total of 140 cash awards: (3) first awards $125, (3) second awards $100, (3) third awards $75 and (5) fourth awards $50 per category.
Deadline:	Mid-January. Students participating from certain counties of Pennsylvania have an earlier deadline. Write to the address below for details.
Address:	Ms. Lori Maccione, Awards Coordinator Scholastic Magazine's Writing Awards Scholastic Inc., Awards Program 730 Broadway, P.O. Box 731 New York, NY 10003
Telephone:	(212) 505-3566

SCIENTIFIC GRANT PROPOSAL WRITING CONTEST   261

Type:	Contest
Focus:	Science
Eligibility:	Illinois high school students and college freshmen and sophomores.
Description:	For writing a scientific research proposal and conducting the proposed research. Proposals don't need to be completely original — they can be a spin-off from a class lab experiment or a hobby. Selection is on the basis of the five-page proposal and an application form.
Awards:	(4) $100 awards for research supplies and a certificate.
Deadline:	February 1, May 1, August 1, and November 1.
Address:	Illinois State Academy of Science Illinois State Museum Springfield, IL 62706
Telephone:	(217) 782-6436

YOUNG PLAYWRIGHTS FESTIVAL | 262

Type:	Awards
Focus:	Script Writing
Eligibility:	High school students
Address:	Dramatists Guild
	234 West 44th Street
	New York, NY 10036
Telephone:	(212) 398-9366

Chapter 8

Internships
and Summer Employment

Type:	Employment
Focus:	Employment by A.I.D as a form of financial aid. Internship opportunities include Business, Economics, Political Science, International Relations, Agriculture, Environmental Sciences, and Public Health.
Eligibility:	High school and college students. Must be a U.S. citizen, enrolled in school full-time, be certified under the economic guidelines, and be able to pass a background security investigation.
Description:	This program offers employment to students who may not be able to continue their education without paid employment. Appointments are made for one year, and students work a maximum of 20 hours per week at A.I.D.
Awards:	Appointments for a renewable position of grades GS-1 through GS-4 at an A.I.D. office for paid work, with pay depending on educational background and experience.
Deadline:	Rolling admissions for school year employment, January 31 for summer employment.
Address:	Student Programs Director Office of Human Resources Development and Management Agency for International Development Office of Personal Management 2401 E Street, NW, Room 1127 Washington, DC 20523-0116

| AMERICAN GEOLOGICAL INSTITUTE (AGI) | 264 |

Type: Internship Program

Focus: Geosciences, including Geology, Geophysics, Hydrology, Meteorology, Physical Oceanography, Planetary Geology, and Earth Sciences

Eligibility: Provides summer employment in geoscience-related industries for college juniors, seniors, and graduate students. Must be a member of one of the ethnic minority groups that are underrepresented in the geosciences — Black Americans, Hispanic Americans, and Native Americans.

Description: The summer internships expose the students to a variety of geoscience occupations and provides them with specialized training in applied geoscience. Interns are matched with companies according to skills/expertise and geographic location.

Awards: Interns receive a salary from the employer.

Address: AGI Special Programs
American Geological Institute
4220 King Street
Alexandria, VA 22302-1507

Telephone: (703) 379-2480, FAX (703) 379-7563

AMERICAN HEART ASSOC. STUDENT RESEARCH PROGRAM | 265

Type:	Research Internship
Focus:	Cardiovascular and Cerebrovascular Research
Eligibility:	Undergraduate juniors and seniors. Must either be a California resident or attending school in California. Students must have completed courses in organic chemistry, biochemistry or biological sciences, physics, and calculus.
Description:	Students work in California laboratories during the summer (10 weeks starting July 1) under the direction of lab scientists. Students are selected on the basis of an application, academic records, and faculty recommendations.
Awards:	$2,500 stipend for the summer.
Deadline:	December 15. Notification April 15.
Address:	American Heart Association/California 805 Burlway Road Burlingame, CA 94010
Telephone:	(415) 342-5522, FAX (415) 579-5701

AMERICAN MUSEUM OF NATURAL HISTORY	266

Type: Internships

Focus: General Science, Evolutionary Biology, Entomology, Ichthyology, Invertebrates, Mammalogy, and Molecular Laboratory

Eligibility: Undergraduate students

Description: The Museum's "Research Experiences for Undergraduates" program offers students a chance to conduct research on projects in evolutionary biology and other museum-related scientific disciplines, under the direction of museum scientists. The program includes an orientation to the museum, biweekly meetings in which the students discuss their research, present informal progress reports, and participate in discussions and seminars on graduate and research career opportunities. At the conclusion of the internship the students submit publication quality research papers and deliver oral presentations of their work to the museum staff. The program runs from the beginning of June through the end of August. Selection is on the basis of an application, a list of the science courses taken by the student, three letters of recommendation, and a statement of interest in a particular project.

Awards: Interns receive a stipend of $2,000 to $2,500 for the summer.

Deadline: April 29

Address: Office of Grants and Fellowships
American Museum of Natural History
Central Park West at 79th Street
New York, NY 10024-5192

Telephone: (212) 769-5000

ANL STUDENT RESEARCH PARTICIPATION PROGRAM | 267

Type:	Summer Internship
Focus:	Basic Physical and Life Sciences, Mathematics, Computer Science, Engineering, applied research relating to Coal, Conservation, Environmental Impact and Technology, and Fission and Fusion Energy
Eligibility:	Students who will be undergraduate juniors or seniors and first year graduate students. U.S. citizenship or permanent residency required.
Description:	11-week summer program allows students to participate in the research activities at Argonne National Laboratory.
Awards:	$200 per week plus round-trip travel and housing.
Deadline:	February 1
Address:	Argonne National Laboratory Division of Educational Programs 9700 South Cass Avenue Argonne, IL 60439
Telephone:	(708) 972-3366, FAX (708) 972-3193

ASM MSSCSP SUMMER RESEARCH PROGRAM   268

Type:	Summer Internships
Focus:	Microbiology Research, including Biology, Chemistry and Biochemistry.
Eligibility:	Undergraduate sophomore, junior, and senior minority students. Eligible minorities include Black Americans, Hispanic Americans, Native Alaskans, Native American Indians, and Native Pacific Islanders. U.S. citizenship required. Students must be planning to attend graduate school in chemical or biological science.
Description:	The ASM Minority Student Science Careers Support Program provides minority undergraduates with 8–10 weeks of basic science research laboratory experience during the summer. Participants write abstracts summarizing their research projects at the conclusion of the program.
Awards:	(20–24) $800 monthly stipend, travel to and from the host institution, and housing costs.
Deadline:	March 1
Address:	MSSCSP Summer Research Program American Society for Microbiology 1325 Massachusetts Avenue, NW Washington, DC 20005-4171
Telephone:	(202) 737-3600, FAX (202) 737-0233

AT&T SUMMER RESEARCH PROGRAM 269

Type:	Summer Employment
Focus:	Chemistry, Chemical Engineering, Communications Science, Computer Science & Engineering, Electrical Engineering, Information Science, Materials Science, Mathematics, Mechanical Engineering, Operations Research, Physics, and Statistics
Eligibility:	Outstanding female and minority college juniors (and seniors not graduating by May).
Description:	The program provides summer employment for outstanding women and minority students under the guidance of Bell Laboratories scientists as mentors.
Awards:	(60–100) summer employment opportunities, providing a stipend, housing arrangements, transportation, a well-defined project, and the guidance of a mentor.
Deadline:	December 1, with notification by March 15.
Address:	AT&T Summer Research Program (SRP) SRP Administrator AT&T Bell Laboratories 101 Crawfords Corner Road Holmdel, NJ 07733-1988
Telephone:	(908) 949-3728

AT&T UNIVERSITY RELATIONS SUMMER PROGRAM	270

Type: Summer Employment

Focus: Chemistry, Chemical Engineering, Communications Science, Computer Science & Engineering, Electrical Engineering, Information Science, Materials Science, Mathematics, Mechanical Engineering, Operations Research, Physics, and Statistics

Eligibility: Outstanding B.S., M.S., and Ph.D. students and faculty.

Description: The program provides summer employment for outstanding B.S., M.S., and Ph.D. candidates who are within two years of graduation. An AT&T Member of Technical Staff is assigned to each student as a mentor. This program is also open to university faculty members.

Awards: (200–300) summer employment opportunities, providing a stipend, housing arrangements, transportation, a well-defined project, and the guidance of a mentor.

Deadline: February 15, with notification by April 15.

Address: University Relations Summer Program (UR)
               UR Administrator
               AT&T Bell Laboratories
               101 Crawfords Corner Road
               Holmdel, NJ 07733-1988

Telephone: (908) 949-5592

AWU U.S. DEPARTMENT OF ENERGY FELLOWSHIPS	271

Type:	Fellowships
Focus:	Energy research at laboratories and centers in the western U.S.
Eligibility:	At least two years of college preferred. Undergraduate, graduate, and postgraduate students.
Description:	The U.S. Department of Energy provides stipends and other necessary renumeration to teaching faculty members and student participants involved in energy-related research projects at cooperative laboratories in the western U.S.
Awards:	Stipends and other necessary renumeration.
Deadline:	February 1 and March 1 for others (write to address below for more information).
Address:	Associated Western Universities, Inc. AWU U.S. Department of Energy Fellowships 4190 South Highland Drive, Suite 211 Salt Lake City, UT 84124
Telephone:	(801) 278-0799

DOW JONES EDITING INTERNSHIPS	272

Type:	Internships
Focus:	General
Eligibility:	Undergraduate juniors and seniors and graduate students
Description:	Work as copy editors at daily newspapers.
Awards:	(45) internships pay $1,000 scholarships plus regular wages.
Deadline:	November 15
Address:	Dow Jones Newspaper Fund P.O. Box 300 Princeton, NJ 08543-0300
Telephone:	(609) 452-2820

| FAES SUMMER STUDENT GRANTS AT THE NIH | 273 |

Type: Summer Employment

Focus: Biomedical Research

Eligibility: High school, college, graduate and medical/dental students. Must be at least 16 years of age.

Description: Students participate in original scientific research projects in NIH facilities for a period of at least 8 weeks during the summer months. The student's application must identify an NIH sponsor/laboratory. Students must meet requirements to be a volunteer at the NIH and must receive no other salary, stipend, or grant for his/her work at the NIH. Selection is on the basis of an application, transcripts, GPA, and a list of all math and science courses taken during the past four years.

Awards: Monthly stipends are based on the education level of the student, and range from $600 to $675 for high school students, $750 to $900 for undergraduate students, and $1,050 for graduate students.

Deadline: April 3 (March 27 postmark)

Address: Foundation for Advanced Education in the Sciences (FAES), Inc.
                 One Cloister Court, Box 101
                 Bethesda, MD 20814-1460

Telephone: (301) 496-7976, FAX (301) 402-0174

FIELD MUSEUM OF NATURAL HISTORY

| | | 274 |

Type: Fellowships and Internships

Focus: Anthropology, Botany, Geology, and Zoology. For research associated with the museum.

Eligibility: Undergraduate and graduate students. Graduate students are expected to have formal involvement with the museum (e.g., have a curator serve on the student's committee), be in residence in the Chicago area, and spend a significant portion of their research time at the museum.

Awards: Seven internships are available each year for undergraduate students or recent graduates to work directly with a collections and research department staff member at the museum. Stipends of $826/month are awarded for three consecutive months, normally during the summer.

Deadline: February 1

Address: Chairperson, Scholarship Committee
Collections and Research
Field Museum of Natural History
Roosevelt Road at Lake Shore Drive
Chicago, IL 60605-2496

FOSSIL ENERGY PROFESSIONAL INTERNSHIP PROGRAM | 275

Type:	Interships
Focus:	Chemistry, Physics, Engineering, Computer Science, Environmental Sciences, Geology, Mathematics, and Statistics
Eligibility:	Undergraduate students
Description:	Full-time and part-time opportunities for undergraduate students to participate in fossil energy-related research projects that correlate with their academic and career goals.
Awards:	(85) awards per year. Monthly stipend of $1,000 to $1,300; travel (one round trip) to center/campus; off-campus tuition and fees required by the home institution.
Deadline:	January 1, March 1, June 1, and October 1
Address:	Mr. Richard Wiesehuegel Program Manager Oak Ridge Associated Universities P.O. Box 117 Oak Ridge, TN 37831-0117
Telephone:	(615) 576-3383

FOSSIL ENERGY TECHNOLOGY INTERNSHIP PROGRAM | 276

Type:	Internships
Focus:	Chemistry, Physics, Engineering, Mathematics, Computer Science, and Safety and Health
Eligibility:	Undergraduate students and associate degree candidates
Description:	Opportunities for participants to work with technical and administrative staff members engaged in fossil energy research; assignments relate to each student's academic and career goals.
Awards:	(15) awards per year. Monthly stipend of $1,000; transportation to the center; any normal tuition and fees required by the home institution for an off-campus program.
Deadline:	January 1, March 1, June 1, and October 1
Address:	Mr. John T. Crockett Program Manager Oak Ridge Associated Universities P.O. Box 117 Oak Ridge, TN 37831-0117
Telephone:	(615) 576-3253

HEWLETT-PACKARD SEED PROGRAM   277

Type:	Summer Employment
Focus:	Electrical Engineering, Computer Science, Computer Engineering, Mechanical Engineering, Industrial Engineering, Information Technology, Finance, and Business Administration
Eligibility:	Undergraduate students who have completed their freshman year in college and graduate students. Women, minorities, and students with disabilities are encouraged to apply.
Description:	HP's Student Employment and Educational Development (SEED) program provides a minimum of 10 weeks of full-time summer employment for students with a strong interest in a technical or business curriculum. For more information, check with your campus placement office or write to the address below for an application.
Awards:	Salary, round-trip transportation from the student's campus to the work site, and an allowance to defray initial relocation costs.
Deadline:	April 30
Address:	SEED Hewlett-Packard Company 3000 Hanover Street Mail Stop 20AC Palo Alto, CA 94304-1181
Telephone:	(415) 857-2092

MARCH OF DIMES BIRTH DEFECTS FOUNDATION   278

Type:	Research Internship
Focus:	Birth Defects
Eligibility:	Medical students
Description:	The Summer Science Research Program for Medical Students lets medical students spend 3 months during the summer conducting research on birth defects in a laboratory or clinical setting.
Awards:	(50) $2,000 awards
Deadline:	February 15
Address:	March of Dimes Birth Defects Foundation 1275 Mamaroneck Avenue White Plains, NY 10605
Telephone:	(914) 428-7100, FAX (914) 428-8203

MASS MEDIA SCIENCE & ENGINEERING FELLOWSHIP 279

Type:	Internships
Focus:	Science Journalism internships in the natural and social sciences and engineering.
Eligibility:	Priority given to graduate students, but outstanding undergraduate and postdoctoral students will also be considered. Applicants must be enrolled as students in the natural or social sciences or engineering in order to qualify.
Description:	Provides support for 15-20 graduate students as intern reporters, researchers, and production assistants in the mass media for 10 weeks during the summer. Applicants must submit an application form, a current resumé, brief writing samples directed to the general public, transcripts of undergraduate and graduate work, and three letters of recommendation, one of which should be a personal reference.
Awards:	A $400/week stipend is included to help cover living and travel expenses for the duration of the fellowship.
Deadline:	January 15. Notification March 15.
Address:	Ms. Donna R. Kepler American Association for the Advancement of Science Mass Media Science and Engineering Fellowship 1333 H Street, NW, 10th Floor Washington, DC 20005
Telephone:	(202) 326-6600

MINORITY TRAINEESHIPS IN OCEANOGRAPHY	280

Type: Research Internships

Focus: Oceanography and related fields in the Physical and Natural Sciences, Mathematics, and Engineering, including Chemistry, Geology, Geophysics, Meteorology, Physics, and Biology

Eligibility: Undergraduate minority juniors and seniors

Description: This program offers minority undergraduates the opportunity to learn about and conduct research in oceanography at the Woods Hole Oceanographic Institution. Traineeships run for a 10 or 12 week period in the summer or for a semester during the school year, and may be renewed the following year. Trainees conduct research under the direction of a mentor from the WHOI research staff, and also participate in a supervised program of supplemental study. Trainees may participate in the WHOI's seminars and colloquia. The traineeship experience often involves field work, so trainees may have the opportunity to participate in research cruises.

Awards: Trainees are paid the same salary as other employees with similar experience. In addition, they receive the cost of round-trip travel to Woods Hole.

Address: Woods Hole Oceanographic Institution
                 Woods Hole, MA 02543

Telephone: (508) 548-1400 x2219

NATIONAL WILDLIFE FEDERATION

281

Type:	Research Internships
Focus:	Science, Wildlife, and Biology
Eligibility:	Upperclass undergraduate students and graduate students
Description:	Paid research internships run for 24 weeks during the year. Unpaid summer internships run for 12 weeks during the summer. All internships are in the Washington, DC area. Some internships involve a moderate amount of clerical grunge work. Recipients are selected on the basis of a resume, including three to five references, and a cover-letter describing their interests.
Awards:	$265/week
Deadline:	January 1 and August 1
Address:	National Wildlife Federation 1412 16th Street, NW Washington, DC 20036-2266
Telephone:	(202) 797-6800, FAX (202) 797-6646

NATIONAL ZOOLOGICAL PARK

282

Type:	Research Internships
Focus:	Science, Wildlife, and Biology
Eligibility:	Undergraduate students and graduate students
Description:	Paid research internships of 12 weeks duration during the summer or fall. Interns conduct animal research in behavior and ecology, reproduction and nutrition, genetics and husbandry, exotic animal medicine, or veterinary pathology. Selection is on the basis of a 500–1,000 word statement of interest, an application, transcripts, a description of relevant experience, and two letters of recommendation.
Awards:	$2,400 stipend
Deadline:	February 22. Notification by the end of April.
Address:	National Zoological Park Washington, DC 20008
Telephone:	(202) 673-4950, FAX (202) 673-4738

NCAR MINORITY SUMMER EMPLOYMENT PROGRAM   283

Type:	Internship
Focus:	Science and Engineering. Atmospheric Research.
Eligibility:	Minority undergraduate sophomores, juniors, and seniors. The academic background of the applicant should include courses in at least one of the following areas of study: chemistry, biology, meteorology, physics, mathematics, computer science, electrical engineering, social science, environmental issues, and technical writing.
Description:	Students are assigned positions within a scientific research project at the National Center for Atmospheric Research. They also participate in a specially designed course in technical writing. At the conclusion of the summer, each student presents a paper summarizing his or her work at NCAR.
Awards:	Participants receive travel to and from Boulder, a housing allowance, and a monthly stipend.
Deadline:	March 5
Address:	NCAR Minority Summer Employment Program University Corporation for Atmospheric Research P.O. Box 3000 Boulder, CO 80307-3000
Telephone:	(303) 497-8706/1000

NIEHS PROFESSIONAL INTERNSHIP PROGRAM   284

Type:	Internship
Focus:	Environmental Sciences, Biomedical Sciences, and Life Sciences
Eligibility:	Graduate students who have not yet begun thesis or dissertation research.
Awards:	Stipend based on research area and degree; reimbursement for inbound and outbound travel.
Deadline:	Ongoing
Address:	Mr. Richard Wiesehuegel Program Manager Oak Ridge Associated Universities P.O. Box 117 Oak Ridge, TN 37831-0117
Telephone:	(615) 576-3383

NIEHS Summer Intramural Research Training Awards | 285

Type:	Internship
Focus:	Biomedical Research, including Neurosciences, Biophysics, Genetics, Carcinogenesis, Reproductive and Developmental Biology, Chemistry, Pharmacology, Pulmonary Pathobiology, Statistics, Biomathematics, Computer Science, Epidemiology, and Toxicology
Eligibility:	High school, undergraduate and graduate students. Must be at least 16 years of age. U.S. citizenship or permanent residency required.
Description:	Each student works on a structured research project under the supervision of senior laboratory researchers who serve as their mentors. Students may also attend the NIEHS summer seminar series. The internships are held at the NIEHS facility in Research Triangle Park, NC. Interns are selected on the basis of a cover letter, resume, transcripts, and two letters of recommendation.
Awards:	Stipend based on student's educational level, ranging from $800 for high school students to $2,000 for graduate students who have completed three or more years of graduate work.
Deadline:	February 15
Address:	National Institute of Environmental Health Sciences Personnel Officer P.O. Box 12233 Research Triangle Park, NC 27709
Telephone:	(919) 541-3315

NSA SUMMER EMPLOYMENT PROGRAM | 286

Type:	Summer Employment
Focus:	Electrical Engineering, Mathematics, and Computer Science, or Asian, Middle Eastern, and Slavic languages
Eligibility:	Undergraduate juniors and graduate students. Students must possess at least a 3.0 GPA on a 4.0 scale. U.S. citizenship required for applicant and immediate family members.
Description:	Participants work full-time during the summer break for a minimum of 12 weeks. Assignments are chosen on the basis of the student's background, interest, and academic status. Apartments at the University of Maryland, Baltimore County Campus and Capitol College are available at special rates. All assignments are at the NSA facilities located in/around Fort George G. Meade, Maryland. Applicants must submit a completed Application for Federal Employment (SF-171).
Deadline:	November 15
Address:	National Security Agency Coordinator, Summer Employment Program Attn: M322 (SEP) Ft. George G. Meade, MD 20755-6000
Telephone:	1-800-962-9398

PROFESSIONAL INTERNSHIP PROGRAM/ORNL   287

Type:	Internships
Focus:	Chemistry, Geology, Chemical Engineering, Hydrogeology, Mechanical Engineering, Computer Science, and Environmental Sciences
Eligibility:	Undergraduate students
Description:	Opportunities for undergraduate students to participate in energy-related research projects that correlate with their academic and career goals.
Awards:	(15) awards: a monthly stipend of $1,000 to $1,300; travel (one round trip) to center/campus; off-campus tuition and fees required by the home institution.
Deadline:	January, March, June, and October
Address:	Mr. Richard Wiesehuegel Program Manager Oak Ridge Associated Universities P.O. Box 117 Oak Ridge, DC 37831-0117
Telephone:	(615) 576-3383

RESOURCES FOR THE FUTURE   288

Type:	Internships
Focus:	Research concerning natural resources and environmental issues
Eligibility:	Undergraduate and graduate students
Description:	Interns assist staff members and resident scholars with ongoing research projects and the development of new areas of research. Internships commence June 1 and end August 31. Students should submit a letter of interest along with a resume, a recent transcript, and a letter of recommendation from a faculty member.
Awards:	Stipends are based on experience and length of stay.
Deadline:	March 15
Address:	Resources for the Future 1616 P Street, NW Washington, DC 20036
Telephone:	(202) 328-5000/5022, FAX (202) 939-3460

SMITHSONIAN INSTITUTION INTERNSHIPS   289

Type:	Internships
Focus:	General. Science, Library Science, Photography, History, Art, and other museum-related fields
Eligibility:	High school seniors
Description:	40 high school seniors from across the U.S. will serve as interns, spending 35 hours per week working with a Smithsonian professional. The interns as a group also tour sites that many visitors to Washington, DC do not see. Students are selected on the basis of an application, essay, and three recommendations.
Awards:	Each intern will receive a living allowance of $550. Interns from outside the Washington metropolitan area will be provided with housing in a university residence hall and transportation to and from the Smithsonian. Round-trip air tickets will be provided to students living more than 400 miles outside of Washington, DC.
Deadline:	March 15. Notification by early May.
Address:	INTERN '93 Office of Elementary and Secondary Education Arts and Industries Building, Room 1163 Mail Stop 402 Smithsonian Institution Washington, DC 20560
Telephone:	Voice: (202) 357-3049, TDD: (202) 357-1696

SOUTHWESTERN RESEARCH STATION VOLUNTEER PROGRAM	290

Type: Volunteer Program

Focus: Natural History, including Biological, Paleontological, Geological, and Archaeological Research

Eligibility: Advanced undergraduate and graduate students

Description: The Southwestern Research Station is a private preserve in the Chiricahua Mountains, set in the middle of well-protected national forest. The diverse range of biotypes in the vicinity of the Station make it an ideal location for natural history research. The Station is owned and operated by the American Museum of Natural History. Approximately 20 volunteers reside at the Station each year, for a period of 6 to 12 weeks. Volunteers receive room and board and work for the Station on a wide variety of chores. During their spare time, volunteers assist graduate student and faculty researchers with scientific investigations.

Awards: Room and board only.

Address: Resident Director
Southwestern Research Station
Portal, Arizona 85632

Telephone: (602) 558-2396

STUDENT INTERNSHIP PROGRAMS/ORNL   291

Type:	Internships
Focus:	Biological Sciences, Medical Sciences, Physical Sciences, and other related scientific disciplines
Eligibility:	Baccalaureate degree candidates
Description:	Provides opportunities and support for research in exposure and disease registries, health assessments, health effects, toxicological profiles, emergency response, and health education.
Awards:	Monthly stipend of $1,350 to $2,150 (full-time) depending on academic status and research area; limited travel reimbursement; off-campus tuition and fees required by home institution.
Deadline:	Ongoing
Address:	Ms. Linda McCamant Program Manager Student Internship Programs Oak Ridge Associated Universities P.O. Box 117 Oak Ridge, TN 37831-0117
Telephone:	(615) 576-1089

TECHNOLOGY INTERNSHIP PROGRAM/ORNL   292

Type:	Internships
Focus:	Chemical, Electrical, Health Physics, and Mechanical Engineering Technology
Eligibility:	Associate degree students
Description:	Provides opportunities for participants to work with technical and administrative staff members engaged in energy research; assignments appropriately relate to each student's academic goals.
Awards:	Monthly stipend of $1,000
Deadline:	January 1, April 1, July 1, and November 1
Address:	Mr. Richard Wiesehuegel Program Manager Oak Ridge Associated Universities P.O. Box 117 Oak Ridge, TN 37831-0117
Telephone:	(615) 576-3383

UNDERGRADUATE SUMMER INSTITUTES 293

Type:	Research Internship
Focus:	Physics, Chemistry, Materials Science, and Engineering
Eligibility:	Undergraduate juniors. U.S. citizenship required.
Description:	The program is held at Lawrence Livermore National Laboratory. Students have the choice of two 12-day sessions, one in June and one in August. The program is co-sponsored by UC/Davis and the Hertz Foundation.
Awards:	Participants receive travel and living expenses and a $500 award.
Deadline:	January 29
Address:	Undergraduate Summer Institutes Lawrence Livermore National Laboratory The Department of Applied Science University of California, Davis/Livermore P.O. Box 808, L-725 Livermore, CA 94551
Telephone:	(510) 423-9756, Kristin Haworth

U.S. DEPARTMENT OF ENERGY STUDENT EMPLOYMENT 294

Type:	Summer Employment
Focus:	Summer employment and CO-OP programs
Eligibility:	High school students and undergraduate freshmen and sophomores. Must be at least 16 years of age.
Description:	The U.S. Department of Energy publishes a booklet describing the various programs available, which may be obtained by writing to the address below. Most jobs require education or experience appropriate to the type of work for which you apply.
Awards:	Applicants are paid according to educational background and experience. Amounts range from $184 to $254 per week.
Address:	U.S. Department of Energy U.S. Department of Energy Student Employment 1000 Independence Avenue, SW Washington, DC 20595

WOODS HOLE OCEANOGRAPHIC INSTITUTION (WHOI) | 295

Type:	Summer Research Program
Focus:	Oceanography and related fields, such as Chemistry, Engineering, Geology, Geophysics, Mathematics, Meteorology, Physics, Biology, and Marine Policy
Eligibility:	Undergraduate seniors and beginning graduate students
Description:	Each Fellow pursues an independent research project under the guidance of a member of the WHOI's research staff. Fellows may participate in the WHOI's summer seminars and colloquia. Each Fellow writes a research paper and gives an oral presentation of research progress at the conclusion of the 12-week program. Fellows are selected on the basis of their promise as future ocean scientists or ocean engineers, as evidenced by an application, three letters of recommendation, transcripts, and a concise statement of research interests, academic and career plans, and reasons for applying to the WHOI. WHOI also has a summer study program in geophysical fluid dynamics for advanced graduate students.
Awards:	Stipend of $3,600 for the 12-week program. Additional support may be provided for travel.
Deadline:	March 2. Notification mid-April.
Address:	Woods Hole Oceanographic Institution Woods Hole, MA 02543
Telephone:	(508) 457-2000 x 2200, FAX (508) 457-2188

Chapter 9

Study Abroad

Type:	Fellowship
Focus:	Archaeology
Eligibility:	Graduate students in doctoral programs and recent recipients of the Ph.D. Applicant must apply concurrently to the American School of Classical Studies at Athens for Associate Membership or Student Associate Membership and is contingent on their acceptance. U.S. and Canadian citizens and permanent residents are eligible.
Description:	Other major fellowships may not be held during the tenure of the Colburn award.
Awards:	$5,500 fellowship
Deadline:	February 1
Address:	Archaeological Institute of America 675 Commonwealth Avenue Boston, MA 02215-1401
Telephone:	(617) 353-9361, FAX (617) 353-6550

AIA HARRIET AND LEON POMERANCE FELLOWSHIP | 297

Type:	Fellowship
Focus:	Archaeology of the Aegean Bronze Age
Eligibility:	Graduate students in doctoral programs and recent recipients of the Ph.D. Applicants must be residents of the United States or Canada.
Description:	Preference will be given to candidates whose project requires travel to the Mediterranean. Previous Harriet Pomerance Fellows are not eligible.
Awards:	$3,000 fellowship
Deadline:	November 15
Address:	Archaeological Institute of America 675 Commonwealth Avenue Boston, MA 02215-1401
Telephone:	(617) 353-9361, FAX (617) 353-6550

AIA HELEN M. WOODRUFF FELLOWSHIP | 298

Type:	Fellowship
Focus:	Archaeology and Classical Studies
Eligibility:	Graduate students in doctoral programs. U.S. citizenship or permanent residency required.
Awards:	The fellowship, together with other funds from the American Academy in Rome, will support a Rome Prize Fellowship for study at the American Academy in Rome.
Address:	American Academy in Rome 41 East 65th Street New York, NY 10021-6508

AIA Kenan T. Erim Award | 299

Type:	Award
Focus:	Archaeology
Eligibility:	Graduate students in doctoral programs and recent recipients of the Ph.D.
Description:	The award is given to an American or international research and/or excavating scholar working on Aphrodisias material. If the project involves work at Aphrodisias, candidates must submit written approval from the Field Director with their applications. Recipients of the Erim Award must submit a final report to the President of the Archaeological Institute of America and to the President of the American Friends of Aphrodisias, Box 989, Lenox Hill Station, New York, NY 10021.
Awards:	$4,000 award
Deadline:	November 15
Address:	Archaeological Institute of America 675 Commonwealth Avenue Boston, MA 02215-1401
Telephone:	(617) 353-9361, FAX (617) 353-6550

AIA Olivia James Traveling Fellowship | 300

Type:	Fellowship
Focus:	Archaeology, the Classics, Sculpture, Architecture, and History
Eligibility:	Graduate students in doctoral programs and recent recipients of the Ph.D. U.S. citizenship or permanent residency required.
Description:	Preference is given to projects of at least a half year's duration. The award is to be used for travel and study in Greece, the Aegean Islands, Sicily, Southern Italy, Asia Minor, or Mesopotamia. The award is not intended to support field excavation projects. Recipients may not hold other major fellowships during the tenure of the award.
Awards:	$15,000 fellowship
Deadline:	November 15
Address:	Archaeological Institute of America 675 Commonwealth Avenue Boston, MA 02215-1401
Telephone:	(617) 353-9361, FAX (617) 353-6550

AMERICAN-SCANDINAVIAN FOUNDATION   301

Type:	Fellowships and Grants
Focus:	Study or research in Scandinavia (Denmark, Finland, Iceland, Norway, Sweden)
Eligibility:	Applicants must be U.S. citizens or permanent residents and have completed their undergraduate education by the time the overseas project is to begin.
Description:	Language competence, financial need, and merit are considered in making awards.
Awards:	Grants of $2,500 are for short visits and fellowships of $15,000 are intended for a full academic year of research or study.
Deadline:	November 1
Address:	The American-Scandinavian Foundation Exchange Division 725 Park Avenue New York, NY 10021
Telephone:	(212) 879-9779, FAX (212) 249-3444

BUDAPEST SEMESTERS IN MATHEMATICS   302

Type:	Study Abroad
Focus:	Mathematics and Computer Science
Eligibility:	Undergraduate sophomores, juniors, and seniors
Description:	A one or two-semester study abroad program for English-speaking students of mathematics and computer science. The program, founded by Paul Erdős, is held in Hungary, and all classes are taught in English by some of Hungary's best mathematicians. Hungary has one of the best educational systems in pure mathematics in the world.
Awards:	The program charges tuition, but the total costs are about half of what a student would expect to pay at a U.S. private institution like MIT or Stanford.
Address:	Dr. Paul D. Humke North American Director Budapest Semesters in Mathematics Department of Mathematics St. Olaf College Northfield, MN 55057
Telephone:	(507) 645-6440, E-mail: humke@stolaf.edu

BUNDESKANZLER SCHOLARSHIPS FOR GERMANY 303

Type:	Study Abroad
Focus:	For study in Germany. Study may be in any field, but the Humanities, Social Sciences, Law, and Economics are preferred.
Eligibility:	U.S. citizens aged 30 or under, including undergraduate, graduate, and postgraduate students as well as young professionals.
Description:	The Alexander Von Humboldt Foundation awards the Bundeskanzler scholarships in an effort to strengthen transatlantic ties. The emphasis is on future U.S. leaders in the academic world, business, and politics. Candidates must be nominated by the presidents and deans of leading American universities and by the presidents of the American Council of Learned Societies and the American Association of Universities.
Awards:	(10) twelve-month scholarships, providing a monthly allowance of DM 5,500 for housing and living expenses. Participants will also receive intensive German language training. Scholarship holders may be accompanied by their spouses and dependent children.
Deadline:	March 15
Address:	Alexander von Humboldt Foundation Jean-Paul Strabe 12 D5300 Bonn 2, Germany Association of American Universities One Dupont Circle, Suite 730 Washington, DC 20036
Telephone:	228-833-0, FAX 228-833-1; (202) 466-5030, FAX (202) 775-9242

FULBRIGHT-HAYS PROGRAM   304

Type:	Fellowships
Focus:	For graduate study in any field in which the project can be profitably undertaken abroad.
Eligibility:	Applicants must be U.S. citizens, hold a bachelor's degree, and have language proficiency sufficient to carry out the proposed study and to communicate with the host country.
Awards:	Approximately (670) grants are available for graduate study abroad in over seventy countries.
Deadline:	Varies but typically includes round-trip transportation, tuition, and maintenance for one academic year (write to address below for exact details).
Address:	Institute of International Education U.S. Student Programs Division Fulbright-Hays Program 809 United Nations Plaza New York, NY 10017-3580
Telephone:	(212) 984-5330

GERMAN ACADEMIC EXCHANGE SERVICE (DAAD)	305

Type:	Fellowships
Focus:	For graduate study in any field at German institutions of higher education.
Eligibility:	For American graduate, doctoral, or postdoctoral students. U.S. citizenship required. Candidates must be 32 years of age or younger, have a bachelor's degree, and have a good working knowledge of German.
Description:	Recipients must not hold a Fulbright grant, another DAAD grant, or a grant from any other German organization during the duration of the fellowship. For more information, write to the IIE, U.S. Student Programs, 809 United Nations Plaza, New York, NY 10017, or the address given below.
Awards:	Round-trip travel to Germany, tuition, and a stipend. Duration is from 7 to 10 months during the academic year.
Deadline:	October
Address:	German Academic Exchange Service (DAAD) 950 Third Avenue, 19th floor New York, NY 10022

INDO-AMERICAN FELLOWSHIP PROGRAM	306

Type:	Fellowships
Focus:	For advanced research in India during the academic year.
Eligibility:	Applicants must be U.S. citizens
Awards:	Approximately 12 grants are available to U.S. citizens for advanced research in India. In addition to a basic grant there are travel, dependents, and research allowances. Write to address below for details.
Deadline:	June 15
Address:	Council for the International Exchange of Scholars Attn: Indo-American Fellowship Program 3400 International Drive, NW, Suite M-500 Washington, DC 20008-3097

ITALIAN NATIONAL RESEARCH COUNCIL FELLOWSHIPS   307

Type:	Fellowships
Focus:	Mathematics
Eligibility:	U.S. citizenship required
Description:	Offered by the Italian National Research Council (*Consiglio Nazionale delle Ricerche*) to foster collaboration between U.S. and Italian mathematicians.
Awards:	Stipend of 2,200,000 Italian *lire* per month, for a maximum of 12 months, plus travel expenses to and from the country of residence.
Address:	Prof. Carlo M. Scoppola C.N.R. via Santa Marta 13A 50139 Firenze, Italy

JAPAN–U.S. JAMS SEMINAR   308

Type:	Travel
Focus:	Mathematics, Science, and Engineering. Cultural exchange.
Eligibility:	Undergraduate students
Description:	The Japan–U.S. Mathematical Sciences (JAMS) seminar consists of lectures by distinguished guests and talks by the participants. Students are selected on the basis of an application, essay, and letters of recommendation.
Awards:	Sixty students will participate — 25 from Japan, 25 from the U.S., and 10 from other countries. An understanding of Japanese is not required. JAMS will provide full transportation (including round-trip airfare from the U.S.) and living costs within Japan.
Deadline:	February 1
Address:	Japan–U.S. JAMS Administrator Beatrice Spencer Kleppner 19 Beatrice Circle Belmont, MA 02178
Telephone:	(617) 484-6472

KENNEDY SCHOLARSHIPS	309

Type:	Fellowships
Eligibility:	Citizens of the United Kingdom
Description:	Provides support for postgraduate study at Harvard University or the Massachusetts Institute of Technology.
Deadline:	October 18
Address:	Secretary Kennedy Memorial Trust 16 Great College Street London SWIP 3RX, England

KOSCIUSZKO FOUNDATION	310

Type:	Scholarships
Focus:	Scholarships for Americans of Polish descent
Eligibility:	Americans or Canadians of Polish descent with a minimum completed M.A./M.S. degree. Priority is given to doctoral or postdoctoral students and scholars.
Description:	The Foundation sends a number of students to Poland for one year of study of the Polish language, literature, history, and culture.
Awards:	Tuition and housing in addition to a monthly stipend in Polish currency for food and miscellaneous expenses. Transportation to and from Poland is at the expense of the participant.
Deadline:	November 15
Address:	The Kosciuszko Foundation 15 East 65th Street New York, NY 10021-6595
Telephone:	(212) 734-2130, FAX (212) 628-4552

LADY DAVIS FELLOWSHIP TRUST   311

Type:	Fellowships
Focus:	All fields
Eligibility:	For graduate study and/or research at Hebrew University of Jerusalem and the Technion (Israel Institute of Technology), Haifa.
Description:	Lady Davis Fellows are selected on the basis of demonstrated excellence in their studies, promise of distinction in their chosen fields of specialization, and qualities of mind, intellect, and character.
Awards:	Fellowships are tenable for one year. They may be renewed for a second year and in special circumstances awarded for the third year. The grant for fellows defrays the costs of travel, tuition fees (where applicable), and reasonable living expenses.
Deadline:	November 30
Address:	Lady Davis Fellowship Trust P.O. Box 1255 Jerusalem, Israel 91904
Telephone:	02-663-848

MARSHALL SCHOLARSHIPS 312

Type:	Scholarships
Focus:	Field Unrestricted
Eligibility:	U.S. graduates. Age limit of 25 years. Minimum cumulative GPA of 3.7 (A-).
Description:	Up to 40 scholarships are offered by the British government to U.S. graduates, tenable at any university in the United Kingdom. Recipients of awards are required to take a degree at their British University. Apply through British Consulates-General for more information. These include: Northeast – Suite 4740, Prudential Tower, Prudential Center, Boston, MA 02199; Mideast – 3100 Massachusetts Avenue, NW, Washington, DC 20008; South – Suite 912, 225 Peachtree St., NE, Atlanta, GA 30303; Central – 33 North Dearborn St., Chicago, IL 60602; Pacific – 1 Sansome St., San Francisco, CA 94104.
Awards:	Approximately $11,000 per year for a maximum of two years.
Deadline:	October 15
Address:	Marshall Scholarships Suite 4740 Prudential Tower Prudential Center Boston, MA 02199

RHODES SCHOLARSHIP   313

Type:	Fellowships
Focus:	General. For study at Oxford University for up to three years of postbaccalaureate study in any field.
Eligibility:	Unmarried U.S. citizens of age between 18 and 24 on October 1 of year of application. (Scholarships are also granted to citizens of Australia, Bermuda, Canada, Caribbean, Germany, Hong Kong, India, Jamaica, Kenya, Malaysia, New Zealand, Nigeria, Pakistan, Singapore, South Africa, and Zimbabwe, but by a different procedure.)
Description:	Deferment not allowed. Must remain unmarried during the first year of residence at Oxford. Selection is on the basis of an application, transcripts, proof of citizenship, a 1,000-word essay describing applicant's interests, a brief summary of college honors and activities, five to eight references, four of whom are college faculty who have taught the applicant.
Awards:	Provides stipend, tuition, and travel assistance. 32 American students are selected each year.
Deadline:	October 1
Address:	Rhodes Scholarship Trust American Secretary Pomona College Claremonth, CA 91711-6305

ROTARY FOUNDATION SCHOLARSHIPS | 314

Type:	Study Abroad
Focus:	General. All fields are eligible, but not unsupervised research or medical internships or residencies.
Eligibility:	Undergraduate and graduate students. Applicants can be any age over 18 as long as they have completed two years of university work or appropriate professional experience by the time they wish to begin scholarship studies. Scholars may be married or single. Applicants must be citizens of a country in which there is a Rotary club, including the United States.
Description:	Contact your local Rotary club for application materials. Applications must be endorsed by the local club and district to be considered by the Rotary Foundation. Not all Rotary clubs will offer scholarships every year.
Awards:	(1,000) one-year awards, including round-trip transportation and up to $20,000 for tuition, room and board, books and supplies, a small contingency allocation, and language training if necessary. The Rotary Foundation also offers a new multi-year scholarship for study abroad with a flat grant of $10,000 a year for up to three years.
Deadline:	July 15. Local Rotary clubs may set local deadlines as early as March. Notification by December 15.
Address:	Rotary Foundation of Rotary International One Rotary Center 1560 Sherman Avenue Evanston, IL 60201
Telephone:	(708) 866-3000, FAX (708) 328-8554

SOCIAL SCIENCES RESEARCH COUNCIL 315

Type:	Fellowships
Focus:	Social Sciences
Eligibility:	Graduate students. U.S. citizenship required.
Description:	Provides support for doctoral candidates at U.S. universities to conduct thesis research in Africa, the Middle East, Asia, Western Europe, Berlin, Japan, the Soviet Union, Latin America, and the Caribbean.
Deadline:	Deadlines vary from program to program.
Address:	Social Science Research Council Fellowships and Grants 605 Third Avenue New York, NY 10158
Telephone:	(212) 661-0280

| SUMMER INSTITUTE IN JAPAN | 316 |

SUMMER INSTITUTE IN JAPAN 316

Type: Work Abroad

Focus: Science and Engineering, including Biomedical Science and Engineering.

Eligibility: Graduate students. Must be enrolled in a U.S. institution for a science or engineering Ph.D. program or a M.D. program with an interest in biomedical research. U.S. citizenship or permanent residency required. Women, minorities, and persons with disabilities are encouraged to apply.

Description: This program provides 60 U.S. graduate students with first-hand experience in a Japanese research laboratory. Internships are held at government, corporate, and university laboratories in Tokyo and Tsukuba. Students also receive intensive Japanese language training and lectures on Japanese science, history, and culture. The program runs 8 weeks, from the end of June to the end of August. For more information, request NSF publication 92-105 "Summer Institute in Japan" from NSF's Publications Office at pubs@nsf.gov or (202) 357-7668. Be sure to give your name and complete mailing address. Application materials may also be obtained by sending an E-mail message to stisserv@nsf.gov with message body "get nsf92105". You will receive a copy of publication 92-105 by return E-mail.

Awards: NSF pays travel costs to and from Japan and an allowance of $2,000. This allowance is meant to compensate in part for the loss of summer employment. The Japanese government will provide dormitory accommodations, food, and professional travel allowances.

Deadline: December 1, with notification in March.

Address: Japan Program, Room V-501
Division of International Programs
National Science Foundation
1800 G Street, NW
Washington, DC 20550
E-mail: NSFJinfo@nsf.gov

Telephone: (202) 653-5862, FAX (202) 653-5929

THOMAS J. WATSON FELLOWSHIP PROGRAM   317

Type:	Study Abroad
Focus:	World Affairs. General.
Eligibility:	College graduates
Description:	The program gives Fellows the opportunity for a focused and disciplined *Wanderjahr* of their own devising and lets them immerse themselves in cultures other than their own for an entire year. The experience should not involve extended formal study at a foreign university. Fellows are required to submit quarterly progress reports while abroad and a final evaluation and accounting for Fellowship funds when they return. Candidates must be nominated by their university. Selection is on the basis of an application, project description, and an interview.
Awards:	(65) $15,000 grants. If the Fellow will be accompanied by and will support a spouse or dependent child, the grant is $21,000.
Deadline:	Early November. Notification in mid-March.
Address:	The Thomas J. Watson Foundation 217 Angell Street Providence, RI 02906
Telephone:	(401) 274-1952, FAX (401) 274-1954

WINSTON CHURCHILL FOUNDATION 318

Type: Fellowships

Focus: Engineering, Mathematics, and Science

Eligibility: Must be between the ages of 19 and 26 and hold a bachelor's degree or its equivalent from a U.S. college. Must not hold a Ph.D. Must also be a U.S. citizen and enrolled in one of the 50 participating colleges or universities.

Description: For graduate work at Churchill College, Cambridge University, England. A list of participating schools is available from the foundation. An application can be obtained from the foundation representative at your school.

Awards: 10 full tuition and fees fellowships of approximately $16,000. Students will receive an allowance of $4,000 for 9-months or $5,000 for 12-months and a travel allowance of $500.

Deadline: November 15, with notification by April 15.

Address: Winston Churchill Foundation
of the United States
P.O. Box 1240, Gracie Station
New York, NY 10028

Telephone: (212) 879-3480

Chapter 10

Other Resources

Electronic Bulletin Boards

FEDIX

FEDIX is an on-line service which provides accurate and timely information about federal agencies. There are no registration fees and no access charges for using FEDIX.

FEDIX provides daily information updates on:

- Scholarships, fellowships, and grants
- Federal education and research programs
- Availability of used government research equipment
- Minority assistance research and education programs
- News and general information within participating agencies.

FEDIX is accessible through the NSF Internet using the `telnet` program at the address:

```
fedix.fie.com [192.11.228.1]
```

At the login prompt, type `fedix`. When connected, type NEW at the USERID prompt and follow the instructions provided.

For modem access to FEDIX dial 1-800-783-3349 or (301) 258-0953. Use the following settings on your modem: 1200, 2400 or 9600 baud, 8 databits, no parity, and 1 stopbit. Once connected, type NEW at the USERID prompt and follow the instructions provided. Files may be downloaded using the Xmodem or Ymodem protocols, or through screen capture. You may also use `ftp` to get files from `fedix.fie.com`.

Copies of the free FEDIX User's Guide are available online in FEDIX, or by calling (301) 975-0103. Send E-mail to `comments@fedix.fie.com` for more information.

NSF STIS

STIS is an electronic dissemination system that provides fast, easy access to National Science Foundation (NSF) publications. Publications available through STIS include

265

the *NSF Bulletin*, NSF program announcements, press releases, general publications and reports, and award abstracts. The goal of STIS is to make all printed NSF publications available electronically.

STIS may be accessed through several methods, including E-mail, anonymous FTP, WAIS, and on-line access through telnet or modem dialup:

- *E-mail*. Send a message to `stisserv@nsf.gov` with the body of the message as follows:

  ```
  Request:  stis
  Topic:  index
  ```

  You will receive a list of documents available on STIS and instructions for retrieving them.
- *E-mail notification of new documents*. To receive a weekly summary of new documents on STIS (or the full text of all documents added to STIS), send a message to `stisserv@nsf.gov` with the body of the message as follows:

  ```
  Request:  stis
  Topic:  stisdirm
  ```

  You will receive instructions for this service.
- *Anonymous FTP*. Connect via anonymous FTP to `stis.nsf.gov`. Use the userid `anonymous` and enter your E-mail address as the password. The file `ftpindex` contains a list of the files available on STIS and additional instructions.
- *On-Line via Telnet*. Telnet to `stis.nsf.gov`. At the login prompt, enter `public`. Documents may be browsed online, or downloaded using Kermit.
- *On-Line via Modem*. Use the following settings on your modem: 1200, 2400, or 9600 baud, 7-E-1. Dial (202) 357-0359 or (202) 357-0360. When connected, press the Enter (Return) key. At the login prompt, enter `public`. Documents may be browsed online, or downloaded using the Kermit protocol.
- *WAIS*. The NSF WAIS server is `stis.nsf.gov`. You can get the `.src` file from the "Directory of Servers" at `quake.think.com`.

For more information, send E-mail to `stis-request@nsf.gov`, phone (202) 357-7555, or TDD (202) 357-7492. Requests for *printed* publications may be sent to `pubs@nsf.gov`.

The BITNET equivalents for the Internet E-mail addresses given above are the same, but with `@NSF` instead of `@nsf.gov`. The IP address for `stis.nsf.gov` is `[128.150.195.40]`.

ASM BIOFAX

The Biological Careers Factual Exchange (BIOFAX) is an electronic bulletin board which lists over 600 scholarship, fellowship, grant, and training programs of interest to undergraduate and graduate students who are pursuing biological science careers. The focus of the bulletin board is on Microbiology Research, including Biology, Chemistry, and Biochemistry. The information contained in BIOFAX is also available by mail.

To gain access to BIOFAX, set your computer modem for 2400 baud, 8 bits data, 1 stop bit, and no parity, and call 1-800-445-8949 ((202) 737-0254 in Washington, DC).

For more information, write to Christina M. Johnson, Coordinator–MSSCSP, American Society for Microbiology, 1325 Massachusetts Avenue, NW, Washington, DC 20005-4171, call (202) 737-3600 x 295, or fax (202) 737-0233.

Government Aid Programs

Federal Programs

The U.S. Department of Education offers several student aid programs for U.S. citizens. Some provide grants and some provide loans. Graduate students and undergraduate students who already have a bachelor's degree are not eligible for the grants.

The grant programs include:

- **Pell Grant Program** (formerly the Basic Grant Program): Pell Grants are based on financial need for half-time and full-time students at participating schools. Obtain the proper form from the financial aid office at the school you plan to attend. You can apply either by filling out the Federal form, "Application for Federal Student Aid" or by checking off the Pell Grant box on one of the nonfederal forms. The Pell Grant provides up to $2,300 per year.

- **Supplemental Education Opportunity Grant (SEOG) Program**: SEOG Grants are based on financial need with similar eligibility requirements as the Pell Grant Program. They are awarded by the financial aid offices at participating schools. The SEOG Grant provides up to $4,000 per year.

The loan programs include:

- **Stafford Loans** (formerly Guaranteed Student Loans (GSL)): There are now two types of Stafford Loans, subsidized and unsubsidized. The subsidized loans are based on financial need and have a 5% origination fee. The federal government pays the interest on the subsidized loans until graduation or termination of studies. The unsubsidized loans are not based on financial need and have a 6.5% origination fee. The government does *not* pay the interest on the unsubsidized loans, so the interest begins to accrue immediately, but the student has the option of deferring the interest payments while in school by capitalizing them (adding them to the principal). Capitalizing the interest payments effectively compounds the interest rate. Undergraduates may borrow up to $2,625 during the freshman year, up to $3,500 during the sophomore year, and up to $5,500 per academic year during the junior and senior years (and 5th year, if applicable), with a cumulative limit for undergraduate study of $23,000. Graduate students may borrow up to $8,500 per academic year with a cumulative limit of $65,500, including any undergraduate Stafford Loans. The interest rate for new borrowers changes each July 1 and is pegged to the three-month Treasury bill rate plus 3.1%, with a 9% cap. The interest rate for repeat borrowers is the same as the rate for prior Stafford Loans.

- **Parent Loans for Undergraduate Students (PLUS)**: The natural or adoptive parents or legal guardians of undergraduate students may borrow up to the full cost of their children's education, less any financial aid. Repayment commences 60 days after funds disbursal. The interest rate is variable, but will not exceed 10%. PLUS loans are not based on financial need and have a 5% origination fee. PLUS loans are administered by each state's local guarantee agency. Call the Federal Student Aid Information Center at 1-800-4FED-AID for the address and phone number of the guarantee agency in your state.

- **Supplemental Loans for Students (SLS)**: Graduate students and independent undergraduate students may borrow up to $4,000 per academic year during their first and second years and $5,000 per academic year during their third, fourth, and fifth years ($23,000 total). Applicants for an SLS loan must also apply for the Pell Grant (if an undergraduate) and Stafford Loan. SLS loans are not based on financial need. Repayment begins upon graduation, termination of studies, or if the student falls below full time. The interest rate is variable, but will not exceed 11%. The borrower is charged interest from the day the loan is disbursed.

- **Perkins Loan** (formerly National Direct Student Loan Program): Full-time and part-time students may borrow up to $3,000 per year for undergraduate study ($15,000 total) and $5,000 per year for graduate study ($30,000 total). Repayment begins 9 months after the student either graduates, leaves school, or drops below half-time, and may be extended over a ten-year period. The interest rate is 5%.

The federal government also funds College Work Study (CWS), a cooperative education program which provides part-time employment to students at eligible colleges and universities. Students must demonstrate financial need and must maintain good academic standing while participating in the program. CWS jobs are typically for 10 hours of work each week and may not exceed 20 hours per week. Ideally the jobs should match the student's academic interests and career goals, but this doesn't always occur.

For further information on the Stafford, SLS, or PLUS loans, call 1-800-LOAN-USA (1-800-562-6872). For information on any federal financial aid program, call the Federal Student Aid Information Center at 1-800-4FED-AID (1-800-433-3243). You can write to them at *Federal Student Aid Information Center*, P.O. Box 84, Washington, DC 20044-0084. Ask for a copy of "The Student Guide." You can also get information from the financial aid office at the school you plan to attend.

The Higher Education Act, signed into law by President Bush on July 16, 1992, includes a pilot program that provides "direct loans" to students at several hundred schools, starting in 1994. Under the "IDEA Credit" plan, students will be able to borrow directly from the Department of Education, with each student having a lifetime loan account. Some novel repayment possibilities include variable installments based on after-college income and repayment through IRS withholding.

If your parents are considering a PLUS loan, they should also investigate home-equity loans. Home-equity loans let them borrow up to 80% of the appraised value of their home less the mortgage, using the home as collateral. The interest rate is currently in the same ballpark as the PLUS loans (in fact, in some cases it's lower) and the interest can be deducted on their income tax return.

State Programs

Every state has one or more scholarship and loan programs for students who are residents of the state. The programs vary from state to state, with some based solely on need and others taking academic merit into account. Some have special restrictions — minorities, children of veterans, or career goal of teaching — and some are for in-state public institutions only. In some states the state office serves as a clearinghouse for aid provided to residents by local corporations. Write to the addresses given below for the information you need. You can call the Federal Student Aid Information Center at 1-800-4FED-AID for the address and phone number of the guarantee agency in your state.

Alabama
Alabama Commission on Higher Education
One Court Square, Suite 221
Montgomery, AL 36104
(205) 269-2700

Alaska
Alaska Comm. on Postsecondary Educ.
State Office Building, Pouch F
Juneau, AK 99801
(907) 465-2962

Arizona
Arizona Comm. for Postsecondary Educ.
2020 North Central Avenue, Suite 275
Phoenix, AZ 85004
(602) 229-2590

Arkansas
Arkansas Department of Higher Education
1301 West Seventh Street
Little Rock, AR 72201
(501) 371-1441

California
Student Aid Commission
1515 S Street, Box 510845
Suite 500, North Building
Sacramento, CA 94245-0845
(916) 445-0880

Colorado
Colorado Commission on Higher Education
Colorado Heritage Center
1300 Broadway, Second Floor
Denver, CO 80203
(303) 866-2723

Colorado
Colorado Student Loan Program
999 18th Street, Suite 425
Denver, CO 80202-2440
(303) 294-5050

Connecticut
Connecticut Department of Higher Education
61 Woodland Street
Hartford, CT 06105
(203) 566-2618

Delaware
Delaware Postsecondary Educ. Comm.
820 West French Street, 4th Floor
Wilmington, DE 19801
(302) 577-6055

District of Columbia
Office of Postsecondary Education Research
and Assistance (OPERA)
2100 M.L. King Avenue, SE, Suite 401
Washington, DC 20020-5732
(202) 727-3685/3688

Florida
Office of Student Financial Assistance
Florida Department of Education
1344 Florida Education Center
Tallahassee, FL 32399-0400
(904) 487-0049

Georgia
Georgia Student Finance Authority
2082 East Exchange Place, Suite 200
Tucker, GA 30084
(404) 393-7108

Georgia
Georgia State Regents Scholarship
244 Washington Street, SW
Atlanta, GA 30334
(404) 656-2272

Hawaii
Hawaii State Postsecondary Educ. Comm.
2444 Dole Street
Honolulu, HI 96822
(808) 948-8213/8294

Idaho
Office of the State Board of Education
Len B. Jordan Building, Room 307
650 West State Street
Boise, ID 83720
(208) 334-2270

Illinois
Illinois State Scholarship Commission
500 West Monroe, 3rd Floor
Springfield, IL 62704
(217) 782-6767

Illinois
Illinois State Scholarship Commission
106 Wilmont Road
Deerfield, IL 60015
(708) 948-8500

Illinois
Illinois State Scholarship Commission
State of Illinois Center
100 West Randolph, Suite 3-200
Chicago, IL 60601
(312) 814-3745

Indiana
State Student Assistance Commission
150 W Market Street, 5th Floor
Indianapolis, IN 46204
(317) 232-2350

Iowa
Iowa College Aid Commission
914 Grand Avenue
Des Moines, IA 50309
(515) 281-3501

Kansas
Board of Regents
400 SW 8th Avenue, Suite 609
Topeka, KS 66603-3925
(913) 296-3517

Kentucky
Kentucky Higher Educ. Assistance Auth.
1050 US 127 South
Frankfort, KY 40601
(502) 564-7990

Louisiana
Office of Student Financial Assistance
P.O. Box 91202
Baton Rouge, LA 70821-9202
(504) 922-1011

Maine
Department of Educ. and Cult. Srvcs.
Education Building, Station 23
Auguste, ME 04330
(207) 289-2321

Maryland
Maryland State Scholarship Board
2100 Guilford Avenue
Baltimore, MD 21218
(301) 659-6420

Massachusetts
Massachusetts State Scholarship Office
Board of Regents of Higher Education
330 Stuart Street
Boston, MA 02116
(617) 727-9420

Massachusetts
Massachusetts Higher Educ. Assistance Corp.
1010 Park Square Building
Boston, MA 02116
(617) 426-9796

Michigan
Michigan Higher Educ. Assistance Auth.
P.O. Box 30008
Lansing, MI 48909
(517) 373-3399

Michigan
Michigan Department of Education
Michigan Guarantee Agency
P.O. Box 30047
Lansing, MI 48909
(517) 373-0760

Minnesota
Minnesota Higher Education Coord. Board
Suite 400, Capitol Square Building
550 Cedar Street
St. Paul, MN 55101
(612) 296-3974

Mississippi
Board of Trustees of State Institutions of
Higher Learning
3825 Ridgewood Road
Jackson, MS 39211-6453
(601) 982-6570

Missouri
Coordinating Board for Higher Education
P.O. Box 1438
Jefferson City, MO 65102
(314) 751-3940

Montana
Montana Guaranteed Student Loan Program
2500 Broadway
Helena, MT 59620-3104
(406) 444-6594

Nebraska
Nebraska Coord. Comm. for Postsec. Educ.
P.O. Box 95005
301 Centennial Mall South
Lincoln, NE 68509-5005
(402) 471-2847

Nevada
University of Nevada Board of Regents
405 Marsh Avenue
Reno, NV 89509
(702) 784-4958

New England
New England Board of Higher Education
45 Temple Place
Boston, MA 02111
(617) 357-9620

New Hampshire
New Hampshire Postsecondary Educ. Comm.
61 South Spring Street
Concord, NH 03301
(603) 271-2555

New Jersey
New Jersey Department of Higher Education
Office of Student Assistance
4 Quakerbridge Plaza, CN 540
Trenton, NJ 08625
(609) 292-8770

New Mexico
Board of Educational Finance
1068 Cerrillos Road
Santa Fe, NM 87501
(505) 827-7383

New Mexico
New Mexico Educ. Assist. Foundation
P.O. Box 27020
3900 Osuna, NE
Albuquerque, NM 87125-7020
(505) 345-3371/8821

New York
New York Higher Educ. Services Corp.
99 Washington Avenue
Albany, NY 12255
(518) 473-8567

New York
New York State Assembly
Legislative Office Building 829-A
Albany, NY 12248

North Carolina
North Carolina State Educ. Assistance Auth.
P.O. Box 2688
Chapel Hill, NC 27515
(919) 549-8614

North Carolina
North Carolina College Foundation, Inc.
P.O. Box 12100
2100 Yonkers Road
Raleigh, NC 27605
(919) 834-2893

North Dakota
Student Financial Assistance Program
State Capitol, 10th Floor
600 E Boulevard Avenue
Bismarck, ND 58505-0230
(701) 224-4113

Ohio
Ohio Board of Regents
3600 State Office Tower
30 East Broad Street
Columbus, OH 43215
(614) 466-1190

Oklahoma
Oklahoma State Regents for Higher Education
500 Education Building
State Capitol Complex
Oklahoma City, OK 73105
(405) 524-9100

Oregon
Oregon State Scholarship Commission
1445 Willamette Street
Eugene, OR 97401
(503) 345-7318

Pennsylvania
Pennsylvania Higher Educ. Assist. Agency
Harrisburg, PA 17105-8114
(717) 975-3320

Rhode Island
Rhode Island Higher Educ. Assistance Auth.
274 Weybosset Street
Providence, RI 02903
(401) 277-2050

South Carolina
South Carolina Higher Education Tuition
Grants Agency
P.O. Box 12159
1310 Lady Street, Keenan Bldg., 1st Floor
Columbia, SC 29211
(803) 734-1200

South Dakota
Department of Education and Cultural Affairs
700 Governors Drive
Pierre, SD 57501-2291
(605) 773-3134

South Dakota
South Dakota Board of Regents
207 E Capitol Avenue
Pierre, SD 57501-2408
(605) 773-3455

South Dakota
South Dakota Education Assistance
Corporation
115 First Avenue, SW
Aberdeen, SD 57401
(605) 225-5722

Tennessee
Tennessee Student Assistance Corporation
Parkway Towers, Suite 1950
404 James Robertson Parkway
Nashville, TN 37219-5097
(615) 741-1346

Texas
Texas Higher Education Coordinating Board
P.O. Box 12788, Capitol Station
Austin, TX 78711-2788
(512) 483-6340

Utah
Utah State Board of Regents
No. 3 Triad, Suite 550
355 W. N. Temple
Salt Lake City, UT 84180-1205
(801) 538-5247

Vermont
Vermont Student Assistance Corporation
P.O. Box 2000, Champlain Mill
Winooski, VT 05404
(802) 655-9602

Virginia
Virginia Education Loan Authority
State Education Assistance Authority
411 E Franklin Street, Suite 300
Richmond, VA 23219
(804) 775-4000

Virginia
State Council of Higher Education
Office of Financial Aid
James Monroe Building
101 North 14th Street
Richmond, VA 23219
(804) 225-2137

Washington
Washington State Higher Education
Coordinating Board
P.O. Box 43430
917 Lakeridge Way
Olympia, WA 98504-3430
(206) 753-3571

West Virginia
West Virginia Board of Regents
950 Kanawha Boulevard, East
Charleston, WV 25301
(304) 558-2101

West Virginia
West Virginia College and University Systems
West Virginia Higher Educ. Grant Program
P.O. Box 4007
Charleston, WV 25364
(304) 347-1211

Wisconsin
Wisconsin Higher Education Aids Board
131 West Wilson Street, P.O. Box 7885
Madison, WI 53707
(608) 266-0888

Wyoming
Wyoming Community College Commission
122 W 25th Street, Herschler Bldg., 1 West
Cheyenne, WY 82002
(307) 777-7763

Puerto Rico
Council on Higher Education
Box F, UPR Station
Rio Piedras, Puerto Rico 00931
(809) 751-1136

Virgin Islands
Virgin Islands Board of Education
P.O. Box 11900
St. Thomas, Virgin Islands 00801
(809) 774-4546

Miscellaneous Programs

National Merit Scholarship Program

The *National Merit Scholarship Corporation* annually awards approximately 1,800 nonrenewable awards of $2,000 and 4,200 renewable undergraduate scholarships ranging from $250 to $2,000 or more per year. To enter the competition, take the PSAT/NMSQT (Preliminary Scholastic Aptitude Test/National Merit Scholarship Qualifying Test) in October of your junior year in high school. Recipients must score within the top 1/2 of 1% on the test. For more information, write to the National Merit Scholarship Corporation, 1560 Sherman Avenue, Suite 200, Evanston, IL 60201-4897.

Veterans Programs

Contact the *Department of Veteran Affairs*, Veterans Benefits Administration, Washington, DC 20420, if you are a veteran or the child or spouse of a veteran.

The *Aerospace Education Foundation*, 1501 Lee Highway, Arlington, VA 22209-1198, (703) 247-5839, publishes a listing of organizations that provide financial assistance for those with an aviation or military affiliation.

Woodrow Wilson Foundation

The Woodrow Wilson National Fellowship Foundation runs Science and Mathematics Leadership Institutes for high school teachers. Each year, 50 top high school teachers in mathematics, chemistry, and physics are selected to attend the intensive four-week program held on the Princeton University campus. With the help of distinguished college and university faculty, they take a fresh look at recent research and methods.

For more information, write to the *Woodrow Wilson National Fellowship Foundation*, P.O. Box 642, Princeton, NJ 08542, call (609) 924-4666, or fax (609) 497-2939.

The Charlotte W. Newcombe Doctoral Dissertation Fellowships provide annual stipends of $11,500 for research on ethical and religious values in all fields. Students must have completed all predoctoral requirements and be enrolled at an American university. The deadline is December 1.

The Woodrow Wilson Foundation also runs programs in education research (Spencer Dissertation Year Fellowships), women's studies, historical research, and public policy.

Science Honor Societies

Mu Alpha Theta

Mu Alpha Theta is a mathematics club and honor society for high school and junior college students. It publishes a journal, *The Mathematical Log*, which contains articles, puzzles, and problems of interest to high school and junior college mathematics students. Mu Alpha Theta also sponsors an annual mathematics competition. The organization has over 1,200 chapters in the United States, Canada, Japan, Switzerland, and Germany. Local chapters hold monthly meetings.

The national organization sells a variety of inexpensive enrichment materials, including back issues of the Mathematical Log and Math Buds, a book of cryptarithms, a book of logical puzzles, and a collection of problems and solutions from the NYSML-ARML mathematics competition.

There are no annual dues, but full members pay a $2 initiation fee.

Mu Alpha Theta is sponsored by the Mathematical Association of America and the National Council of Teachers of Mathematics.

For more information, write to Mu Alpha Theta, 601 Elm Avenue, Room 423, Norman, Oklahoma 73019-0315, or call (405) 325-4489.

Sigma Xi

Sigma Xi, the Scientific Research Society, is an honor society for scientists and engineers. There are more than 500 chapters and clubs across North America with the majority located at universities. Members receive the Sigma Xi newsletter and a subscription to *American Scientist*, a bimonthly publication. (Nonmember subscriptions to *American Scientist* are available by calling 1-800-282-0444.)

An individual may be elected as an associate member if he or she is at the outset of their career and demonstrates an aptitude for research (usually evidenced by a written report of an independent investigation). The purpose of associate membership is to encourage promising young investigators to continue careers in scientific research. It is anticipated that an associate member's research achievement will eventually lead to eligibility for promotion to full membership. An individual may be elected to full membership after demonstrating a noteworthy achievement through published refereed papers, patents, Ph.D. thesis, or similar means.

For more information, write to Sigma Xi Headquarters, 99 Alexander Drive, Box 13975, Research Triangle Park, NC 27709, or call 1-800-243-6534 or (919) 549-4691.

Tau Beta Pi

Tau Beta Pi is the national engineering honor society and the world's largest engineering society. There are more than 208 chapters on university campuses across the U.S., and over 369,000 members have been initiated since the society's founding in 1885.

In addition to recognizing engineering students of superior scholarship, Tau Beta Pi runs a large fellowship program, described on page 193.

For more information, write to The Tau Beta Pi Association, Inc., P.O. Box 8840, University Station, Knoxville, TN 37996-0002, or call (615) 546-4578.

Sources of Career Information

Write to these organizations for scholarships and fellowships, career information, and other opportunities in your field. Also ask about student membership in the organization, where applicable. Note that many national organizations provide travel grants for student members to enable them to attend the national meeting or conference, especially if they are presenting a paper or participating in the conference's volunteer program.

Accounting
American Accounting Association
5717 Bessie Drive
Sarasota, FL 34233-2399

Acoustics
Acoustical Society of America
500 Sunnyside Boulevard
Woodbury, NY 11797
(516) 349-7800

Actuarial Science
Society of Actuaries
475 N. Martingale Road, Suite 800
Schaumburg, IL 60173-2226
(708) 706-3500

Actuarial Science
American Academy of Actuaries
1720 I Street, NW, 7th Floor
Washington, DC 20006
(202) 223-8196

Actuarial Science
Casualty Actuarial Society
1100 N. Glebe Road, Suite 600
Arlington, VA 22201
(703) 276-3100

Aeronautical Engineering & Avionics
Academy of Aeronautics
LaGuardia Airport
Flushing, NY 11371

Aeronautics and Astronautics
Amer. Inst. of Aeronautics and Astronautics
Student Programs
The Aerospace Center
370 L'Enfant Promenade, SW
Washington, DC 20024-2518
(202) 646-7458/7444

Aerospace Engineering
Institute of Aeronautics and Astronautics
Director of Student Programs
1633 Broadway
New York, NY 10019

Astronautics
American Astronautical Society
6352 Rolling Mill Place, Suite 102
Springfield, VA 22152
(703) 866-0020

Agricultural Engineering
American Society of Agricultural Engineers
2950 Niles Road
St. Joseph, MI 49085-9659
(616) 429-0300

Agricultural Research
U.S. Department of Agriculture
Agricultural Research Service
Personnel Division, Room 107, Building 003
Beltsville, MD 20705

Agronomy
American Society of Agronomy
677 South Segoe Road
Madison, WI 53711
(608) 273-8080

Anthropology
American Anthropological Association
1703 New Hampshire Avenue, NW
Washington, DC 20009
(202) 232-8800

Anthropology
Society for Applied Anthropology
P.O. Box 24083
Oklahoma City, OK 73124-0083
(405) 232-4902

Archaeology
Society for American Archaeology
808 17th Street, NW, Suite 200
Washington, DC 20006
(202) 223-9774

Archaeology
Archaeological Institute of America
675 Commonwealth Avenue
Boston, MA 02215-1401
(617) 353-9361

Artificial Intelligence
American Assoc. for Artificial Intelligence
445 Burgess Drive
Menlo Park, CA 94025
(415) 328-3123

Astronomy
American Astronomical Society
University of Texas, Astronomy Department
Austin, TX 78712-1083
(512) 471-1309
E-mail: aas@astro.as.utexas.edu

Biochemistry
American Society for Biochemistry and
Molecular Biology
9650 Rockville Pike
Bethesda, MD 20814
(301) 530-7145

Biology
American Institute of Biological Sciences
730 11th Street NW
Washington, DC 20001-4521
(202) 628-1500

Biology Teaching
National Association of Biology Teachers
11250 Roger Bacon Drive, Suite 19
Reston, VA 22090
(703) 471-1134

Biomedical Engineering
Biomedical Engineering Society
P.O. Box 2399
Culver City, CA 90231
(213) 206-6443

Biometrics
Biometrics Society
1429 Duke Street, Suite 401
Alexandria, VA 22314
(703) 836-8311

Biophysics
Biophysical Society
9650 Rockville Pike, Suite 512
Bethesda, MD 20814
(301) 530-7114

Biotechnology
Industrial Biotechnology Association
1625 K Street, NW, Suite 1100
Washington, DC 20006-1604
(202) 857-0244

Broadcasting Technology
Society of Broadcast Engineers, Inc.
P.O. Box 20450
Indianapolis, IA 46220
(317) 253-1640, FAX (317) 253-0418

Cardiology
American College of Cardiology
9111 Old Georgetown Road
Bethesda, MD 20814
(301) 897-5400

Cell Biology
American Society for Cell Biology
9650 Rockville Pike
Bethesda, MD 20814
(301) 530-7153

Cereal Chemistry
American Association of Cereal Chemists
3340 Pilot Knob Road
St. Paul, MN 55121
(612) 454-7250

Chemical Engineering
American Institute of Chemical Engineers
345 East 47th Street
New York, NY 10017
(212) 705-7660/7338

Chemistry
American Chemical Society
Education Division
1155 Sixteenth Street, NW
Washington, DC 20036
(202) 452-2127/872-4600

Chemistry
American Institute of Chemists
7315 Wisconsin Avenue
Bethesda, MD 20814
(301) 652-2447

Civil Engineering
American Society of Civil Engineers
345 East 47th Street
New York, NY 10017
1-800-548-ASCE
(212) 705-7496

Computer Science
Association for Computing Machinery
11 W. 42nd Street, 3rd Floor
New York, NY 10036
(212) 869-7440

Computer Science
IEEE Computer Society
1730 Massachusetts Avenue, NW
Washington, DC 20036
(202) 371-0101

Dentistry
American Dental Association
211 East Chicago Avenue
Chicago, IL 60611
(312) 440-2500

Ecology
The Ecological Society of America
9650 Rockville Pike, Suite 2503
Bethesda, MD 20814
(301) 530-7005

Economics
American Economic Association
2014 Broadway, Suite 305
Nashville, TN 37203-2418
(615) 322-2595

Electrical Engineering
IEEE Service Center
445 Hoes Lane
P.O. Box 1331
Piscataway, NJ 08854-1331
(908) 562-5523

Electrochemistry
The Electrochemical Society, Inc.
10 South Main Street
Pennington, NJ 08534-2896
(609) 737-1902

Engineering
JETS, Inc.
345 East 47th Street
New York, NY 10017

Engineering
National Society of Professional Engineers
1420 King Street
Alexandria, VA 22314
(703) 684-2800

Engineering
American Society for Engineering Education
Eleven Dupont Circle, Suite 200
Washington, DC 20036
(202) 293-7080

Entomology
American Entomological Association
1900 Race Street
Philadelphia, PA 19103
(215) 561-3978

Entomology
Entomological Society of America
9301 Annapolis Road
Landham, MD 20706-3115
(301) 731-4535

Fisheries
American Fisheries Society
5410 Grosvenor Lane, Suite 110
Bethesda, MD 20814-2199
(301) 897-8616

Forensics
American Academy of Forensic Sciences
218 E Cache La Poudre, P.O. Box 669
Colorado Springs, CO 80901-0669
(719) 636-1100

Fungi/Mycology
Mycological Society of America
Mary E. Palm, Secretary
Room 329, Bldg 011A
Beltsville Agricultural Research Center
Beltsville, MD 20705
(301) 344-2327

Genetics
American Society of Human Genetics
9650 Rockville Pike
Bethesda, MD 20814
(301) 571-1825

Genetics
American Genetic Association
P.O. Box 39
Buckeystown, MD 21717
(301) 695-9292

Genetics
Genetic Society of America
9650 Rockville Pike
Bethesda, MD 20814
(301) 571-1825

Geography
American Geographical Society
156 Fifth Avenue, Suite 600
New York, NY 10010-7002
(212) 242-0214

Geography
The Association of American Geographers
1710 Sixteenth Street, NW
Washington, DC 20009-3198
(202) 234-1450

Geological Sciences
American Geological Institute
4220 King Street
Alexandria, VA 22302-1507
(703) 379-2480

Geological Sciences
American Assoc. of Petroleum Geologists
P.O. Box 979
Tulsa, Oklahoma 74101-0979
(918) 584-2555

Geological Sciences
Geological Society of America
3300 Penrose Place
P.O. Box 9140
Boulder, CO 80301
(303) 447-2020

Geological Sciences
Society of Petroleum Engineers
P.O. Box 833836
Richardson, TX 75083-3836
(214) 669-3377, FAX (214) 669-0135

Geophysics
Society of Exploration Geophysicists
P.O. Box 702740
Tulsa, OK 74170-2740
(918) 493-3516

Geophysics
American Geophysical Union
2000 Florida Avenue, NW
Washington, DC 20009
(202) 462-6900

History of Science
History of Science Society
35 Dean Street
Worcester, MA 01609
(508) 831-5712

Horticulture
American Society for Horticulture Science
113 S West Street
Alexandria, VA 22314-2824
(703) 836-4606

Human Factors
Human Factors Society
P.O. Box 1369
Santa Monica, CA 90406
(213) 394-1811

Industrial Engineering
Institute of Industrial Engineers
25 Technology Park/Atlanta
Norcross, GA 30092
(404) 449-0460

Information Science
American Society for Information Science
8720 Georgia Avenue, Suite 501
Silver Spring, MD 20910-3602
(301) 495-0900

Journalism
The Dow Jones Newspaper Fund Inc.
P.O. Box 300
Princeton, NJ 08540

Linguistics
Linguistics Society of America
1325 18th Street, NW, Suite 211
Washington, DC 20036
(202) 835-1714

Manufacturing Engineering
Society of Manufacturing Engineers
1 SME Drive, P.O. Box 930
Dearborn, MI 48121
(313) 271-1500

Mass Spectrometry
American Society for Mass Spectrometry
P.O. Box 1508
East Lansing, MI 48823-1508
(517) 337-2548

Materials Science
Materials Research Society
9800 McKnight Road
Pittsburgh, PA 15237
(412) 367-3003, FAX (412) 367-4373

Mathematics
Mathematical Association of America
1529 Eighteenth Street, NW
Washington, DC 20036
(202) 387-5200

Mathematics
American Mathematical Society
P.O. Box 6248
Providence, RI 02940
(401) 455-4000

Mathematics Teaching
National Council of Teachers of Mathematics
1906 Association Drive
Reston, VA 22091
(703) 620-9840

Mechanical Engineering
American Society of Mechanical Engineers
1825 K Street, NW, Suite 218
Washington, DC 20006-1202
(202) 785-3756

Medical Physics
American Assoc. of Physicists in Medicine
335 East 45th Street
New York, NY 10017
(212) 661-9404

Medicine
American Medical Association
515 North State Street
Chicago, IL 60610

Metallurgy
American Society for Metals
9639 Kinsman
Metals Park, OH 44073
(216) 338-5151

Meteorology
American Meteorology Society
45 Beacon Street
Boston, MA 02108
(617) 227-2425

Microbiology
American Society for Microbiology
1325 Massachusetts Avenue, NW
Washington, DC 20005
(202) 737-3600

Mineralogy
Mineralogical Society of America
1625 I Street, NW, Suite 414
Washington, DC 20006
(202) 775-4344

Neuroscience
Society for Neuroscience
11 Dupont Circle, Suite 500
Washington, DC 20036
(202) 462-6688

Nuclear Engineering
American Nuclear Society
555 North Kensington Avenue
LaGrange Park, IL 60525
1-800-323-3044
(708) 352-6611

Nutrition
American Institute of Nutrition
9650 Rockville Pike
Bethesda, MD 20814-3990
(301) 530-7050

Oceanography
Marine Technology Society
1828 L Street, NW, Suite 906
Washington, DC 20036-5104
(202) 775-5966

Operations Research
Operations Research Society of America
Mt. Royal and Guilford Avenues
Baltimore, MD 21202
(301) 528-4146

Optics
Optical Society of America
2010 Massachusetts Avenue, NW
Washington, DC 20036
(202) 416-1960

Optics
Society of Photo-Optical Instr. Eng. (SPIE)
1000 20th Street
Bellingham, WA 98225
(206) 676-3290

Ornithology
American Ornithologists' Union
National Museum of Natural History
Smithsonian Institution
Washington, DC 20560
(202) 357-1970

Ornithology
Cooper Ornithological Society
2933 Third Avenue, West
Dickinson, ND 58601
(701) 225-9148

Paleontology
The Paleontological Society
Attn: Dr. John Pojeta, Jr.
USGS Room E-501
U.S. National Museum
Washington, DC 20560

Pharmacology
American Society of Pharmacology
& Experimental Therapeutics Inc.
9650 Rockville Pike
Bethesda, MD 20814

Pharmacy
American Pharmaceutical Association
2215 Constitution Avenue, NW
Washington, DC 20037

Pharmacy
American Assoc. of Colleges of Pharmacy
1426 Prince Street
Alexandria, VA 22314
(703) 739-2330

Photogrammetry
American Society for Photogrammetry and
Remote Sensing
5410 Grosvenor Lane, Suite 210
Bethesda, MD 20814-2160
(301) 493-0290, FAX (301) 493-0208

Physics
American Physical Society
335 East 45th Street
New York, NY 10017-3483
(212) 682-7341

Physics
American Institute of Physics
335 East 45th Street
New York, NY 10017-3483
(212) 661-9404

Physics Teaching
American Association of Physics Teachers
5112 Berwyn Road
College Park, MD 20740
(301) 345-4200

Physiology
American Physiological Society
9650 Rockville Pike
Bethesda, MD 20814
(301) 530-7164

Planetary Sciences
The Planetary Society
65 North Catalina Avenue
Pasadena, CA 91106
(818) 793-5100

Plant Physiology
American Society of Plant Physiologists
15501 Monona Drive
Rockville, MD 20855
(301) 251-0560

Plastics Engineering
Society of Plastics Engineers
c/o Jack Contessa, Education Director
14 Fairfield Drive, P.O. Box 0403
Brookfield, CT 06804-0403
(203) 775-0471

Political Science
American Political Science Association
1527 New Hampshire Avenue, NW
Washington, DC 20036
(202) 483-2512

Psychiatry
American Psychiatric Association
1400 K Street, NW
Washington, DC 20005
(202) 682-6000

Psychoanalysis
American Academy of Psychoanalysis
30 East 40th Street, Suite 206
New York, NY 10016
(212) 679-4105

Psychoanalysis
American Psychoanalytic Association
309 East 49th Street
New York, NY 10017
(212) 752-0450

Psychology
American Psychological Association
750 First Street, NE
Washington, DC 20002-4242
(202) 336-5500

Radiology
American College of Radiology
1891 Preston White Drive
Reston, VA 22091
1-800-227-5463, (703) 648-8900

Robotics
Machine Vision Association
1 SME Drive, P.O. Box 930
Dearborn, MI 48121
(313) 271-1500

Safety Engineering
American Society of Safety Engineers
1800 East Oakton Street
Des Plaines, IL 60018-2187
(708) 692-4121

Science Journalism
Council for the Advancement of Science
Writing, Inc.
P.O. Box 404
Greenlawn, NY 11740
(516) 757-5664

Science Teaching
National Science Teachers Association
1742 Connecticut Avenue, NW
Washington, DC 20009
(202) 328-5800

Seismology
Seismological Society of America
El Cerrito Professional Building, Suite 201
El Cerrito, CA 94530
(415) 525-5474

Sociology
American Sociological Association
1722 N Street, NW
Washington, DC 20036-2981
(202) 833-3410

Solar Energy
American Solar Energy Society
2400 Central Avenue, B-1
Boulder, CO 80301
(303) 443-3130

Space Science
National Aeron. and Space Admin. (NASA)
Educational Publications Library
400 Maryland Avenue, SW
Code LEP
Washington, DC 20546

Space Science
General Aviation and Manufacturers
Association (GAMA)
1400 K Street, NW, Suite 801
Washington, DC 20005
(202) 393-1500

Space Science
University Aviation Association
P.O. Box 2321
Auburn, AL 36830

Space Science
National Space Society
922 Pennsylvania Avenue, SE
Washington, DC 20003
(202) 543-1900

Speleology
National Speleological Society
Cave Avenue
Huntsville, AL 35810
(205) 852-1300

Speleology
Cave Research Foundation
4074 W Redwing Street
Tucson, AZ 85741
(602) 744-2243

Statistics
American Statistical Association
1429 Duke Street
Alexandria, VA 22314-3402
(703) 684-1221

Toxicology
Society of Toxicology
1101 14th Street, NW, Suite 1100
Washington, DC 20005
(202) 371-1393

Zoology
The American Society of Zoologists
Box 2739
104 Sirius Circle
California Lutheran College
Thousand Oaks, CA 91360
(805) 492-3585

State Science Talent Searches

Since 1946, State Talent Searches have been held concurrently with the national competition by special arrangement with Science Service. Anyone desiring information on the State Science Talent Searches should send their inquiries to the directors in the respective states. For a prompt reply, please send a stamped, self-addressed envelope with your inquiry.

Alabama
The Gorgas Scholarship Foundation, Inc.
Dr. Leven S. Hazlegrove
Professor & Chairman, Dept. of Chemistry
Samford University
800 Lakeshore Drive
Birmingham, AL 35229

Arkansas
Arkansas Academy of Science
Dr. John D. Peck
Department of Biology
University of Central Arkansas
Conway, AR 72032

Colorado-Wyoming
Colorado-Wyoming Academy of Science
Elemer Bernath
Executive Secretary, C-WJAS
803 Ensign
Fort Morgan, CO 80701

Connecticut
The University of Connecticut
John Tanaka
Director, Honors Program
Professor of Chemistry
Storrs, CT 06268

District of Columbia
Washington Academy of Sciences
Mrs. Edythe Durie
5011 Larno Drive
Alexandria, VA 22310

Florida
Florida Academy of Sciences
Tom DeRosa
Westminster Academy
5620 NE 22nd Avenue
Ft. Lauderdale, FL 33308

Georgia
Georgia Junior Academy of Science
Dr. Don A. Berkowitz
Director, GJAS
P.O. Box 684
Social Circle, GA 30279

Illinois
Illinois State Academy of Science
Dr. Donald R. Dickerson and Dr. Dorothy Martin
Illinois State Museum
Spring and Edwards Streets
Springfield, IL 62706

Indiana
Indiana Academy of Science
Walter Cory
Coordinator for School Science
Wright Education Building, Room 153
Indiana University
Bloomington, IN 47405

Iowa
Iowa Junior Academy of Science
Dr. Gary E. Downs
Chairman of Students' Programs
Iowa State University
N126 Quadrangle
Ames, IA 50011

Kansas
Kansas Academy of Science
Dr. Leland E. Keller
Professor of Physiology
Kansas State University
Pittsburg, KS 66762

Kentucky
Kentucky Junior Academy of Science
Dr. John Wernegreen
Associate Professor of Physical Science
Eastern Kentucky University
220 Memorial Science Building
Richmond, KY 40475

Louisiana
University of Southwestern Louisiana
Dr. Duane Blumberg
Department of Mathematics and Statistics
Lafayette, LA 70504

Maryland
Maryland Academy of Sciences
Mary Reyko
Education Dept., Maryland Science Center
601 Light Street
Baltimore, MD 21230

Massachusetts
Massachusetts Science Talent Search
Dr. Mary H. Laprade
Director, Clarke Science Center
Smith College
Northampton, MA 01603

Michigan
Michigan Science Talent Search
Dr. Eldon L. Graham
Associate Professor
Department of Engineering and Technology
Saginaw Valley State College
University Center, MI 48710

Minnesota
Minnesota Science Talent Search
Dr. Adela S. Elwell, Field Director
Opportunities, Science Division
Minnesota State University
Bemidji, MN 56601

Mississippi
Mississippi State Science Talent Search
Don Cotten
University of Southern Mississippi
P.O. Box 8414, Southern Station
Hattiesburg, MS 39406

Nebraska
Nebraska Academy of Sciences, Inc.
Dr. Don Woodburn, Science Consultant
Nebraska Department of Education
301 Centennial Mall South, Box 94987
Lincoln, NE 68509

New Jersey
New Jersey Academy of Science
Douglas Garatina
13 West 50th Street
Bayonne, NJ 07002

New Mexico
New Mexico Inst. of Mining and Tech.
M. Jimmie Killingsworth
Assistant Professor of English
CS Box A
Socorro, NM 87801

North Carolina
North Carolina Student Academy of Science
Dr. Jonathan Franz, Executive Director
St. Andrews Presbyterian College
Laurinburg, NC 28352

Ohio
Ohio Academy of Science
Lynn Edward Eifner
Executive Officer
445 King Avenue
Columbus, OH 43201

Oklahoma
Northeastern Oklahoma State University
Dr. Joe M. Anderso
Professor of Botany
Division of Natural Science and Mathematics
Tahlequah, OK 74464

Oregon
Oregon Museum of Science and Industry
David Heil
Science Education Manager
4015 SW Canyon Road
Portland, OR 97221

Pennsylvania
Pennsylvania Academy of Science
Dr. Kurt C. Schreiber, Professor
Department of Chemistry
Duquesne University
Pittsburgh, PA 15282

Texas
Science Teachers Association of Texas
Dr. Virginia Rawlins
Assistant Professor of Physics
North Texas State University
Denton, TX 76203

Utah
Utah Academy of Sciences, Arts, and Letters
Junior Academy Division
Richard S. Peterson
State Spec. in Science Ed.
Utah State Office of Education
250 East 500 South
Salt Lake City, UT 84111

Vermont
American Chemical Society
Green Mountain Section
Dr. George C. Crooks
74 Spear Street
South Burlington, VT 05401

Virginia
Virginia Junior Academy of Science
Mrs. Luella VanNewkirk,
Science Teacher Thomas Jefferson
Intermediate School
125 Old Glebe Road
Arlington, VA 22204

Washington
Washington State Science Talent Search
Donald G. Dietrich
Professor of Chemistry
Seattle Pacific University
Seattle, WA 98118

West Virginia
West Virginia Science Talent Search
Joseph F. Glencoe, Jr.
Department of Biology
West Virginia Wesleyan College
Buckhannon, WV 26201

Wisconsin
University of Wisconsin-Eau Claire
Dr. Dean Nelson
Professor of Chemistry
Eau Claire, WI 54701

Wyoming
(See Colorado-Wyoming)

State Societies of Professional Engineers

Each state and province of the United States has a Society of Professional Engineers, through which many scholarships and internships are available for students interested in pursuing a career in engineering. Each state has a different program available, so it is best to contact your state office directly for current information. The following are the addresses of the headquarters of the member state societies of the National Society of Professional Engineers.

Alabama Society of Professional Engineers
George E. Shofner, Jr., P.E.
Business/Engineering Bldg., Suite 255 ERG
1000 Eleventh Way, South
Birmingham, AL 35294
(205) 934-8470

Alaska Society of Professional Engineers
John E. Johansen, P.E.
406 Eureka Avenue
Fairbanks, AK 99701

Arizona Society of Professional Engineers
Ms. Janice L. Rizer
2415 West Colter, #4
Phoenix, AZ 85015
(602) 249-0963

Arkansas Society of Professional Engineers
Ms. Ann Hamilton
One Union Station, Suite 409
Markham & Victory Streets
Little Rock, AR 72201
(501) 376-4128

California Society of Prof. Engineers
Ms. Carol A. Taugher
1005-12th Street, Suite J
Sacramento, CA 95814
(916) 442-1041

Professional Engineers of Colorado
Richard L. Bogdanovich, P.E.
2755 South Locust #214
Denver, CO 80222
(303) 756-8840

Connecticut Society of Prof. Engineers
2600 Dixwell Avenue
P.O. Box 4499
Hamden, CT 06514
(203) 281-4322

Delaware Society of Professional Engineers
Ms. Margaret Wise
P.O. Box 2865, Suite 218
Wilmington, DE 19805
(302) 656-7311

District of Columbia
Society of Professional Engineers
Helen E. Collins
315 Lewis Street, NW
Vienna, VA 22180

Florida Engineering Society
Charles E. Cook
P.O. Box 750
Tallahassee, FL 32302

Georgia Society of Professional Engineers
Ms. Jackie Kimberly
One Park Place, Suite 226
1900 Emery Street, NW
Atlanta, GA 30318
(404) 355-0177

Guam Society of Professional Engineers
Jose Gutierriez, Jr.
P.O. Box 6857
Tamuning, Guam 96911
(671) 632-2815

Hawaii Society of Professional Engineers
Howard T. Hanzawa, P.E.
P.O. Box 86, Puunene
Maui, Hawaii 96784
(808) 877-5068

Idaho Society of Professional Engineers
Ms. Jacquelyn K. Fuller
842 LaCassia Drive
Boise, ID 83705
(208) 345-1730

Illinois Society of Professional Engineers
Gary Crites, CAE
1304 South Lowell
Springfield, IL 62704
(217) 544-7424

Indiana Society of Professional Engineers
Ms. Laura Howe
P.O. Box 20806
Indianapolis, IN 46220
(317) 255-2267

Iowa Engineering Society
Mr. David H. Scott
1051 Office Park Road, #2
West Des Moines, IA 50265
(515) 223-0309

Kansas Engineering Society
Mr. William M. Henry
627 South Topeka, P.O. Box 477
Topeka, KS 66601
(913) 233-1867

Kentucky Society of Prof. Engineers
Joseph Dougherty
Rt. 3, Box 96F
Frankfort, KY 40601
(502) 695-5880

Louisiana Engineering Society
Mrs. Leta G. Bueto
P.O. Box 2683
1213 Nicholson Drive
Baton Rouge, LA 70821
(504) 344-4318

Maine Society of Professional Engineers
Gerard H. Chabot, P.E.
RR 2, Box 5760
Oxford, ME 04270
(207) 998-2730

Maryland Society of Professional Engineers
Ms. Carol T. Shaner
113 West Franklin Street
Baltimore, MD 21201
(301) 752-3318

Massachusetts Society of Prof. Engineers
Mrs. Carol Fitzgerald
555 Huntington Avenue
Roxbury, MA 02115
(617) 442-7745/46

Michigan Society of Professional Engineers
Harry R. Ball, P.E.
P.O. Box 10214
Lansing, MI 48901
(517) 487-9388

Minnesota Society of Prof. Engineers
Mr. Donald W. Hassenstab
Professional Building, Suite 130
555 Park Street
St. Paul, MN 55103
(612) 292-8860

Mississippi Engineering Society
Mrs. Mary Ellen Odom
5425 Executive Place, Suite D
Jackson, MS 39206
(601) 366-1312

Missouri Society of Prof. Engineers
Mr. Paul E. Jobe
330 East High Street, 2nd Floor
Jefferson City, MO 65101
(314) 636-4861

Montana Society of Engineers
Ms. JoAnn Harris
1629 Avenue D
P.O. Box 20996
Billings, MT 59104
(406) 259-7300

Nebraska Society of Prof. Engineers
Fred E. Anderson, Jr., P.E.
1630 K Street, Suite D
Lincoln, NE 68508
(402) 476-2572

Nevada Society of Professional Engineers
Barbara J. Gilson
1050 E. Flamingo Road, Suite 367
Las Vegas, NV 89119

New Hampshire Society of Prof. Engineers
David Provan, P.E.
Provan & Lorbor Inc.
P.O. Box 389
Contoocook, NH 03229

New Jersey Society of Prof. Engineers
Mr. Joseph A. Simonetta
407 West State Street
Trenton, NJ 08618
(609) 393-0099

New Mexico Society of Prof. Engineers
Ms. Kate Warder
1615 University Boulevard, NE
Albuquerque, NM 87102
(505) 247-9181

New York State Society of Prof. Engineers
Ms. Christine M. Sikora
150 State Street
Albany, NY 12207
(518) 465-7386

Prof. Engineers of North Carolina
Mr. Roy L. Baber, Jr.
4000 Wake Forest Road, Suite 116
Raleigh, NC 27609
(919) 872-0683

North Dakota Society of Prof. Engineers
Guilford O. Fossum, P.E.
P.O. Box 1031
Grand Forks, ND 58206-1031
(701) 777-3782

Ohio Society of Professional Engineers
Edward E. Fanning, CAE
445 King Avenue, Room 103
Columbus, OH 43201
(614) 424-6640

Oklahoma Society of Prof. Engineers
Mr. Ira T. Oliver
Oklahoma Engineering Center
201 N.E. 27th Street, Room 125
Oklahoma City, OK 73105
(405) 528-1435

Professional Engineers of Oregon
Ms. Bernie Taylor
1423 S.W. Columbia
Portland, OR 97201
(503) 228-2701

Pennsylvania Society of Prof. Engineers
Mr. John P. Seeley
4303 Derry Street
Harrisburg, PA 17111
(717) 561-0590

Puerto Rico Society of Prof. Engineers
Emilio Arsuaga
Asuaga - Hurtado, G.P.O. Box 4432
San Juan, PR 00936
(809) 825-1125

Rhode Island Society of Prof. Engineers
Ms. Marsha Cain
Charles Orms Building
10 Orms Street
Providence, RI 02904
(401) 751-3200

South Carolina Society of Prof. Engineers
Mr. Joe S. Jones, II
P.O. Box 11937
Columbia, SC 29211
(803) 771-4271

South Dakota Society of Prof. Engineers
Derek Hazeltine
Hazeltine & Associates
P.O. Box 1037
Pierre, SD 57501-1037
(605) 224-1591

Tennessee Society of Prof. Engineers
Ms. Mary D. Shahan
206 Capitol Boulevard, Suite 301
Nashville, TN 37219
(615) 242-2486

Texas Society of Professional Engineers
Mr. Gerhardt Schulle, Jr.
P.O. Box 2145
3501 Manor Road
Austin, TX 78768
(512) 472-9286

Utah Society of Professional Engineers
Chuck Lush, P.E.
9913 Pinehurst Drive
Sandy, UT 84092-0434
(801) 572-3055

Vermont Society of Prof. Engineers
David H. Bartlett, P.E.
RE #1, Box 1051
Williamstown, VT 05769

Virginia Society of Professional Engineers
Ms. Lisa Scott Schroeder
116-118 E. Franklin Street, Suite 601
Richmond, VA 23219
(804) 780-2491

Washington Society of Prof. Engineers
Mrs. Colleen Yuhl
12828 Northrup Way
Bellevue, WA 98005
(206) 885-2660

West Virginia Society of Prof. Engineers
John R. Martin, Jr., P.E.
The Peoples Building, Room 804
179 Summers Street
Charlestown, WV 25301-2131
(304) 346-2100

Wisconsin Society of Prof. Engineers
Judith A. Whalen
6325 Odana Road
Madison, WI 53719
(608) 274-8555

Wyoming Society of Professional Engineers
Deb Schultz, P.E.
Meheen Engineering
5920 Yellowstone Road, Suite 2-C
Cheyenne, WY 82009

Student Research Conferences and Journals

AAAS Student Poster Session

The American Association for the Advancement of Science (AAAS) has a special paper poster session for research by undergraduate and graduate students at its annual meeting in February. The students with the best presentations in their fields receive cash awards and are recognized at the AAAS awards ceremony during the annual meeting. Instructions on how to submit abstracts are published in a "Call for Papers" in the first September issue of *Science*. The deadline for submission of abstracts is November 1. For more information, write to AAAS Meetings, Department SM, 1333 H Street, NW, Washington, DC 20005.

Student Research Journals

These publications either publish high school student research papers or are targeted to an audience of high school science and mathematics students.

Journal of Student Research
Gerry Roe, Editor
20110 Canyon Road
Sheridan, OR 97378
(503) 843-4214

Journal of High School Science Research
Mike Farmer, Editor
P.O. Box 193
Tigerville, SC 29688

Quantum
Phyllis Marcuccio
National Science Teachers Association
3140 North Washington Boulevard
Arlington, VA 22201
(703) 243-7100

Student Research Programs

This section describes some of the more well-known summer research programs for students. Other programs are listed in Science Service's *Directory of Science Training Programs for Precollege Students* and in the Duke University Talent Identification Program's directory of programs for the gifted (see the bibliography on page 309 for information on both of these publications). Other internship and summer employment programs are listed in Chapter 8, pages 221–246.

Duke University Talent Identification Program

Duke University's Talent Identification Program offers a summer residential program for high school students who are talented in math and science. Courses are offered in precalculus, math problem solving, number theory, logic, computer science, chemistry, physics, astronomy, marine biology, animal behavior, and psychology. To qualify for the program, students must meet certain SAT/ACT score cutoffs. The program has four 3-week terms during the summer and costs approximately $2,000. Scholarships are available, based on need. The application deadline is May 1.

For more information, write to Tom Ulmet, Assistant Director, Educational Programs, Talent Identification Program, Duke University, P.O. Box 40077, Durham, NC 27706-0077, or call (919) 684-3847.

Earthwatch

Earthwatch matches paying volunteers with field research expeditions. Participants help with the research activities of the expeditions and are given hands-on training at the research site. Volunteers pay a portion of the costs, including transportation, room, board, and field equipment, with a typical expedition costing the volunteer around $1,200. There are a limited number of scholarships for students and teachers. Fields of research include art and archaeology, geosciences, life sciences, marine studies, social sciences, and rain forest conservation and ecology.

Write Earthwatch, The Center for Field Research, 680 Mt. Auburn Street, P.O. Box 403, Watertown, MA 02172, call (617) 926-8200, or fax (617) 926-8532 for more information.

Foundation for Field Research

The Foundation for Field Research is similar in concept to Earthwatch. Fields of research include archaeology, botany, entomology, folklore, herpetology, marine archaeology, historic architecture, marine biology, ornithology, paleontology, prehistoric rock art, primatology, sea turtle research, and wild mammal research. A limited number of partial scholarships for students are available.

Write to the Foundation for Field Research, P.O. Box 2010, Alpine, CA 91903-2010, or call (619) 445-9264 for more information.

Hampshire College Summer Studies in Mathematics

Hampshire College offers the Summer Studies in Mathematics program for high school students of high ability and motivation in mathematics. Students investigate problems from number theory, combinatorics, chaos theory, topology, and other fields in small classes and seminars. The program's faculty live in the same dormitory as the students to create a cohesive community centered around mathematics. Selection is on the basis of an application and an interesting test (which is mailed after the application is received) and other evidence of ability in mathematics. The six-week program costs approximately $1,250, including tuition, room, board, and fees. Scholarships are available, based on need. The application deadline is May 1.

For more information, write to Prof. David C. Kelly, Summer Studies in Mathematics, Hampshire College, Box NS, Amherst, MA 01002, or call (413) 549-4600 x 375.

International Summer Institute

Middle school and high school students from around the world participate in laboratory and classroom instruction in science, mathematics, and the humanities. The campus-based program also includes recreational and enrichment activities.

Write International Summer Institute, Carl Berkowitz, Director, P.O. Box 843, Bowling Green Station, New York, NY 10274, or call (212) 747-1755 for more information.

Johns Hopkins Center for Talented Youth

The Johns Hopkins Center for Talent Youth provides mathematically precocious youth with the opportunity to take advanced science and math courses during two 3-week summer sessions. The summer programs are held at Loyola Marymount University in Johns Hopkins University, Baltimore, Maryland; Los Angeles, California; Skidmore College, Saratoga Springs, New York; Dickinson College, Carlisle, Pennsylvania; Hampshire College, Amherst, Massachusetts; Franklin and Marshall College, Lancaster, Pennsylvania; and College du Leman, Geneva, Switzerland.

To qualify, students must take the SAT during the 7th grade and score greater than 500 on the math and 950 on math and verbal combined. A sliding scale is used for scores of older students. Courses are offered in precalculus, calculus, chemistry, biology, genetics, astronomy, marine ecology, paleobiology, and computer science. The program costs approximately $1,750 for tuition, room, board, books, supplies, lab fees, and registration fees. Scholarships are available, based on need. The application deadline is in early to mid-April.

For more information, write to Dr. Luciano Corazza, The Johns Hopkins University, 2701 North Charles Street, Baltimore, MD 21218, or call (410) 516-8427. You can also write to William Durden, Director of the Center for Talented Youth at the address given above, or call (410) 338-8427.

Ohio State University, Ross Young Scholars Program

The Ohio State University offers the Arnold Ross Young Scholars Program for talented students who are interested in pursuing careers in mathematics, science, or technology. Students participate in research apprenticeships during the 8-week program and are exposed to creativity in math and science. Participants are selected on the basis of an application, essay, problem set, and letters of recommendation. The program costs approximately $1,200, including tuition, room, and board. Scholarships are available, based on need. The application deadline is May 15.

For more information, write to Prof. Arnold Ross, Department of Mathematics, The Ohio State University, 231 West 18th Avenue, Columbus, OH 43210, or call (614) 292-1569.

Research Science Institute

The Research Science Institute (RSI) is an intensive six-week summer program for academically talented science and mathematics students who have completed their third year of high school or the equivalent. Selection of participants is based solely on academic excellence. Students engage in scientific research under the guidance of mentors at corporations, universities, research organizations, and government agencies. The research internships, which form the core of the program, are augmented by classroom lectures in science, mathematics, and the humanities by distinguished professors from leading universities during the first week of the program, field trips on weekends, and a guest lecture series in the evenings. During the last week of RSI the students prepare reports on their research for oral and written presentation. There is no cost to participants, except for transportation to and from the program at the beginning and end. The Research Science Institute is one of the few programs to expose young students to scientific research and has consistently had a greater percentage of its alumni/ae win academic awards such as the Westinghouse Science Talent Search Scholarships and the National Science Foundation Graduate Fellowships than any other educational organization.

RSI is also described in the preface to this book. For more information, write to the Center for Excellence in Education, Research Science Institute, 7710 Old Springhouse Road, McLean, VA 22102, or call (703) 448-9062. You can also send E-mail to center@rsi.cee.org.

Space Life Sciences Training Program

The Space Life Sciences Training Program is an intensive six-week program held at the Kennedy Space Center, Florida, from mid-June through the end of July. In the mornings, students attend lectures by leading research scientists, managers, engineers, and astronauts from NASA Centers, universities, and industry. In the afternoons, students participate in the planning and execution of experiments that span the range of life sciences research and space flight experiments of current interest to NASA. Students are involved in the conceptualization, preparation, preflight and postflight testing, data analysis, and report preparation phases of the experiments. Evening and weekend activities include informal discussions with visiting lecturers and astronauts and work on special projects. Students also tour the Kennedy Space Center shuttle and payload facilities. Participants will receive five semester hours of tuition-free college credit through Florida A&M University, one of the program sponsors. There is no cost to the participants for this program — students receive round-trip transportation between their home and the Orlando International Airport in Florida, free accommodations in the Cocoa Beach area near Kennedy Space Center, local transportation to and from the space center, and a daily meal allowance.

To be eligible, candidates must be undergraduate students pursuing their first undergraduate degree and must have a minimum cumulative GPA of 3.00 or higher at the time of application. Students in the last year of undergraduate school are not eligible to apply (i.e., graduating seniors may not apply, but fourth year seniors who will be continuing on for a fifth year are eligible). Participants must be 16 years of age or older. U.S. citizenship is required. Eligible majors include animal sciences, biochemistry, biology, biophysics, biostatistics, chemistry, computer science, ecology, engineering, geology, life sciences, mathematics, pharmacy, physics, plant sciences, pre-medicine, and psychology. Previous SLSTP participants are not eligible.

Approximately 40 students are selected each year on the basis of an application, official college transcripts, three letters of recommendation, and a 500-word essay. In the essay, the applicant describes past classroom, laboratory and research experiences in the science, and briefly discusses future career goals. The (post-mark) deadline is January 31, with notification by March 31.

For further information, write to Program Director, SLSTP, Florida A&M University, College of Pharmacy and Pharmaceutical Sciences, 106 Honor House, Tallahassee, FL 32307, or call (904) 599-3636.

Chapter 11

Taxability of Scholarships and Fellowships

This chapter discusses the taxability of various kinds of scholarships and fellowships. We are not offering tax advice and make no warranties as to the accuracy of this information.

If you have questions about your case after reading the relevant IRS publications you should consult the IRS or an accountant. Individuals should always seek personal professional tax advice since each case may be different.

Federal Tax Reform Act of 1986

The Federal Tax Reform Act of 1986 changed the rules for the taxability of scholarships and fellowships, making them much more severe. We assume in this chapter that all scholarships and fellowships under discussion were granted on or after August 17, 1986.

If the student in question is a degree candidate, amounts used for tuition and course-related expenses (fees, books, supplies, and equipment required for courses)[1] are exempt from federal income tax.[2] The scholarship or fellowship must not be in exchange for teaching and research services performed by the student; if teaching, research, or other services are required for receipt of a degree, they must be required of all degree candidates. Amounts used for other expenses (e.g., room and board, computers,[3] and

---

[1] Some doctoral programs do not require graduate students to take courses. For graduate students in such degree programs, it isn't necessary that educational expenses be related to a specific course, so long as you can demonstrate that they are necessary for the completion of your degree and no reasonable alternative exists. This is especially true if you register for a catch-all "Reading and Research" course.

[2] Note that if the award letter states that the stipend is for living expenses but doesn't mention educational expenses, educational expenses paid out of the stipend may not necessarily be excludable from taxable income. The same thing may apply if the award letter doesn't provide any details on the purpose of the stipend and an amount has been designated for tuition. Many students will exclude educational expenses from the stipend income anyway, since this is a gray area in the tax code. If the award letter specifies that the stipend may be used for educational expenses, or if it doesn't differentiate between tuition and stipend, excluding educational expenses is easier to defend during an audit.

[3] The IRS is very strict about excluding or deducting expenses associated with the purchase of a computer or software. If you can justify the computer as a tool that is absolutely necessary for your education and

non-required expenses) are *not* exempt from tax. If the student is not a degree candidate, the full amount of the fellowship or scholarship is subject to federal income tax.

Note that an excludable expense is used to reduce the taxable income before any deductions. So when you pay for an excludable expense using your scholarship or fellowship, you can still take advantage of the standard deduction (assuming that you aren't claimed as a dependent on another person's return). In contrast, claiming a deductible expense usually requires you to itemize your deductions. Itemizing your deductions is worthwhile only if the sum of your itemized deductions exceeds the standard deduction. For most students the standard deduction is larger. If you itemize your deductions, however, you *cannot* both exclude and deduct the same educational expense.

The full amount of a scholarship or fellowship is generally exempt from FICA (social security tax). This is true whether or not the student is a degree candidate.

Prizes are no longer exempt from tax. Cash scholarship prizes won in a contest are not considered scholarships or fellowships unless the recipient is required to use them for educational purposes as a degree candidate enrolled at an educational institution.

Teaching and Research Assistantships

For the purposes of the tax code, a scholarship or fellowship is an amount paid to the student to enable him or her to pursue studies or conduct research at an educational institution. In addition, a grant paid as compensation for services or primarily for the benefit of the grantor is not considered a scholarship or fellowship and hence represents taxable income.

Thus if a teaching and research assistantship requires teaching or research services as a condition for receiving the grant, the grant is taxable, even if used for tuition. If, however, the TA/RA's tuition is waived, that portion of the grant is exempt from income tax, provided that the rest of the stipend represents fair pay for the services rendered. If the research performed by the RA is chosen by the RA and is performed for the purpose of writing a thesis, the amount of the grant may be considered a fellowship. Thus tuition-waivers are usually tax-exempt, but stipends aren't.

If a portion of the grant represents payment for services, the grantor (e.g., the university) is required to report the taxable portion on a W2 form as wages and do appropriate withholding. Otherwise there is currently no requirement that the amounts be reported to the IRS on a W2 or otherwise, even if they are taxable. Likewise there is no requirement that income tax be withheld from your stipend, so you may have to pay estimated tax on the taxable portion of your scholarship or fellowship grant.

---

there are no alternative equivalent facilities available (e.g., a workstation provided by your advisor or a campus computer cluster), it is possible that the IRS will allow it. Consult the IRS or a tax professional about your specific circumstances.

Reporting Scholarships and Fellowships on a Tax Return

The IRS does not fully specify how to report scholarships and fellowships on the income tax return. It is not sufficient to just subtract the nontaxable amounts[4] from the income reported on line 7 of Form 1040 (wages, salaries, tips, etc.), because the IRS computers will detect a discrepancy between the amounts reported on line 7 of Form 1040 and the amounts reported on your W2 forms. This will force a human being to look at your return and can result in an audit.

Regardless of whether the tax-free grant was reported to the IRS on a W2 form, you should exclude the tax-free portion of the grant (including any amounts spent on course-related expenses) from the amount reported on line 7 of Form 1040[5] and write in the space to the left "See attached letter." Attach an explanatory letter to the Form 1040 that specifies the amount subtracted, states that the amount excluded is for educational and course-related expenses from a scholarship or fellowship, and itemizes those expenses. You may want to describe the expenses in detail in order to justify them as part of your educational program. The letter should also include your name and social security number. Be sure to keep a copy of your return and letter, in case the IRS happens to "lose" the letter and audits you. To include taxable scholarship income which has not been reported to the IRS on a W2, write "SCH" and the taxable amount not reported on a W2 in the space to the left of line 7.

Be sure to keep receipts for any course-reported expenses, in case you are audited.

Get Current Information

The taxability status of scholarships and fellowships is constantly changing, so the information in this chapter may quickly become out of date. Request a copy of IRS Publication 520 "Scholarships and Fellowships" and Publication 508 "Educational Expenses" from the IRS Forms Distribution Center at 1-800-TAX-FORM (1-800-829-3676) and read it carefully. The IRS taxpayers' assistance number is 1-800-829-1040.

Be sure to consult the latest tax guides and your financial aid office for any last-minute changes, since tax laws tend to change around December. Keep up with the financial press and write your congressman.

A good tax guide to read is J. K. Lasser's *Your Income Tax 1993* from Prentice Hall. New editions come out every year in November-December and sell for around $14. A free supplement is available in January-February.

Another useful tax guide is Allen Bernstein's *Tax Guide for College Teachers and Other College Personnel 1993*, available for $27.95 from Academic Information Service, Inc., P.O. Box 929, College Park, MD 20741. Although intended primarily for college faculty and staff, much of the material is also relevant to graduate students.

---

[4]More accurately, such amounts should be referred to as *excludable*, not nontaxable or tax-free.

[5]You can either subtract the amount of educational expenses from your stipend and write the result on line 7, or you can list the educational expenses as a negative amount on line 22 (Other income). Somehow the latter seems safer. In any event, you should attach an explanatory letter to the Form 1040.

Chapter 12

Suggested Readings

This guide gathers together many of the scholarship and fellowship programs and contests of interest to science and mathematics students. It is by no means complete. Should you wish to look for additional resources and opportunities, this chapter lists many useful references and publications. You can find a selection of them in the reference section of your local library. Others are inexpensive enough that you can purchase them at your local bookstore or through the mail.

Those books which are extraordinarily good have been marked with a diamond ($\diamond$) at the end of their entry.

Undergraduate Scholarships

This section lists references that are primarily for undergraduate students.

1. **Don't Miss Out: The Ambitious Student's Guide to Financial Aid** ($6.00 + $1.25 p&h). 16th Edition, 1992, 120 pages. A guide to the financial aid game and strategies for getting the most support possible. Revised annually. Available from *Octameron Associates, Inc.*, P.O. Box 2748, Alexandria, VA 22301. (703) 836-5480.

2. **The Scholarship Book. A Comprehensive Guide to Private-Sector Scholarships, Grants and Loans for Undergraduates** ($14.95). 1987. 373 pages. By Daniel J. Cassidy and Michal J. Alves. Published by Prentice Hall, Englewood Cliffs, NJ. A comprehensive listing of basic information about several thousand scholarship and grant programs. Essentially a printout of the National Scholarship Research Service's database. Quality variable. The scholarship search service is available for a fee from *National Scholarship Research Service*, P.O. Box 2516, San Rafael, CA 94912. (415) 456-1577.

3. **Educational Awards Handbook** (free). Available from *Rotary Foundation of Rotary International*, One Rotary Center, 1560 Sherman Avenue, Evanston, IL 60201. (708) 866-3000.

4. **Financial Aid for College Through Scholarships and Loans: FACTS** ($7.95). 4th edition, 1985, 169 pages. By Elizabeth Hoffman and Kathleen Gladstone. Includes step-by-step instructions for filling out the financial aid forms. Written from a Massachusetts orientation. Available from *FACTS*, Box 208, Wellesley Hills, MA 02181.

5. **AFL-CIO Guide to Union Sponsored Scholarships, Awards, and Student Financial Aid** ($3.00). Available from *AFL-CIO Department of Education*, 815 Sixteenth Street, NW, Washington, DC 20006.

6. **Science Education for You** ($2.00). Available from *National Science Teachers Association*, 1742 Connecticut Avenue, NW, Washington, DC 20009.

7. **Financial Aids for Higher Education** ($45). By Oreon P. Keeslar. Available from *Wm. C. Brown Company Publishing*, 2460 Kerper Boulevard, Dubuque, IA 52001.

8. **Scholarship Programs Using the Location Service Offered by Educational Testing Service** (free). Describes 70 scholarship programs. Available from *Educational Testing Service*, 20 Nassau Street, Princeton, NJ 08450.

9. **College Check Mate: Innovative Tuition Plans That Make You a Winner** ($6.00 + $1.25 p&h). 5th Edition, 1992. Describes a variety of innovative tuition assistance plans offered by U.S. educational institutions, including installment plans, prepayment discounts, tuition freezes, tuition equalization, family plans, academic incentives, tuition remission for student leaders, off-hour rates, guaranteed tuition plans, and moral obligation scholarships. Available from *Octameron Associates, Inc.*, P.O. Box 2748, Alexandria, VA 22301. (703) 836-5480.

10. **The College Financial Aid Emergency Kit** ($4.95 plus 55 cents p&h). 1992. Pocket guide to financial aid for college. Available from *Sun Features, Inc.*, Box 368-II, Cardiff, CA 92007.

Scholarships and Fellowships

This section lists references for undergraduate and graduate students.

1. **Chronicle Student Aid Annual** ($19.95 + $2.00 p&h). Describes 2,050 financial aid programs available to undergraduate, graduate, and postgraduate students, including programs sponsored by both public and private organizations. Also includes programs offered by AFL-CIO affiliated unions. Revised annually. Available from *Chronicle Guidance Publications, Inc.*, 66 Aurora Street, P.O. Box 1190, Moravia, NY 13118-1190, as Catalog No. 502A. (315) 497-0330.

2. **Need a Lift?** ($2.00). 39th edition, 1990, 120 pages. A comprehensive guide to educational opportunities, careers, loans, scholarships, and employment for undergraduate and graduate students. Contains quite a bit of information about

programs for children of veterans. Includes an extensive annotated bibliography. Revised annually. Available from *The American Legion*, National Emblem Sales, P.O. Box 1055, Indianapolis, IN 46206. ◇

3. **Scholarships, Fellowships, and Loans** ($80.00). By S. Norman Feingold and Marie Feingold. Provides detailed coverage about fellowships, assistantships, scholarships, and research opportunities. Available from *Bellman Publishing Company*, P.O. Box 34937, Bethesda, MD 20817. Newer editions (1992 and onward) are now published by Gale Research (see below).

4. **Scholarships, Fellowships, and Loans: News Service and Counselors Information Services** ($35.00 per year). Published quarterly, provides up-to-date information regarding student financial aid. Includes annotated bibliography of books and professional journals. Available from *Bellman Publishing Company*, P.O. Box 34937, Bethesda, MD 20817.

5. **Scholarships, Fellowships, and Loans**. 9th edition, 1992, 769 pages. By Debra M. Kirby. (Previous editions by Norman and Marie Feingold, Bellman Publishing Company.) Comprehensive listing of scholarships, fellowships, loans, and grants. Includes several indexes, and charts for quickly identifying programs of interest. A significant improvement over previous editions, which were repetitious database printouts. Available from *Gale Research, Inc.*, 835 Penobscot Building, Detroit, MI 48226-4094. 1-800-347-GALE, (313) 961-2242, FAX (313) 961-6815. ◇

6. **College Scholarship Guide**. By Clarence E. Lovejoy and Theodore S. Jones, 125 pages. Describes scholarships, fellowships, and loan funds sponsored by educational and fraternal groups and by government and industry. Available from *Simon & Schuster, Inc.*, 630 Fifth Avenue, New York, NY 10020.

7. **The College Blue Book — Scholarships, Fellowships, Grants and Loans** ($48.00). 23rd edition, 1991, 855 pages. Essentially a database printout that repeats the same programs under each area, field, or subject. Available from *Macmillan Publishing Company*, 866 Third Avenue, New York, NY 10022. ◇

8. **How To Find Out About Financial Aid**. 1987, 334 pages. By Gail A. Schlacter. A guide to over 700 directories listing scholarships, fellowships, loans, grants, awards, and internships. Available from *Reference Service Press*, 1100 Industrial Road, Suite 9, San Carlos, CA 90010. (415) 594-0743.

Graduate Fellowships

This section lists references that are primarily for graduate students.

1. **Annual Register of Grant Support** ($149.00 + $6.75 p&h). 1992, 25th edition. Extensive directory of fellowship and grant support programs of government agencies, private foundations, businesses, and professional organizations. Available from *National Register Publ. Co.*, 3004 Glenview Road, Wilmette, IL 60091. ◇

2. **Annual Register of Grant Support** ($165.00 + $6.75 p&h). 1993, 26th edition. By R.R. Bowker. Extensive directory of fellowship and grant support programs of government agencies, private foundations, businesses, and professional organizations. Available from *Reed Reference Publishing Company*, 121 Chanlon Road, New Providence, RI 07974. ◇

3. **The Grants Register** ($89.95). Lisa Williams, editor. 1993-95. Lists scholarships, fellowships, and grants for graduate study. Biennial. Available from *St. Martin's Press*, 175 Fifth Avenue, New York, NY 10010.

4. **Guide to Programs – National Science Foundation** ($4.75). List of programs of the National Science Foundation, include graduate fellowship programs. Available from *Superintendent of Documents*, U.S. Government Printing Office, Washington, DC 20402, as order S/N 038-000-00577-4.

5. **A Selected List of Fellowship Opportunities and Aids to Advanced Education for U.S. Citizens and Foreign Nationals** (free). 1988. 60 pages. Available from Publication Office, *National Science Foundation*, 1800 G Street, NW, Washington, DC 20550. ◇

6. **The Graduate Scholarship Book** ($29.95). 1990, 2nd edition. 441 pages. By Daniel J. Cassidy. Published by Prentice Hall, Englewood Cliffs, NJ. Guide to scholarships, fellowships, grants, and loans for graduate and professional study. Essentially a printout of the National Scholarship Research Service's database. Quality variable. The scholarship search service is available for a fee from *National Scholarship Research Service*, P.O. Box 2516, San Rafael, CA 94912. (415) 456-1577.

7. **Free Money for Graduate School** ($35.00). By Laurie Blum, 1990, 1st edition, 288 pages. A directory of private grants and fellowships for graduate students. Available from *Henry Holt & Co.*, 115 West 18th Street, New York, NY 10011.

8. **Grants for Graduate Study** ($59.95). 3rd edition, 1992. 365 pages. Revised about every 3 years. Compiled by the University of Massachusetts at Amherst. Includes over 700 programs of interest to graduate students sponsored by over 400 organizations. Includes an excellent general introduction to the grant seeking process by Risa Sodi and Andrea Leskes. Data was gathered by a survey conducted during the first half of 1991. Available from *Peterson's Guides*, Box 2123, Princeton, NJ 08543-2123. 1-800-EDU-DATA. ◇

9. **Assistantships and Graduate Fellowships in the Mathematical Sciences** ($15 plus $2 p&h). Free for members of the American Mathematical Society (AMS). Lists graduate student assistantships and fellowships in the mathematical sciences at U.S. educational institutions. See also *Notices of the American Mathematical Society*, which publishes a monthly column entitled "Funding Information for the Mathematical Sciences" and a column entitled "Stipends for Study and Travel" in the October issue. The latter focuses on support for postdoctoral students.

Available from the *American Mathematical Society*, P.O. Box 6248, Providence, RI 02940-6248. ◇

10. **Foundation Grants to Individuals** ($40). 7th edition, 1991. Available from *The Foundation Center*, 79 Fifth Avenue, New York, NY 10003. 1-800-424-9836. (212) 620-4230. The Foundation Center maintains two national libraries of information on philanthropic organizations, one in New York and one in Washington, DC. The DC library is located at 1001 Connecticut Avenue, NW, Suite 938, Washington, DC 20036. (202) 331-1400.

11. **Graduate Assistantship Directory in the Computer Sciences** (free). Description of computer science departments and financial assistance at over 100 universities in the U.S. Available from *Association for Computing Machinery (ACM)*, 11 West 42nd Street, 3rd Floor, New York, NY 10036. ◇

12. **Directory of Computer and High Technology Grants** ($44.50 plus $4 p&h). By Richard Eckstein. Lists over 600 funding sources for computer hardware and software and other high-tech related grants. Available from *Research Grant Guides*, Department 4B, P.O. Box 1214, Loxahatchee, FL 33470. (407) 795-6129.

13. **Encyclopedia of Associations**. 27th edition, 1993. A guide to more than 23,000 national and international organizations. Volume I: National Organizations of the U.S. Volume V: Research Activities and Funding Programs. Available from *Gale Research, Inc.*, 835 Penobscot Building, Detroit, MI 48226-4094. 1-800-347-GALE, (313) 961-2242, FAX (313) 961-6815. ◇

Federal Aid Programs

1. **The Student Guide: Five Federal Financial Aid Programs** (free). Available from *Federal Student Aid Information Center*, P.O. Box 84, Washington, DC 20044-0084. 1-800-4FED-AID (1-800-433-3243). Alternate address: *Consumer Information Center*, Student Guide, Pueblo, CO 81009. 1-800-333-INFO. ◇

2. **Financial Aid for Higher Education** ($1.00). Available from *Superintendent of Documents*, U.S. Government Printing Office, Washington, DC 20402.

3. **A Guide to Student Assistance** ($0.60). Available from *Superintendent of Documents*, U.S. Government Printing Office, Washington, DC 20402 as House Document #9-221.

4. **College Grants from Uncle Sam: Am I Eligible and for How Much?** ($3.00 + $1.25 p&h). 11th Edition, 1992, 32 pages. Short sketches of all government grant programs. Includes worksheet for determining eligibility for federal aid and estimating the size of the award. Available from *Octameron Associates, Inc.*, P.O. Box 2748, Alexandria, VA 22301. (703) 836-5480.

5. **College Loans from Uncle Sam: The Borrower's Guide that Explains It All** ($3.00 + $1.25 p&h). 11th Edition, 1992, 32 pages. Describes government loan programs in depth. Includes directory of state-guaranteeing agencies, and the PLUS and GSL programs. Available from *Octameron Associates, Inc.*, P.O. Box 2748, Alexandria, VA 22301. (703) 836-5480.

6. **How the Military Will Help You Pay for College** ($9.95). 1985. Written by Don M. Betterton. Available from *Peterson's Guides*, Box 2123, Princeton, NJ 08543-2123. 1-800-EDU-DATA.

7. **Getting Yours: The Complete Guide to Government Money** ($8.95 plus $1.50 p&h). Available from *Penguin Books*, Order Department, 299 Murray Hill Parkway, East Rutherford, NJ 07073-2112.

Women and Minorities

1. **Directory of Special Opportunities for Women** ($18.00). 290 pages. Listings of national, state, county, city, and private organizations, associations, programs, and agencies where women can find educational and career opportunities. Available from *Garrett Park Press*, P.O. Box 190, Garrett Park, MD 20896.

2. **Directory of Special Programs for Minority Group Members** ($30.00). 5th edition, 1990, 348 pages. Listing of over 4,000 career information services and financial aid sources for members of underrepresented minority groups. Available from *Garrett Park Press*, P.O. Box 190, Garrett Park, MD 20896.

3. **Financial Aid Unscrambled: A Guide for Minority Engineering Students** (free). 1990, 24 pages. Guide to financial aid for minority engineering students. Available from *National Action Council of Minorities in Engineering (NACME)*, 3 West 35th Street, Third Floor, New York, NY 10001-2281. (212) 279-2626.

4. **Financial Aid for Minorities in Engineering and Science** ($4.95). 1991, 70 pages. List of financial aid, scholarship, and fellowship programs for members of underrepresented minority groups. Available from *Garrett Park Press*, P.O. Box 190, Garrett Park, MD 20896.

5. **Directory of Federal R&D Agencies' Programs to Attract Women, Minorities, and the Physically Handicapped to Careers in Science and Engineering** (free). Directory listing over 40 federally sponsored programs at government agencies. Available from *National Science Foundation*, 1800 G Street, NW, Washington, DC 20550. (202) 357-9496. ◇

6. **Directory of Financial Aid for Minorities** ($47.50 + $4 p&h). 530 pages. By Gail A. Schlacter and Sandra E. Goldstein. A guide to over 2,000 scholarships, fellowships, loans, and grants for minority students. Includes a breakdown by type of minority. Available from *Reference Service Press*, 1100 Industrial Road, Suite 9, San Carlos, CA 90010. (415) 594-0743.

7. **Directory of Financial Aid for Women** ($45 + $4 p&h). 466 pages. By Gail A. Schlacter. A guide to over 1,000 scholarships, fellowships, loans, and internships for female students. Available from *Reference Service Press*, 1100 Industrial Road, Suite 9, San Carlos, CA 90010. (415) 594-0743.

8. **Grants at a Glance — A Directory of Funding and Financial Aid Resources for Women in Science**. 78 pages, 1987. By Julie Goodman. Provides information on research grants, fellowships, scholarships, and awards geared toward female scientists and science students in the life sciences, physical sciences, social sciences, and engineering. Predominantly postdoctoral and beyond, although there are a few listings for predoctoral and undergraduate programs. Published by the *Association for Women in Science (AWIS)*, 2401 Virginia Avenue, NW, Suite 303, Washington, DC 20037. (202) 833-1998. ◇

9. **Higher Education Opportunities for Minorities and Women: Annotated Selection, 1989** ($4.25). 1988, 96 pages. Describes educational opportunities for minorities and women. Includes annotated bibliography. Available from *Superintendent of Documents*, U.S. Government Printing Office, Washington, DC 20402.

10. **Bureau of Indian Affairs Higher Education Grants and Scholarships** (free). Available from *Office of Indian Education Programs*, Code 522 – Room 3512, 19th and C Streets, NW, Washington, DC 20240.

Financial Aid Advice

1. **Meeting College Costs**. Gives examples and general guidelines for estimating college expenses and determining the expected contributions from parents and students. Available free of charge from your high school guidance counselor. Schools may purchase them in packages of 50 for $6 from *College Board Publications*, P.O. Box 886, New York, NY 10101. ◇

2. **Financial Aid Fin-Ancer: Expert Answers to College Financing Questions** ($3.50 + $1.25 p&h). 1992. Discusses unusual circumstances, such as divorce and job loss, and how they impact the financial aid process. Includes step-by-step instructions for filling out the financial aid forms. Available from *Octameron Associates, Inc.*, P.O. Box 2748, Alexandria, VA 22301. (703) 836-5480. ◇

3. **Applying for Financial Aid** (free). Available from *American College Testing Program Publications*, P.O. Box 186, Iowa City, IA 52243.

4. **How to Pay for Your Children's College Education** ($12.95). Available from *College Board Publications*, Box 886, New York, NY 10101.

Cooperative Education Programs

1. **Cooperative Education Undergraduate Program Directory** (free). Annual directory of the colleges and universities that participate in co-op programs. Explains what cooperative education is and how it works. Available from *National Commission of Cooperative Education*, 501 Stearns Center, 360 Huntington Avenue, Boston, MA 02115. ◇

2. **Earn & Learn: Cooperative Education Opportunities Offered by the Federal Government** ($3.50 + $1.25 p&h). 13th edition, 1992, 36 pages. Directory of federal agencies that sponsor cooperative education and work-study programs and the schools that participate in the program. Available from *Octameron Associates, Inc.*, P.O. Box 2748, Alexandria, VA 22301. (703) 836-5480.

College Costs and College-Controlled Aid

1. **The A's and B's of Academic Scholarships** ($6.00 + $1.25 p&h). 14th edition, 1992, 144 pages. A comprehensive listing of college-controlled academic (merit) scholarships in the U.S. Available from *Octameron Associates, Inc.*, P.O. Box 2748, Alexandria, VA 22301. (703) 836-5480.

2. **The College Money Handbook** ($9.95). 1983. By Karen C. Hegener and Eric A. Suber. Guide to expenses, scholarships, loans, jobs, and special aid programs at over 1,700 four-year colleges. Includes some merit awards. Available from *Peterson's Guides*, Box 2123, Princeton, NJ 08543-2123. 1-800-EDU-DATA.

3. **College Costs** ($1.50 plus 15% p&h, minimum order 10). 1991. Provides data on enrollment and costs (tuition, fees, and room and board) at U.S. four-year colleges and universities. Available from *Life Insurance Marketing and Research Association*, Box 208, Hartford, CT 06141.

4. **The College Cost Book** ($14.95). Lists student expenses at postsecondary institutions. Annual publication. Available from *College Board Publications*, P.O. Box 886, New York, NY 10101.

5. **The College Planning Search Book** ($6). Available from *American College Testing Program Publications*, P.O. Box 186, Iowa City, IA 52243.

6. **The Best Buys in College Education** ($10.95). By Edward B. Fiske and Joseph M. Michalak. 1987, 473 pages. Available from *Times Books*, New York, NY.

7. **The Ultimate College Shopper's Guide** ($12.95). 1992. By Heather Evans and Deidre Sullivan. Contains numerous lists of rankings and comparisons of schools by cost and financial aid packages. Published by Addison-Wesley, Reading, MA.

Contests and Competitions

1. **Advisory List of National Contests and Activities** ($3.00). Fairly good list of national competitions in mathematics, the sciences, and the humanities. Available from *National Association of Secondary School Principals*, 1904 Association Drive, Reston, VA 22091. ◇

2. **Winning Money for College: The High School Student's Guide to Scholarship Contests** ($8.95). Available from *Peterson's Guides*, Box 2123, Princeton, NJ 08543-2123. 1-800-EDU-DATA.

Summer Programs

1. **Directory of Science Training Programs for Precollege Students** ($3.00). List of summer and academic year programs in the mathematical, physical, medical, biological, social, and engineering sciences. Available from *Science Service, Inc.*, 1719 N Street, NW, Washington, DC 20036. (202) 785-2255. ◇

2. **1992 Educational Opportunity Guide** ($13.00). Directory of Programs for the Gifted. List of summer and academic year programs for gifted students. Broken down by state. Also includes a list of regional talent searches such as the Johns Hopkins Program, and a list of academic competitions and activities. Available from *Talent Identification Program*, Duke University, Box 40077, Durham, NC 27706-0077. ◇

3. **Young Scholars Program**. The National Science Foundation funds a variety of summer and academic-year enrichment programs in science, mathematics, and engineering at colleges and universities for high school students. Write to Young Scholars Program, Division of Research Career Development, *National Science Foundation*, 1800 G Street, NW, Washington, DC 20550, or call (202) 357-7536 for more information.

4. **1988 Internships** ($10.95). Annual publication. Available from *Writer's Digest Books*, 9933 Alliance Road, Cincinnati, OH 45242.

5. **National Directory of Internships** ($24.50). Biannual publication. Directory of over 800 internship programs. Available from *National Society for Experiential Education*, 3509 Hayworth Drive, Suite 207, Raleigh, NC 27609, (919) 787-3263.

6. **Federal Job Information Center**. The U.S. Office of Personnel Management (OPM) runs an information line, (202) 653-8468, which includes recorded messages on job listings and other federal employment-related information. You can obtain a "Career America" information packet and a copy of form SF-171, the Personnel Qualifications Statement, by writing to *U.S. Office of Personnel Management*, 1900 E Street, NW, Washington, DC 20415, or calling (202) 632-6118. In addition, commercial job-listing publications are available from *Federal Jobs Digest*, 325 Pennsylvania Avenue, SE, Washington, DC, 20003, 1-800-824-5000,

Federal Times, 6883 Commercial Drive, Springfield, VA 22159, (703) 750-8600, and *Federal Career Opportunities*, Federal Research Service, Inc., P.O. Box 1059, Vienna, VA, 22183, 1-800-822-JOBS or (202) 333-5627.

Study and Travel Abroad

1. **Academic Year Abroad** ($39.95, plus $3 p&h). Sarah Steen, editor. 1992/93. Describes over 2,000 undergraduate and graduate study-abroad programs conducted during the academic year. Annual; new editions are published each January. Available from *Institute of International Education*, Publications Service, 809 United Nations Plaza, New York, NY 10017. ◇

2. **Fulbright and Other Grants for Graduate Study Abroad** (free). List of grants for graduate study and research abroad, administered by the IIE for U.S. citizens. Available from *Institute for International Education*, U.S. Student Programs, 809 United Nations Plaza, New York, NY 10017-3580. (212) 984-5330, (212) 883-8200. ◇

3. **Study in the United Kingdom and Ireland** ($14.95, includes p&h). E. Marguerite Howard, Editor. Describes over 800 postsecondary study programs in Britain and Ireland, sponsored by U.S. and foreign universities and other organizations. Biennial. Available from *Institute for International Education*, 809 United Nations Plaza, New York, NY 10017. (212) 984-5330.

4. **Basic Facts on Foreign Study** (free). 1992, 40 pages. Basic information on what to expect from study abroad programs and sources of further information. Single copies are free, but bulk copies cost $35 per 100 plus $3 s&h. Available from *Institute for International Education*, U.S. Student Programs, 809 United Nations Plaza, New York, NY 10017-3580. (212) 984-5330, (212) 883-8200.

5. **Work, Study, Travel Abroad: The Whole World Handbook** ($12.95 plus $1.50 p&h). Available from *CIEE Publications*, 205 East 42nd Street, New York, NY 10017. (212) 661-1414.

6. **Vacation Study Abroad** ($26.95, plus $3 p&h). E. Marguerite Howard, Ed. Annual publication. A guide to over 1,300 summer and short-term study programs conducted around the world by U.S. colleges and universities, foreign institutions, and private organizations. Contains information on courses, costs, scholarships, and accommodations. Available from *Institute for International Education*, 809 United Nations Plaza, New York, NY 10017. (212) 984-5330.

7. **U.S. Information Agency (USIA)** (free). For information on USIA's international educational and cultural exchange programs, including the Fulbright Program. Available from *U.S. Information Agency*, Office of Public Liaison, 301 Fourth Street, SW, Washington, DC 20547. ◇

8. **International Research and Exchanges Board (IREX)** (free program announcement). Lists programs administered by IREX, both graduate and postdoctoral, including exchanges for a semester or an academic year with the USSR and socialist countries of Eastern Europe. Available from *International Research & Exchanges Board*, 126 Alexander Street, Princeton, NJ 08540-7102. (609) 683-9500. FAX (609) 683-1511. ◇

9. **Study Abroad**, Vol. 27, 1992-1993 ($24.00). 1,350 pages, paperback. Provides information on several hundred thousand study grants in over 100 countries for the years 1988-1991. Available from *UNIPUB*, 4611-F Assembly Drive, Lanham, MD 20706-4391 as Order No. U7145. (301) 459-7666.

10. **Financial Resources for International Study: A Guide for U.S. Nationals** ($36.95 plus $5.75 p&h). 250 pages. Describes scholarships and fellowships offered by governments, foundations, and other organizations for U.S. nationals to study abroad. Available from *Peterson's Guides*, Box 2123, Princeton, NJ 08543-2123. 1-800-EDU-DATA. ◇

11. **Canadian Studies Graduate Fellowship Program**. Description of programs for U.S. citizens to study in Canada. Available from *Canadian Embassy*, 501 Pennsylvania Avenue, Academic Relations, Washington, DC 20001. (202) 682-1740. You can also get some information from NSERC, Canada's equivalent to the United State's NSF. Write to Scholarships and International Programs Directorate, *National Sciences and Engineering Research Council*, 200 Kent Street, Ottawa, Ontario, K1A 1H5, CANADA, or call (613) 995-6295.

Music

1. **Available Music Scholarships**. Available from *Select Publications, Inc.*, 114 E. 32nd Street, New York, NY 10016.

2. **The Musician's Guide: The Directory of the World of Music**, 7th Edition, 1983. Lists 406 national and international competitions in music and over 600 foundations. Available from *Music Information Service, Inc.*, New York.

Humanities Fellowships

1. **Fellowships and Grants** ($45). In *Publications of the Modern Language Association of America (PMLA)*, Directory Issue, 106(4):912-937, September 1991. Updated periodically. High quality listing of fellowships in the humanities. About half are predoctoral, with the rest postdoctoral and faculty. Many support study abroad. Available from *Modern Language Association of America*, Member and Customer Services Office, 10 Astor Place, New York, NY 10003-6981.

2. **Guide to Grants and Fellowships in Languages and Linguistics** ($3). Available from *Linguistics Society of America*, 1325 18th Street, NW, Washington, DC 20036.

3. **Grants, Fellowships, and Prizes of Interest to Historians**. 1991. 261 pages. Includes over 400 listings of support for individuals, teams, and prizes for books and other published works. Also contains a bibliography of other information sources. Available from *American Historical Association*, Publication Sales Department, 400 A Street, SE, Washington, DC 20003. (202) 544-2422.

4. **Directory of Grants in the Humanities**. 1986. Available from *ORYX Press*, 2214 North Central at Encanto, Phoenix, AZ 85004-1483. (602) 254-6156.

Career Information

1. **Chronicle of Occupational Briefs**. Short descriptions of over 530 occupations. Available from *Chronicle Guidance Publications, Inc.*, P.O. Box 1190, Moravia, NY 11318.

Other Resources

1. **Sourcebook for Science, Mathematics, and Technology Education**, 1992. Compiled and edited by Mary Beth Lennon and Barbara Walthall. Comprehensive listing of state and federal education-related agencies, museums, scientific organizations, and other resources. Includes name, organization, program, geographical, and publications indexes. Published by the *American Association for the Advancement of Science (AAAS)*, 1333 H Street, NW, Washington, DC 20005-4792, AAAS publ. #91-38S. (202) 326-6400. ◇

2. **Science Fairs and Projects**. A book of example science fair projects and other information about science fairs. Available from *National Science Teachers Association*, 1742 Connecticut Avenue, NW, Washington, DC 20009, (202) 328-5800.

3. **Thousands of Science Projects**. This book lists the titles of successful science fair projects from the ISEF and Westinghouse competitions. It is a good source of ideas for science fair projects. Available from *Science Service, Inc.*, 1719 N Street, NW, Washington, DC 20036. (202) 785-2255. ◇

Index

Poetry, 132, 207–8, 210
Polish, 255
Political Science, 109, 140, 158, 187, 199,
          221, 282
Postal employees, 88
Postgraduate Students, 142, 229, 235
          Female, 144
          Minorities, 163
Pre-Medicine, 294
Prepaid tuition plans, 55
Presidential Scholars, 80
Princeton University, 157
Procrastination, 1, 55
Proofreading, 9, 24, 33
Proposal writing, 218
PSAT/NMSQT, 274
Psychiatry, 282
Psychoanalysis, 282
Psychology, 99, 133, 140, 158, 161, 282,
          294
Publications, 43
Public Health, 221
Public Policy, 199
Public Service, 89, 115, 135, 195
Puerto Ricans, 102, 105, 156, 181
Puerto Rico, 273
Pulmonary Pathobiology, 239
Purina Mills, 188

Q

Qualifying exams, 29, 38

R

Race, 3
Radiochemistry, 91
Radioecology, 91
Radiology, 282
Reaching schools, 20
Realistic goals, 19
Recommendations, *see* Letters of recom-
          mendation
Records, 9
References, 301–12
Rejection, 26
Relieving stress, 26
Religion, 57, 216, 274

Religious affiliation, 3
Remote Sensing, 191
Research, 29
Research ability, 32
Research Assistantships, 31
Research Grants, 69, 87, 92, 119, 146, 159,
          189
Research internships, 223–24, 234, 236, 245
Research Science Institute, vii, 293
Residence, 3
Resource Conservation, 183
Respiratory Therapy, 66
Résumé, viii, 3, 6, 8, 23
Retirement funds, 52
Rhode Island, 272
Rhodes Scholarship, 258
Rickover, v, vii
Robotics, 123, 191, 282
Rocketry, 117, 216
Room and board, 47
Rotary Foundation, 301
RSI, v, vii, 293

S

Sacrifices, 51
SAE, 121
Safety and Health, 233
Safety Engineering, 112, 282
Safety schools, 20
Sanitary Engineering, 91
SASE, 5, 8
SAT, 19–20
Savings bonds, 55
Scams, 2, 10
SCEEE, 141
Scholarships, 57–62, 64–67, 69–90, 93–108,
          110–11, 113–25, 127–37, 139–40,
          145–47, 164, 173, 180–81, 187,
          211–18, 255, 257, 266
          Blind Students, 112
          Female, 77, 97, 108
          Minorities, 66, 91, 100, 102, 108, 133,
              136, 145, 181
          References, 301–3
Scholarship search companies, 2
School rankings, 30
School visits, 16, 30